The Metaphysics of Meditation

Bloomsbury Studies in World Philosophies

Series Editor:
Monika Kirloskar-Steinbach

Comparative, cross-cultural and intercultural philosophy are burgeoning fields of research. Bloomsbury Studies in World Philosophies complements and strengthens the latest work being carried out at a research level with a series that provides a home for thinking through ways in which professional philosophy can be diversified. Ideal for philosophy postgraduates and faculty who seek creative and innovative material on non-Euroamerican sources for reference and research, this series responds to the challenges of our postcolonial world, laying the groundwork for a new philosophy canon that departs from the current Eurocentric sources.

Titles in the Series:
Andean Aesthetics and Anticolonial Resistance, by Omar Rivera
Chinese Philosophy of History, by Dawid Rogacz
Chinese and Indian Ways of Thinking in Early Modern European Philosophy, by Selusi Ambrogio
Indian and Intercultural Philosophy, by Douglas Berger
Toward a New Image of Paramārtha, by Ching Keng
African Philosophy and Enactivist Cognition, by Bruce B. Janz
Interrelatedness in Chinese Religious Traditions, by Diana Arghirescu
The Metaphysics of Meditation, by Stephen Phillips

The Metaphysics of Meditation

Sri Aurobindo and Ādi Śaṅkara on the Īśā Upaniṣad

Stephen Phillips

BLOOMSBURY ACADEMIC
LONDON • NEW YORK • OXFORD • NEW DELHI • SYDNEY

BLOOMSBURY ACADEMIC
Bloomsbury Publishing Plc, 50 Bedford Square, London, WC1B 3DP, UK
Bloomsbury Publishing Inc, 1385 Broadway, New York, NY 10018, USA
Bloomsbury Publishing Ireland, 29 Earlsfort Terrace, Dublin 2, D02 AY28, Ireland

BLOOMSBURY, BLOOMSBURY ACADEMIC and the Diana logo
are trademarks of Bloomsbury Publishing Plc

First published in Great Britain 2024
This paperback edition published 2025

Series design by Louise Dugdale
Cover image © Olga Kurbatova/Getty Images

A catalogue record for this book is available from the British Library.

A catalog record for this book is available from the Library of Congress.

ISBN: HB: 978-1-3504-1241-5
PB: 978-1-3504-1244-6
ePDF: 978-1-3504-1242-2
eBook: 978-1-3504-1245-3

Series: Bloomsbury Studies in World Philosophies

Typeset by RefineCatch Limited, Bungay, Suffolk

For product safety related questions contact productsafety@bloomsbury.com.

Dedicated to the memory of
Professor Arabinda Basu

Motto: *Brahma-sūtra-śāṅkara-bhāṣya* 2.1.29: *samānatvāc ca na anyatarasminn eva pakṣa upakṣeptavyo bhavati* | *parihṛtas tu brahma-vādinā sva-pakṣe doṣaḥ* |

Śaṅkara on *Brahma-sūtra* 2.1.29: If the same problem is faced by all views, a position is not to be discarded because only one could be right. Here, then, the current difficulty as applied to Vedānta can be ignored.

Contents

Acknowledgments viii
Sanskrit Transliteration and Pronunciation ix

Introduction: Vedānta and Yoga 1

1 Who is Addressed by Ādi Śaṅkara, Who by Sri Aurobindo? 17

2 "Blocked Out" by the Lord or "Integrated?" (*Īśā* 1, 2, and 3) 29

3 The Whole in the Part (*Īśā* 4 and 5 and the *maṅgala-vācana*) 41

4 Mystical Knowledge of Unity (*Īśā* 6 and 7) 53

5 (K)nots of Metaphysics: The Causal Argument for the "Self-Existent," *svayam-bhū* (*Īśā* 8) 67

6 Knowledge of Self (*ātman*) and Knowledge of the Occult (*Īśā* 9 through 14) 81

7 A Theistic Way to Self-Discovery (*Īśā* 15 and 16) 97

8 Aspiration and Surrender (*Īśā* 17 and 18) 107

Appendix A The *Īśā Upaniṣad* (the two readings and the Sanskrit) 121

Appendix B Śaṅkara's Commentary on the *Īśā Upaniṣad* 131

Appendix C From the *Bhagavad Gītā* 165
Part One: "The Yoga of Meditation" (*Gītā* chapter 6) 165
Part Two: "The Yoga of Action" (*Gītā* chapters 3, 4, and 5) 166

Appendix D: Śaṅkara's Theodicy (from his *Brahma-sūtra Commentary*) 171

Glossary of Sanskrit Words 177
Classical Authors, Schools, and Texts 185
Notes 191
Bibliography 219
Index 229

Acknowledgments

Before the 2020 pandemic, Mousumi Mukherjee invited me to give that year the Arabinda Basu Memorial Lecture held annually in Kolkata at the Sri Ramakrishna Institute of Culture. Unfortunately, I was unable to travel, but preparation for the lecture turned into this book. And so for Mousumi's invitation I am most grateful. Leaving Durham University and the Spalding Professorship of Eastern Philosophy to return to India and Benares Hindu University, Professor Arabinda Basu was a teacher of mine when I attended the Sri Aurobindo International Centre for Education in Pondicherry in the 1970s. From him I learned a lot about the philosophy of Aurobindo and its predecessors. Thanks go to Professor Matthew Dasti of Bridgeport University, my erstwhile student, who is responsible for important improvements, commenting on more than one draft. My long-time friend Colin Foote made many suggestions about parallels in Buddhism that have been incorporated. I thank Professor Nirmalya Guha of the Indian Institute of Technology, Varanasi, who years ago visiting Austin, Texas, inspired me to renew my study of Vedānta and Ādi Śaṅkara in particular. Through video link I presented an overview of the book at a conference organized by Benedetta Zacarello in honor of Sri Aurobindo's 150th birthday, in Paris, École normale supérieure, November 2022, and profited from comments from several participants. And of course I owe a lot to students to whom I had the privilege of teaching classical Indian philosophies for almost forty years at the University of Texas at Austin.

Editor and Publisher Colleen Coalter of Bloomsbury Academic steered this work through the publication process, most graciously, providing wisdom and encouragement. Let me also thank Monika Kirloskar-Steinbach, editor of the Bloomsbury Series in World Philosophies, Suzie Nash, Bloomsbury Philosophy editor, and Judy Tither, copy editor, as well as Mr. Honeywood along with Benedict O'Hagan for the fine points of proofs and printing, and Balsa at Indexbusters for a first-rate index.

Socorro County, New Mexico
July 2023

Sanskrit Transliteration and Pronunciation

Sanskrit words are spelled throughout this book with diacritical marks in standard indological fashion. Proper pronunciation is not necessary in a work of philosophy (pronounce as you like), but here is a guide using well-known English words.

Vowels (omitting two that rarely occur):

a like 'u' in 'mum': *manas* (both vowels: muhnuhs)
ā like 'a' in 'father': Nāgārjuna (naa-gaar-joo-nuh)
i like 'y' in 'baby': *mukti*
ī like 'ee' in 'feed': Śrī (shree)
u like 'u' in 'pull': *mukti*
ū like 'oo' in 'moon': *rūpa* (roo-puh)
ṛ like 'rea' in 'really' (while turning the tip of the tongue up to touch the palate): *Ṛg Veda*
e like 'a' in 'maze': *tejas* (tay-juhs)
ai like 'i' in 'mine': *advaita*
o like 'o' in 'go': *yoga*
au like 'ow' in 'cow': *saucya* (sowch-yuh)

Consonants and semivowels—**y**, **r**, **l**, **v**—are pronounced roughly as in English. Some special cases:

kh exactly like **k** in Sanskrit—that is, like the 'k' in 'kite'— except aspirated, that is, breath out, as with 'keel': *mukha*

All other aspirated consonants follow the same principle: **gh** like **g** except aspirated, **th** like **t**, and so on. Of special note:

c like 'ch' in 'churn'
ch another aspirate, same principle: *sac-chid-ānanda*
ñ like 'n' in canyon
ṭ There is no English equivalent: a 't' sound (as in 'tough') but with the tip of the tongue touching the roof of the mouth:

ṭh aspirated **ṭ**
ḍ like 'd' in 'deer' but "lingualized" as with **ṭ**
ḍh aspirated **ḍ**
ṇ lingualized 'n' sound
ph aspirated **p** as in 'part', not 'f'.

There are three sibilants:

ś like 'sh' in 'shove'
ṣ lingualized 'sh' sound
s like 's' in 'sun': *sūrya*

Other uses of the "dot under":

ḥ calls for breath following a vowel. For example, *duḥkha* is pronounced as follows, 'du', and then breath (very short) and then 'kha'.
ṃ This is shorthand for any nasal, the particular type determined by the class of the following consonant: **ṅ** is guttural, **ñ** palatal, **ṇ** lingual, **n** dental, and **m** labial. For example, the **ṃ** in 'Sāṃkhya' is equivalent to **ṅ**, since **kh** belongs to the guttural class.

Euphonic combination, *sandhi*:

The "hat" symbol ˆ is used for vowel *sandhi*, vowel "combination," when two words are compounded (for instance, *Īśā* + *upaniṣad* = *Īśôpanisad*). The hat shows that a vowel so marked is long, or is the dipthong **e** or **o**, because of *sandhi* in the coming together of the two words.

Introduction: Vedānta and Yoga

Vedāntic meditation

According to an ancient tradition of yoga in India, meditation is antithetical to willful bodily action, mental, too. Breathing is all you do, and hold your back straight, subconsciously or almost subconsciously, relaxing your shoulders. The trick is stillness, including mental stillness, not thinking, not daydreaming, doing nothing, just sitting, self-conscious, awake. Attention, concentration homes in on being "thoughtlessly" aware. This is, paradoxically, a mental act, delicate, with difficulty accomplished, we are told in yoga traditions, coming about when attention (*manas* in Sanskrit) centers on awareness itself.[1]

Gradually, or suddenly, magic happens, a subtle awareness, a new dimension of sensing, visions or a surreal sense of reality, as one lives inside, identity obliterated or expanded. Wonder and awe are common, along with psychic powers in some, which are distractions according to a famous declaration of the *Yoga-sūtra* (*YS* 3.37).[2] We are told that the best that occurs is nothing that we do, apart from our meditation discipline, a ladder pulled up behind. It happens because of what we are, not just a "surface self" with a demonic subconscious full of "asocial instincts," as say the Freudians, but a great self with an angelic superconscious, blissful, generous, creative. Or, in the conception of the *Īśā Upaniṣad*, it happens because of what the "Lord" is, who, in one interpretation, Śaṅkara's, comes to block out the little "you," or, in another, Aurobindo's, comes as a divine connection, an occult "Conscious Force" belonging to truer part of oneself, *ātman*, and an "opening" to that self's native energy. The *Īśā* ("*eeshah*," *c.* 500 BCE) is one of the very earliest teachings of yoga and meditation, an *upaniṣat* (anglicized "Upanishad" or "Upaniṣad"), which is a genre of so-called "psychological" learning, *adhyātmika*—concerning self and consciousness—in early Indian literature.

According to Śaṅkara ("Shankara," *c.* 700 CE), Aurobindo (1872–1950), and many other "Vedāntins" over the centuries, the *Īśā* and other Upaniṣads are guides to transformations of consciousness that are valuable in the extreme. In their telling, Vedānta is at heart a yoga-inspired philosophy of a phenomenological route to the hidden self and "Brahman"—*brahman* is the "Absolute," "the One." With this Vedānta combines an explanatory narrative, a monistic rational theology also put forth first in certain Upaniṣads. These themes converge in several ways, perhaps none more important than with "identity," *abhimāna*, how one "regards" oneself and others.

Upaniṣads

Upaniṣads are among the earliest records of metaphysical speculation and argument in any culture, and that dimension has generated the most interest among both classical philosophers and moderns. But philosophy is hardly all there is to admire. The verses of the *Īśā* are poetry of a high caliber. Meditation makes use of poetic symbols and rhythms, and the *Īśā* is misread as only a philosophic treatise expressing a worldview. The meter of each of the eighteen verses is regular, most verses being made up of two lines of sixteen syllables, dividing into half lines of eight syllables in a pattern that though not absolutely fixed by longs and shorts is sufficiently uniform that variations matter. Some verses are in other meters but are still regular in the distribution of longs and shorts. There are also beautiful images plainly directed to an inner world closer to dreams than to the deliveries of sense experience. Note that mystics perforce use symbols and non-literal language to communicate to non-mystics about mystic discoveries, since the everyday speech had in common does not much cater to the mystical in the denotations of words.[3] We have to expect symbolic language. Furthermore, in the verses of the *Īśā* there are the Vedāntic equivalent of "koans," mantras with apparent contradictions and antinomies that resist rational analysis. This book comprises essays on the short wisdom poem, following the two Vedāntins' comments, ideally with utmost sensitivity to both the meditational phenomenology expressed poetically and the metaphysics of a greater self, *ātman* and *brahman*. The goal is to trace a worldview and consonant yoga teaching common to two authors who are typically taken to be oceans apart, not only chronologically but in intellectual stance, while also attending to the poetic dimension that seems key to the meditations advanced.

From an academic, "Religious Studies" perspective, Upaniṣads form part of an immense sacred literature in Hinduism called "Veda," much of which was transmitted orally for centuries, beginning as far back as 3,500 years. From a

"Philosophy" perspective, Upaniṣads form an early wisdom literature complete with metaphysical and psychological speculation, mainly proto forms of cosmopsychism coupled with an emanationist theism, or panentheism, positing a "God with many faces." To attempt a unified definition, I would say an Upaniṣad is a crisp prose or verse composition suitable for meditation and consciousness discipline—to include a mental (*buddhi*) yoga, something like a panentheistic equivalent of Western natural theology—panentheistic, that is to say, as focused on "Brahman," the "Self," *ātman*, the "Inner Controller," as opposed to "God," *and* on hidden connections among different realms or dimensions of experience. There are a few hundred of the compositions made over the centuries, memorized, and a dozen or so early or "classical" Upaniṣads, at some point about 2,000 years ago, separated out from other Vedic work—hymns, stories, formula for rituals—and collected as a group—the original "Vedānta"—out of distinct genealogical lines (Vedic *śākhā*, "branches"). Inspiring practice lineages called *sampradāya*, they became for "Vedāntins" (Upaniṣad enthusiasts, roughly) the most revered of texts (*śruti*) which, along with more detailed oral teachings, were passed from teachers to students who became themselves teachers, Vedāntic gurus.

It is important to keep in mind that even the classical Upaniṣads hardly speak with one voice. Composed by different people at different times for different audiences, Upaniṣads do not all say the same thing. The most egregious error of classical commentators, according to modern critics, is to insist on consistent teachings throughout the corpus, thus motivating forced readings. The mistake is indeed made, but Śaṅkara, for one, readily admits that many Upaniṣadic passages are not directed to his number-one interest, the way to "self-discovery," to immediate, perception-like knowledge of the Absolute as one's own self, although that is by far the most important topic, he asserts. He points out that some passages are about, for example, occult connections with divinities in rituals. Such passages do not elicit much reflection on his part. Possibly learning from Buddhist hermeneutics that dismisses apparent contradictions in the canonical sermons on the assumption that the Buddha's statements were tailored to different audiences (a Bodhisattva has "skill in means," *upāya-kauśala*), Vedāntins make similar moves, ignoring much in some Upaniṣads. An overly "scripturalist" interpretation rampant in academia misrepresents Śaṅkara's main thrust, which is to teach yoga, the way to self-discovery. But a metaphysical line of argument does indeed occupy him, apparently complementing in his mind the Upaniṣadic meditational teaching. The same goes for Aurobindo. Indeed, while the chief task of the Vedānta school in general may be said to be to frame the teachings of the Upaniṣads intellectually as a yogic path, or paths, to a mystical "knowledge" of self and Brahman, we must not lose sight of certain lines of metaphysical reasoning.

Upaniṣads may be regarded from many points of view, and they do indeed have diverse dimensions, psychological, ethical, metaphysical, aesthetic, and more. But they strike me—in agreement with Aurobindo and other "neo-Vedāntins" along with Śaṅkara (as I shall continue to argue)—to be on the whole meditation manuals, not concerned as much with belief as with consciousness discipline.[4] The hermeneutics of the texts has been much discussed, both in scores of classical Sanskrit works and by modern scholars. Probably since Upaniṣads express seminal views about metaphysical and psychological topics of great interest—the existence and nature of a greater "self," *ātman*, and consciousness, personal identity, and everything's relation to the "One"—this dimension has drawn the most scholarly attention. Puzzles debated in later Sanskrit texts by the dozens do indeed have Upaniṣadic origins. But world-directed explanations and psychology constitute an intellectual yoga pointed mainly, it seems to me, to fostering flexibility in personal regard, how one looks upon oneself and other persons ethically and in other ways.[5] And all that is taken to foster the best sort of meditation, that which leads to self-discovery. In any case, even the prose Upaniṣads contain jokes, false etymologies, punning, parables, many devices common in poetry but not well suited, in sum, for conveying intellectual truth. The "poetry" is, nonetheless, awesome for contemplation. This is a philosophic study, but we have to talk about yoga and meditative means to mystical experience—*sādhana* for short—since, even if mistaken, both Aurobindo and Śaṅkara see that as central in the *Īśā*. History and context are helpful for understanding especially certain Upaniṣadic passages, but the metaphysics and psychology of yoga practice will be our main concerns.

Śaṅkara and Aurobindo

In even broadest historical context, Śaṅkara and Aurobindo are standout writers, Aurobindo in English in several genre, Śaṅkara in Sanskrit commentarial prose along with the *Upadeśa-sahasrī*, "A Thousand Teachings," a text partly in prose, partly in verse, along with—probably, the ascription being controversial—elegant devotional poetry. The two stand at practically the far ends of Vedāntic criticism, engaged Upaniṣadic inquiry, I should say, the bookends of a long shelf of a great literature.[6] Śaṅkara, late seventh century or early eighth century by best estimate, is the author of the oldest Upaniṣadic commentaries extant, and

Aurobindo is a Western-educated Indian intellectual who began learning Sanskrit in England and studying Upaniṣads along with practicing yoga upon returning to India in 1893. Furthermore, both tie Upaniṣadic readings to general outlooks on life, and both now have been studied widely (a large secondary literature now trails each author). Furthermore, Aurobindo commented on Śaṅkara's work on the *Īśā*, and, I shall argue, was influenced by him on crucial points. There has been overemphasis of the nineteenth century "evolutionary" strand in Aurobindo as marking divergence, in my opinion. But now since the *Īśā* dates to about 1,000 years before Śaṅkara and Śaṅkara to more than 1,000 years prior to Aurobindo, we have to expect enormous cultural difference, some of which comprises crucial context for their thought. Nevertheless, yoga practice coupled with Vedānta philosophy effectively links the three. That amazing fact inspires this collection of essays.

Sāṃkhya's *pradhāna* vs Vedānta's *brahman*

Śaṅkara and Aurobindo and all Vedāntins inherit from a few classical Upaniṣads—especially the *Kaṭha*, not so much the *Īśā*—the difficulty of putting together an emanationist theism, a form of cosmopsychism, with a dualist yoga psychology called "Sāṃkhya," roughly "Analysis" (the word capitalized because later there emerges a so-named, minor classical school). Sāṃkhya philosophy stresses disidentification—rejection of all *abhimāna*, all personal regard—in an "enlightenment" experience or state.[7] Sāṃkhya as a worldview (*darśana*) is a negligible player on the later classical scene, but as a model for meditation it is influential across school, religion too (having Buddhist and Jaina influence as well as Vedic/Hindu). A dualist model of the goal of meditation is promulgated, disconnection of consciousness from all physical and mental reality, from everything outside itself, to be the isolated *puruṣa*, the individual "conscious being" separate from *prakṛti*, "nature," as putatively realized in an enlightenment experience. Now there is nary a yogic, spiritual, or religious philosophy rooted in classical India that does not hold some form of the thesis that our ordinary self-concepts are flawed. But Sāṃkhya's version of this is radical. Just about everything about our ordinary identities is wrong, and while Śaṅkara attacks the metaphysics of Sāṃkhya as woefully inadequate, his meditational teaching includes the idea that an ordinary sense of self and identity (*abhimāna*) typically needs deepening through disidentification with the person's active persona, becoming in effect an inactive witness like the *puruṣa* of Sāṃkhya. But Śaṅkara argues vigorously that not Sāṃkhya's primordial nature, *pradhāna*, an original homogeneous form of inconscient stuff, *prakṛti*, but rather *brahman* is the explanatory terminus for all becoming: Brahman is the "self-existent," *svayam-bhū*, cause of the universe to include its persistence and dissolution as well as of us as individual consciousness centers. The first sūtra of the *Brahma-sūtra* announces inquiry into *brahman* and the very second defines Brahman as world-cause: "Whence the world and all originate." Śaṅkara's espousing a phenomenological dualism in the fashion of the Sāṃkhya coupled with Sāṃkhya's materialist view of nature presents philosophic and hermeneutic problems that will occupy us especially in Chapter 5.

Classical Vedānta inherits from the early Upaniṣads central theses about *brahman*. Bracketing concerns with priority, interconnectedness, and compatibility, I find, at a minimum, the following nine:

1. Brahman is self (*ātman*) and consciousness.
2. Brahman is world ground and agential creator, the "inner controller."
3. Brahman is transcendent of "names and forms," *nāma-rūpa*, that is, of finite and mutable particulars.
4. Brahman as Brahman in itself along with its relation to the universe is "inexplicable," *anirvacanīya*, indeterminable in thought.
5. Brahman is unitary, the coincidence of apparent opposites, and omnipresent.
6. Brahman has "non-dual," "self-illumining" (*advaita*, *svayam-prakāśa*) self-awareness.
7. Brahman is the essence of everything.
8. Brahman is the locus of value, and awareness of Brahman is the "supreme personal good," *parama-puruṣârtha*, securing freedom from fear and evil.
9. Brahman is discoverable by yoga and meditation.

The *Bhagavad Gītā*

A few words about the *Gītā*, which is *not* traditionally viewed as belonging to the highest rank of spiritual authority, *śruti*, since it is not found in the core Vedic texts, unlike the *Īśā* and several dozen Upaniṣads. The *Gītā* is a short episode in a massive epic poem, the *Mahābhārata* (*c.* 200 BCE). Despite its "non-*śruti*" standing, every Vedāntin of whom I am aware, classical and modern, regards the text as as much a first-tier authority for philosophy—and all the more for yoga practice—as the plainly argumentative *Brahma-sūtra*. The *Gītā* presents a proto-systematic worldview, although its emphasis, like Śaṅkara's in his *Īśā* commentary, is on yoga, providing psychological and metaphysical propositions apparently as support for consciousness discipline. A key theme here is that Śaṅkara in attacking Mīmāṃsaka ritualism is following Kṛṣṇa's condemnation of "Veda-mongers" in the *Gītā*'s chapter two (2.42–4).[8]

Of course, everyday action has many sources, from long-term projects to pressing desires along with "moving" emotions, all of which need to be made calm according to our two meditation masters—save perhaps the "Godward emotions" of *bhakti* and gratitude, Aurobindo teaches, following the *Gītā*, as does Śaṅkara, too, at least in commenting on *Gītā* chapter nine (esp. 9.12–15).[9] "Good" emotions do not urge the kind of activity that obscures the "self," thus permitting a discipline of stillness and inwardness—both Vedāntins urge in line with the definition of "*yoga*" at *Yoga-sūtra* 1.2 (*yoga* = "stillness of the fluctuations of mentality," *citta-vṛtti-nirodha* = *samādhi*).[10] Vedāntins of all periods and subschools incorporate teachings of the *Yoga-sūtra* (*c.* 400 CE), favorably quoting the text while rejecting its dualism of consciousness and nature.[11] But the *Yoga-sūtra* is hardly original; most of the practices it elaborates are laid out in the *Gītā* (*c.* 200 BCE). The *Gītā*, I repeat, echoes Upaniṣads. That is to say, pretty much the same programs are laid out, with the same goal or goals set forth, psychologically considered—concerning attention, self-consciousness, though not of identity—in the *Yoga-sūtra* as in the classical Upaniṣads and the *Gītā*, that is, in two of the three widely recognized classical authorities (*prasthāna-trāyi*) for Vedānta: the Upaniṣads, the *Gītā*, and the *Brahma-sūtra*.[12] Admittedly, detailing a path of meditational "knowledge" seems far from the purpose of the third of the three, which is rather to lay out a metaphysical system and defend it. But that, too, is a dimension of Vedāntic yoga (*buddhi-yoga*), though not often recognized.

The *Brahma-sūtra* and Vedāntic metaphysics

The *Brahma-sūtra*, also called the *Vedānta-sūtra* (*c.* 200 CE), belongs to a distinct genre as a collection of philosophic tenets formulated aphoristically in "sūtras." This type of text is very different from an Upaniṣad. Ascribed to a legendary "Bādarāyaṇa," the *Brahma-sūtra* takes its task to be theory-building centered on the concept of Brahman as found in certain Upaniṣads—the supreme and original reality, the primeval cause—along with arguments about Brahman found in seed form in the Upaniṣads. The purpose is to formulate Vedānta as a school of philosophy in opposition to other schools that have their own foundational texts. It is not to present a way or ways—other than the intellectual (*buddhi-yoga*)—to progress in meditation but rather to fill out a mental picture of Brahman as the "self-existent" (*svayam-bhū*) origin of everything in opposition to other worldviews including a Sāṃkhya interpretation of certain Upaniṣadic passages. Despite the Upaniṣadic doctrine of *nêti nêti*, "Not this, not that"—Brahman is not commonly known in everyday speech—the *Brahma-sūtra* lays out Vedānta as an intellectual system that is better than other systems, wide-ranging theories of metaphysics, Sāṃkhya, Vaiśeṣika, Cārvāka, Buddhist, and others. To be sure, the *Gītā* has passages explaining the world in relation to Brahman, and so, too, do many Upaniṣads, yet without—in stark contrast of genre—the explicit rhetoric and forms of argument that are hallmarks of a philosophic school. Note that it is Bādarāyaṇa who should get the credit—or blame—for systemization with an eye to consistency, not Śaṅkara (except in explaining the sūtras). And despite the classical error of assuming that there is consistency across the Upaniṣadic corpus, there is, let us acknowledge, philosophic virtue in recognizing consistency as a condition for truth.

A broad-stroke kind of metaphysical speculation and even argument are prominent, however, in many Upaniṣads themselves, somewhat in the fashion of Greek presocratic philosophy. Indeed, in the earliest Upaniṣads—in the *Ṛg Veda* itself, the earliest Sanskrit literature—there is metaphysical speculation.[13] In the Upaniṣads, meditation is sometimes taught together with a cosmology that seems playful in connection with instruction about a greater self ("In the beginning there was the One, who, feeling lonely, desiring a second, from its own self brought out a spouse"). Some Upaniṣads include different creation stories amid myth and ritual teaching. But among all the many dimensions and indeed diverse Upaniṣadic conceptions of Brahman and *ātman*, yoga teaching stands out, not polemics in the manner of the *Brahma-sūtra*. Yoga is the way the self and Brahman are realized, not words, "not captured in speech" (*Kena Upaniṣad* 4).[14] According to Ādi Śaṅkara, who, admitting that this or that passage has a different concern, says the *overriding* Upaniṣadic interest is to teach a path to self-discovery, which is framed as *vidyā*, "knowledge" of a true "self," *ātman*. A lot is packed into the notion of this knowledge, including how one is to think of oneself, and others of course as well.

Thus, for us questions about Brahman and self and identity are primary interests. Is there a hidden self, and, if so, what is its character? Can we learn about the origin of the phenomenal world from yogic experience or from reasoning or both in combination? That is, is Brahman knowable by argument or meditation or in some other way? And what sort of "knowledge?" Much turns on distinguishing different kinds of "knowledge," along with how to understand meditational experiences said to transform one's sense of identity as well as to make known what is not otherwise accessible. There are also questions about Brahman's existence and nature, how evil is possible and, in particular, how Brahman can be "all-inclusive" without losing its essential nature as consciousness and bliss.

Action and "liberation"

Śaṅkara takes the "self," *ātman*, to be incompatible with action, and I take him usually to mean that awareness of cosmic connection inside is incompatible with action as ordinarily understood, that is, as motivated by desire for a certain result.[15] He also ties self-discovery to a peculiar and, Aurobindo would say, philosophically unfortunate cosmological supposition of recurring reincarnation for everyone except those who have achieved self-discovery. This or a similar idea occurs in almost all classical Vedānta and in other schools, including Buddhist. One of the prerequisites Śaṅkara finds is that a yogi should be *mumukṣu*, "intent on liberation," where "liberation" (*mukti*, sometimes *mokṣa*) is understood in terms of reincarnation, at least in part: your current identity is one of a series of embodiments that can—with diligent practice—terminate. This in turn is wedded to an idea of freedom from pain and suffering, *duḥkha*, as the end of the reincarnation series.

There is a moral dimension here. Many on the classical scene consider embodiment a precondition for pleasure (*sukha*) or pain (*duḥkha*), while the universe as a whole is thought to be arranged *justly* such that embodiment reflects "moral payback" (this view is emphasized in the Nyāya school: in your next birth you'll get a body—including a brain—you deserve, a configuration of characteristics such as hardiness or language ability, for instance). Buddhists, too, accept the moral-payback view of reincarnation although they have no governing arbiter of justice.

Aurobindo has his own theory of rebirth to which he gives positive spin, interpreting *mumukṣu*, "desire for liberation," as "aspiration," the desire of an individual for self-knowledge *along with* harmonization of all the parts of her being. This he understands as involved in the emergence of a normally hidden "psychic being," *caitya-puruṣa*, said to survive the body—like, we may note, the *sūkṣma-śarīra*, "subtle body," of classical Vedānta. Aurobindo endorses the idea of self-discovery as "freedom from pain and suffering" but without tying it to the reincarnation thesis.

To take an even broader view, we should note that whether "self," *ātman*, is at all an appropriate way to talk about "enlightenment" is a burning issue, partly because of the Buddhist teaching of "no-self," *an-ātman*, and "*nirvāṇa* experience" understood non-substantively and non-theistically to say the least. However, Vedāntins talk about "identity," *abhimāna*, in yogic practice in much the same way that Buddhists, in a practice context, talk about "no-self," *anātman*, it seems to me. Admittedly, in the arguments of the schools the metaphysics of a self, or of a no-self, is the hottest of issues. The main point for us, however, is that there is nothing negative—according to Śaṅkara and hundreds of other Vedāntins, though not without qualification Aurobindo—in the experience or state that is the goal of yoga practice, self-knowledge, *vidyā*. It doesn't matter what the state is called; it may well entail negation of the scope of words—"from which words turn back" (*Kena Upaniṣad*)—as is often claimed. But a view endorsed in all classical Vedānta is that realization of *ātman*, an inmost or most essential "Self," is entirely positive, a true *summum bonum*. Furthermore, Buddhism presents many parallels with central Vedānta claims, even, with that of *ātman*, the Mahāyāna core idea of *tathā-gata-garbha*, an "embryo" in each of us, or potency, to become enlightened. Aurobindo, for his part, tweaks Vedāntic *vidyā* in the direction of a meliorist metaphysics of embodiment, rejecting classical ideas of *mukti*.

Aurobindo emphasizes the compatibility, indeed the complementarity—according to him the central teaching of the *Īśā*—of self-knowledge and action. Śaṅkara thinks that self-discovery entails the absence of the configuration of desire, goal, effort, and, in particular, egoism—all factors he sees as required, as taught by the rival school of Mīmāṃsā—as making possible any action whatsoever. Note that the disagreement must be nuanced since Śaṅkara teaches the possibility of "living liberation," *jīvan-mukti*. Moreover, his "*mumukṣu*" requirement can be interpreted as a shift of identity to Brahman as self, a position Aurobindo endorses. Śaṅkara does not consider *vidyā* to be incompatible with being a living individual. And the yogic traits he explicitly identifies as conducive to self-discovery—"calm, control, and compassion," *śama-dama-dayâdi-yukta*—do not invariably include "wanting liberation," *mumukṣutva*.[16] It practically goes without saying, moreover, that there is much one has to do to become "calm, controlled, and compassionate." Doubtless, lots of behavior changes as one does *sādhana* (try to be "sattvic" in everything—in the spirit of the *Gītā*'s examples—is the categorical imperative). Still, to achieve true "knowledge" there is *nothing in particular* to do according to Śaṅkara except to do nothing, to be one's own awareness, the rest being taken care of by greater forces.

According to Śaṅkara, a transcendent psychological state is made available by way of a path of "knowledge" which involves a shift in how we think of ourselves. Other yogic prerequisites are identified as the meaning of the very first sūtra of the *Brahma-sūtra*, we learn—somewhat surprisingly, it seems to me, given the genre of the text—from his *Brahma-sūtra* commentary. Furthermore, Śaṅkara uses technical terms of yoga psychology throughout his corpus.[17] Although a commentary on the Vyāsa's *Yoga-sūtra-bhāṣya* (*c.* 500 CE) attributed to a "Śaṅkara" appears *not* to have been written by him before he became a Vedāntin (*Yoga-sūtra-bhāṣya-vivaraṇa*; Rukmani 2001: xi ff.), it is hardly a howler to take it as his, as have several scholars (e.g., Leggett 1981, Mayeda 1992). One task here is to try to parse the reasoning and the experiential accounts in the *Īśā* and in Śaṅkara's commentary, with Aurobindo as well, where the two strands are also intertwined. And both theorists face metaphysical knots, which it is important to identify and comprehend.

Meditation and "knowledge"

Whatever the merits of the metaphysics, the difficulties do not undermine reading particular Upaniṣadic texts as meditation manuals—plainly the *Īśā* and large parts of others, the *Kaṭha*, the *Muṇḍaka*, the *Śvetāśvatara*, the *Māṇḍūkya*, and more—which are yogic texts, indeed, the earliest yogic texts.[18] One can follow a phenomenological strand, although imagery may have to be worked with and the experiential separated out from broad lines of "top-down" reasoning.

It is easy to be misled about Upaniṣadic *vidyā*, "knowledge," as some Advaita subcommentators have been, taking it as an understanding of the worldview presented in the *Brahma-sūtra* and that only. Likewise, several modern scholars have mistakenly viewed the "knowledge" extolled by the Upaniṣads—and in the reading of Śaṅkara in particular—as intellectual, not as yogic and experiential, not something connected with a quiet mind and a shift in identity inwards but rather a mental picture whose sweeping propositions about reality are to be contemplated, elaborated, and defended against other propositions. There is a grain of truth in this perspective, since—again I repeat—Śaṅkara does reproduce lines of metaphysical reasoning that do indeed occur in some Upaniṣadic passages, elaborating at great length, and Aurobindo claims to *base* his metaphysics on meditation and special yogic experiences. With the *ācārya*, too, who conveys a living sense of self-realization, commentarial elucidation and philosophical reasoning are not the main story. Against this emphasis, the strongest evidence may be Śaṅkara's understanding of "scriptural" study as triggering self-knowledge. Possibly that's a mistake on his part, as the astute Rāmānuja (eleventh century) alleges in his own *Brahma-sūtra* commentary.[19] Rāmānuja stresses that the psychological event that is "self-knowledge" is not a matter of testimony, not knowledge brought about by words, but is akin to perception. However, I think Śaṅkara would agree, responding that if yogic prerequisites are in place mental contemplation of an Upaniṣadic *mahā-vākya* ("great statement") such as "You are That" *can* be the trigger although of course it need not be and in any case is hardly sufficient. Intellectual insight facilitates a change of *abhimāna*, "sense of personal identity," and disidentification is an old and important teaching. Clearly, Śaṅkara does not take "knowledge" of a supreme self to be merely intellectual.[20] Thus Rāmānuja's criticism seems unfair.

There is potentially vicious ambiguity in the Sanskrit word *vidyā*, usually translated "knowledge," ambiguity that is too often retained in translations using that English word. Several synonyms present the same problem, such as *jñāna*, sometimes translated "cognition" but in Śaṅkara's Upaniṣadic readings often having the same mystic meaning as *vidyā*. What kind of "knowledge?"—I want to ask those who write on these texts. Intellectual knowledge is hardly the same as the "knowledge" that results from meditation. And does not my cat *know* where the milk is? "Knowledge how" is distinct from "knowledge that," as taught by the later Wittgenstein (1951): the distinction suggests that not all knowledge is propositional, at least not immediately, no thought occurring. And unreflective, "animal" knowledge is now often distinguished from "reflective" knowledge in analytic epistemology, as indeed it is in Nyāya and other classical Indian schools. Appallingly, even some of the the best scholars (Nakamura 1982, 2004; Mayeda 1992; Pande 1994; Rambachan 2006) have failed to point out the ambiguity in their own uses of the word "knowledge," and confuse us with wrong assumptions about what Upaniṣadic *vidyā* is supposed to be.[21]

Sanskrit grammarians distinguish two types of negation: *paryudāsa* and *prasajya*, two senses of the negative particle *na*, "not": broad-scope and narrow-scope. A horse is not a candidate for a "non-*brāhmaṇa*," *a-brāhmaṇa* (narrow scope), but only something that is in the same class: a *kṣayatrīya* warrior is an *a-brāhmaṇa* (a non-priest) but not a horse except in the broad sense which is hardly ever used. But in the first line of the so-called "Hymn of Creation," *Ṛg Veda* 10.129, there is broad scope negation of a radical sort. It reads: "There was then neither being nor non-being," *na asad āsīn nô sad āsīt tadānīṃ*. Like a horse as not a priest but also not a non-priest, whatever there was "then" does not fulfill a condition for being the one way or the other, being and non-being, a pair that would seem to have the widest of applications and thus not admit broad-scope negation. In any case, Śaṅkara says the same thing about action/inaction and knowledge of the true self. Self-knowledge does not fulfill a condition necessary to be connected to agency whether the person be moving or not. The self is "not active" in the broad sense, categorially not connected to action, and not to inaction. Yet—and here may lie an error on Śaṅkara's part (Aurobindo claims it is)—the leap to the transcendent is thought to favor inaction in the narrow sense—to *meditate* is not to *act*—a path of knowledge that Śaṅkara contrasts with a path of "right action," *dharma*, of works. Whether he slides between the two meanings will be taken up in several chapters.

Among those with Vedāntic or neo-Vedāntic sympathies, Aurobindo is the latest of a long line of philosophy-cum-yoga critics of Śaṅkara on action. However, I think Śaṅkara's attacks on action have been misunderstood. And Aurobindo does not, I think, in fact distance his understanding of meditational discipline very far from Śaṅkara's. At least normally, one has to be still to go inside. The traits and abilities he takes to support yogic practice are not so different, at least not as much as he apparently believes. This is a central contention of mine. Convergences are far more significant than differences. There is a big difference in some cosmological theorizing that does ramify all the way down to contradictory yogic advice, I admit (much more about this later). But Śaṅkara should be seen as precursing Aurobindo in most important ways despite the difference. I intend to show major continuities, contrary not only to Aurobindo and his followers' take on Śaṅkara but also much scholarly opinion.

Modern studies of Vedānta

Among academic treatments of Śaṅkara, mine best lines up with that of Sarvepalli Radhakrishnan. The definitive study of the history of scholarship on Śaṅkara, both classical and modern, is Pande (1994), and before that great book Nakamura (1983, 2004; both books earlier in Japanese) and Mayeda (1992, 2006). These scholars, however, tend to get it wrong when it comes to an overview of Śaṅkara's teaching. For example, Mayeda seems to miss Śaṅkara's theism altogether. Although Mayeda and Nakamura do identify psychological themes, they, too, like Pande, fail in many instances to appreciate the difference between the "knowledge" touted in the Upaniṣads and an intellectual understanding of interlocking propositions. Aurobindo is generally sensitive to the difference, but the great poet/yogi himself sometimes misreads Śaṅkara as making a metaphysical claim when the purport can be seen as psychological and practice-oriented. Let me add that Maharaj (2020) is an excellent treatment of Aurobindo's study of the *Īśā Upaniṣad* but draws too sharp a contrast between a hermeneutics attributed to Aurobindo (in five principles discussed in Chapter 4) and an imputed "eisegetic" reading by Śaṅkara (condemned for projecting preconceived views). With painstaking unpacking of the commentaries on verses 6 and 7 in particular, on "self-discovery," we'll see that Maharaj is also unfair to Śaṅkara.

The *Īśā* is a composite work in that at least five of its eighteen verses occur in earlier literature such as the *Ṛg Veda* and the *Bṛhadāraṇyaka Upaniṣad* (some verses also appear in later Upaniṣads as well as the *Bhagavad Gītā*). For this study, the *Īśā* is to be read as a unit since both Śaṅkara and Aurobindo take it that way, not to mention countless others over the centuries. The aim here is not to reconstruct the hoary history of the *Īśā*'s composition but rather to scrutinize how it has been read by the two Vedāntins against the backdrop of modern scholarship.

Aurobindo vs Śaṅkara

Aurobindo attacks an "illusionism" he attributes to Śaṅkara in his *magnum opus* of philosophy, *The Life Divine* (1941/1973, especially Book Two, Part One, Chapter Six, "Reality and the Cosmic Illusion"). But crucial terms such as *vidyā* and *avidyā* in Śaṅkara's usage are mainly psychological as opposed to cosmological in an effort to tell us "the way the world is."[22] Perhaps had Aurobindo studied Śaṅkara's *Brahma-sūtra Commentary* and not just his Upaniṣad work, he would have seen that the philosopher is a realist about the things we encounter in the everyday world, not an illusionist. Illusion is a metaphor used to contrast ordinary experience with self-discovery. Perhaps, as suggested by King (1995) and others, Śaṅkara progressed intellectually and changed his mind. But it is one thing to say that *compared* to "self-discovery" ordinary experience *seems* to be of the unreal; it is quite another to say that it is actually an illusion in the terms of the everyday world. One has to keep in mind a "two-truths" doctrine, ramified in both Buddhist Mahāyāna and Vedānta. To be sensitive to the non-cosmological, to the yogic phenomenology, is a major goal of this book. Śaṅkara seems to say in his *Īśā* commentary that living in the "divine light" there is not much you do, at least by the ordinary (and Mīmāṃsaka) understanding of *doing* something. There is a quantum leap, and I don't think that Aurobindo, *au fond*, much disagrees, despite a rejection of Śaṅkara's notion of "liberation," *mukti*, as the truth of self-discovery cosmologically.

This book is framed around Aurobindo's translation of each of the *Īśā*'s eighteen verses along with a translation of each verse differently following the different reading of Śaṅkara as laid out in his commentary translated in Appendix B. All this is done against the backdrop of modern scholarship. Convergences and divergences of these two, or three, ideative streams are the focus of the essays. Appendix A presents the Upaniṣad with the two readings side by side.

No attempt is made to engage the controversies and advances in Advaita metaphysics by Śaṅkara's followers, although Sureśvara, an immediate disciple, and Vācaspati, a more distant follower who brings out well the theistic as well as the yogic side of Śaṅkara, are truer to the master, in my opinion, than the rival subschool of Padmapāda and Prakāśātman. I agree with Richard King (1995) that the "illusionist" *vivarta* view of Prakāśātman and company is not embraced by Śaṅkara, and insofar as he is committed to a story about the origins of the universe—a case can be made that he is not[23]—it is to a realist monism later dubbed *pariṇāma-vāda*, which is a theistic emanationism in plain view in the *Brahma-sūtra*.[24] Thus, there has to be a "supreme" and "non-supreme" (*para* and *apara*) Brahman, as, I think, Aurobindo has to hold, too, despite protestations to the contrary.

One further figure needs introduction, Gauḍapāda (*c.* 650). Tradition has it that Śaṅkara was a student of one of his students, belonging to the same lineage (*sampradāya*). Gauḍapāda is commonly accused of crypto-Buddhism and of dragging Śaṅkara into a world-denying "idealist" metaphysics. However, King (1995) shows this is wrong, and I find it easy to read Gauḍapāda's elaborations of the *Māṇḍūkya Upaniṣad*'s discourse on states of the self as phenomenological. It is hardly idealism but mystic "anti-intellectualism" (*nêti nêti*)—especially the Vedāntic and Buddhist idea of "two truths"—along with yoga psychology that is of greatest interest with Gauḍapāda along with, historically, a complex relationship to Buddhism, as King shows.[25] In any case, this early Advaitin apparently wrote on the short *Māṇḍūkya* a total of 215 verses, called *kārikā*s, on which Śaṅkara wrote commentary, that is, according to Advaita tradition (some scholars disagree).[26] But whatever is the right view of Śaṅkara's relation to Gauḍapāda, Aurobindo early in his Vedānta study read and translated the first twelve of these *kārikā*s *along with* Śaṅkara's commentary in part.[27] In other words, Gauḍapāda's *kārikā*s were studied by Aurobindo—at least some of them—in his late twenties *along with* the commentary of Śaṅkara, which was, for the first twelve *kārikā*s (matching the verses of the Upaniṣad), in part translated by him in a typed manuscript not published in his lifetime. That the *kārikā*s are an important influence for later Advaita Vedānta is commonly recognized, if not perfectly understood. Fortunately, to focus only on Śaṅkara—and Gauḍapāda as called for—makes it easy to study Aurobindo's criticisms of Śaṅkara without too much digression. The only classical Vedāntins we can be sure Aurobindo read are Gauḍapāda and Śaṅkara along with three much later Vedāntins, Ānandagiri (*c.* 1300) and Vijñānabhikṣu (*c.* 1575)—who wrote subcommentaries on Śaṅkara—and Sadānanda (*c.* 1500), a handful of whose verses from the *Vedānta-sāra*, "Essence of Vedānta," Aurobindo translated in a very early manuscript (1902) left unrevised and unpublished in his lifetime. It may be true that in understanding the *Īśā* he lines up with classical "theists" such as Madhva and Vedānta Deśika (for their *Īśā* commentaries see, especially, Magnone 2012). Placement of Śaṅkara and Aurobindo within the broader history of Vedānta is not the purpose here but rather critical exploration of two readings of the *Īśā Upaniṣad*, one by a famous classical Vedāntin and the second by a famous neo-Vedāntin who took himself to oppose the other but who endorsed much of the upshot of the former's teaching, as will be shown.

1

Who is Addressed by Śaṅkara, Who by Aurobindo?

We begin with contextualization of the two readings of the *Īśā* along with what Upaniṣads are and Vedānta philosophy, along with short bios for the two commentators. It is important to be mindful of certain features of Śaṅkara's audience, Aurobindo's as well, although Aurobindo is practically our contemporary and writes in English.

Ancient and classical India was home to what may be called "yogic" traditions, although *śramaṇa*, "ascetic," is the word used by scholars most prominently. These traditions are of great breadth and duration—Hindu, Buddhist, Jaina—and stretch back here and there to root "Vedic" texts earlier than any Upaniṣad. The *Veda*—the word *veda*, like *vidyā*, is often translated "knowledge"—is enormous, and its main parts, which may be as early as 1500 BCE, are problematically continuous with even the old, classical Upaniṣads, which are centuries later.[1] The range of Vedic topics is vast, and any sweeping characterization is almost bound to be wrong.[2] Nevertheless, the full Vedic corpus contains not only insinuations or traces of asceticism in the oldest hymns but also, in each recension, each *śākhā* ("branch"), one or more Upaniṣad, appended from around 800 BCE. So-called "Vedic" Upaniṣads (others are composed much later, outside Vedic inheritances) form parts of the four Vedas—the *Ṛg*, *Yājur*, *Sāman*, and *Atharva Vedas*—at the "end," *anta*. Hence at least certain Upaniṣads are literally *vedānta*, the "final portions of the Veda" (fusion of the two short vowels '*a*' resulting in the long '*ā*' in "Vedānta"). They are also, according to Vedāntins, the "end" (*anta*) of the Veda in a more profound sense, "the intent," "the Veda's *objective*."

An Upaniṣad may be defined as a crisp prose or verse composition suitable for meditation and consciousness discipline. In the early Upaniṣads themselves, the word "*upaniṣat*" means something like "secret teaching."[3] Śaṅkara wrote commentaries on ten Upaniṣads, which are sometimes called the "principal" Upaniṣads, but there are four or five more that are about as old and as widely cited as some of his set. And he quotes five in addition to the ten. These fifteen or so "classical" Upaniṣads were composed most probably between 800 and 200 BCE. Many more instances of the Upaniṣadic genre appear over the centuries, up to our own day. Deussen counts sixty Vedic, that is to say, "authentic," Upaniṣads; others 108, and still others more than 300.[4] Aurobindo composed in Sanskrit what his followers call an Upaniṣad.[5] But the attention of classical Vedāntins such as Śaṅkara—and also of philosophers in other subschools—remained on fourteen or fifteen early Upaniṣads including the *Īśā*.

Then among these most well-known Upaniṣads, the *Īśā* is not the oldest, nor the most influential for Vedānta philosophy. Popular English translations tend to place it, according to estimation of date relative to other Upaniṣads, in the middle of the old set. But with eighteen verses it is the second shortest, and typically placed first in traditional collections in Sanskrit. We may order Śaṅkara's ten chronologically (although this is not how he thought of them): one Upaniṣad's priority to others is pretty easy to determine but scholars are not so sure about the precise date for any of them out of a range of about six centuries: the *Bṛhadāraṇyaka*, *Chāndogya* (two long, prose Upaniṣads), *Taittirīya* (also prose), *Aitareya* (prose), *Īśā* (verse), *Kena* (verse), *Kaṭha* (verse, with a prose first part), *Muṇḍaka* (verse), *Praśna* (verse), and *Māṇḍūkya* (prose). A commentary on the *Śvetāśvatara* (verse) is traditionally ascribed to Śaṅkara, but it was probably written by someone else, say scholars who count it and also sometimes the *Maitri* (prose) as belonging to a "principal" group.

Ideas from these texts shape not only the Vedānta school but several other philosophies, classical Indian philosophies, that is to say, which are complex, multi-dimensional systems of thought (metaphysics, epistemology, logic, ethics, philosophy of language), expressed in "classical" Sanskrit, which as a language is a little different from the Sanskrit of the early Upaniṣads and quite a bit different from the Sanskrit of the oldest parts of the Veda. Of course, most notably Upaniṣads shape the "Vedānta" school, which is named after them, a worldview centered in "Brahman" considered as an all-constituting but also transcendent reality. Note that the classical school is "Vedānta" in a different sense than when the word is used for the Upaniṣads or their teachings. The philosophic school is defined by the *Brahma-sūtra* (*c.* 200 CE) and commentaries, along with independent treatises by philosophers aware of the *Brahma-sūtra*'s systemization of Upaniṣadic teachings. As a philosophic school with an enormous literature, classical Vedānta runs up to modern times.

The core texts of the philosophic schools originate much later than the early Upaniṣads, from about 200 BCE. Philosophic texts are characterized by assertion and argument, whereas Upaniṣads themselves, though presenting arguments, rarely elaborate except in practice terms (find for yourself this Brahman that is matter, life, mind, etc., as per the *Taittirīya Upaniṣad*). Although the emergence of schools of philosophy stretches back more than 2,000 years in some instances, several schools begin much later. Most flower in the later centuries of the pre-modern age: Mīmāṃsā (the oldest), Vedānta, Nyāya, Vaiśeṣika, Sāṃkhya, and others including important tantric, Buddhist, and Jaina schools, all debating one another on issues of metaphysics and epistemology for as much as 2,000 years. We may note that Vedānta with its subvarieties (Advaita, Viśiṣṭâdvaita, and so on) has of any school by far the most extensive Sanskrit literature, although some of the other schools also have Sanskrit texts in the hundreds.

Ādi Śaṅkara, the "original" Śaṅkara, also referred to as "Śaṅkarâcārya," Śaṅkara the "Great Teacher," a South Indian, lived in a religiously tumultuous seventh or eighth century, after the dissolution of the Gupta empire in the north but before the Chola empire in the south, during a period of cultural and political fragmentation.[6] He is said to have become proficient in Sanskrit grammar and much traditional *śāstra* at a young age, a child prodigy. Ironically, against the backdrop of the grown man's insistence on the incompatibility of "knowledge" and "action," he was apparently a very active person, writing extensively (or dictating) and also travelling to the four corners of the subcontinent—Badrinātha, Dwarkā, Śṛṅgeri, and Puri—where, tradition has it, defeating Buddhists and Mīmāṃsakas in open debate, he established four great temple traditions and yogic lineages, *sampradāya*. Śaṅkara must have had contemporary and near contemporary predecessors in composing Upaniṣadic commentaries, but we have only the short work of Gauḍapāda (*c.* 650), his *Kārikā*s, which purport to explain the twelve sections of the *Māṇḍūkya Upaniṣad* but also add a lot.[7] Śaṅkara's Upaniṣadic commentaries are, unlike the *Kārikā*s, no pithy aphorisms. They are elegant but also laborious, often glossing practically every word in the targeted text. The learned author is said to have died at the young age of thirty-two. Personally, I find this detail of the traditional biographies dubious (as have others, such as Nakamura 1983), since Śaṅkara shows mastery of a large literature including an enormous amount from other schools.

Extensive hagiography prevents real biography, but some things can be surmised from Śaṅkara's writings, and not just from their content but from the fact that they are written in Sanskrit and presuppose an audience that could read the language and follow some complex lines of thought.[8] Śaṅkara's corpus is large, although many works ascribed to him were probably written by people eager to promote his theses or versions of them. There is scholarly consensus that Śaṅkara's long *Brahma-sūtra-bhāṣya* is the touchstone whereby the authenticity of other attributed works is to be judged. Whether or not this is the best policy, I follow Mayeda (1992) in taking the *Upadeśa-sahasrī* along with the *Gītā* commentary and the commentaries on ten Upaniṣads as well as that on the *Brahma-sūtra* to have been composed by the same person. It is more controversial, however, whether this person wrote the *Gauḍapādīya Commentary*. Nevertheless, not only did this the premier Advaita Vedāntin write the oldest Upaniṣadic and *Gītā* commentaries that are extant (excepting Gauḍapāda's brief composition), but he also authored the oldest extant commentary on the *Brahma-sūtra*.[9] And one final note: whatever Śaṅkara's reputation from the perspectives of the warring Vedāntic subschools (and modern critics), it is undeniable that his Sanskrit prose is a model of excellence: a master stylist is he.

Almost all of Vedānta's literature is later than Śaṅkara. In light of the deluge that comes after him, it is tempting to see him as anticipating later quarrels, but we should not think that he has in mind fellow Vedāntins as he addresses his readers, Vedāntins, say, of different persuasions on certain issues. It is wrong to see Śaṅkara as writing for an *intra*scholastic audience. His audience is *inter*scholastic, and his major assumption about his readers is, I think, not that they are already Vedāntins but that they know, or at least know about, the mainstream teachings and practices of Vedic ritualists, the "priests," the *brāhmaṇa*s, who could read Sanskrit (few in lower castes could), many actually performing the rituals as their occupation, so to speak. Often when Śaṅkara denigrates action, it is my view that he has in mind, one, an obvious conflict between meditation and, at the same time, any other goal-directed undertaking, but also, two—and in the larger view of the conduct of one's entire life—Vedic rituals as interpreted by Mīmāṃsakas, rites colloquially referred to as "actions," *kriyā*, sometimes as "what ought to be done," *kārya*. These "Exegetes," I think, he takes to be the "Veda-mongers" condemned in the *Gītā*. Legend has it that the great Mīmāṃsaka writer Maṇḍana was converted to Vedānta by Śaṅkara. Be that as it may, it is easy to imagine a Mīmāṃsaka interlocuter, though no one is mentioned by affiliation or name. For the Mīmāṃsaka, the whole of a person's life is to be regulated by rules prescribing actions to be performed from morning till night, the particular nature of which would depend upon the performer's social circumstances, such as age, sex, and caste. In Sanskrit, you can practically hear a Mīmāṃsaka object to Śaṅkara's extolling meditation that he, or she, or anyone, has *duties* to perform, with no time for "navel-gazing." Doing one's duty as prescribed in the Veda is the way to human felicity, not the meditation on self-awareness required by Śaṅkara's way of "knowledge."

The *Mīmāṃsā-sūtra*, which is early as philosophic *Ür* texts go (c. 200 BCE), provides, with the commentary by Śabara (*c.* 300 CE), a characterization of action in general which is refined by later Mīmāṃsakas such as Kumārila (*c.* 660, a near predecessor of Śaṅkara's) and Prabhākara (reputedly Kumārila's renegade pupil). Now, it is not true that in the Upaniṣadic, *pre*classical literature a call to meditate is ever clearly said to override everyday duties as traditionally enjoined. But Śaṅkara does show by Upaniṣadic citation that a transcendence of the sphere of action to be discovered by "turning within, away from desire and action" is indeed taught, and taught as incompatible especially with the rituals prescribed for and by priests. Again, Śaṅkara did not invent the issue, and it includes but is broader than Mīmāṃsaka positions. It is crystalized in the *Gītā* as the teaching that any sort of action prompted by desire for a selfish end is to be given up in order to take a yogic attitude. This is coupled with the further teaching that to take a yogic attitude is to act "for the good of all beings" (*sarva-bhūta-hīte ratāḥ*). "Disciplined in yoga, fight" (*yoga-yukto yudhyasva*) is a refrain of Kṛṣṇa, the yoga teacher, and perform acts effectively ("yoga is skill in action," *yogaḥ karmāsu kauśalam*). And whether Śaṅkara is right about how the *Gītā* purports to harmonize its teaching of *karma-yoga*, the "yoga of action," with the way of knowledge he finds extolled in the *Īśā* and elsewhere, the Advaitin is pellucid on one point: the yoga of works *prepares* one for the path of knowledge.[10] Works build character, especially the works done as *karma-yoga*, which demands sacrifice for the general good (*loka-saṅgraha*). The most dramatic difference between Śaṅkara and Aurobindo may well be Aurobindo's insistence that certain character traits are good in themselves and not just in their instrumental value for self-discovery. But is it really true that Śaṅkara sees a trait such as *ahiṃsā*, "non-injury," as valuable *only* as instrumental? In his *Gītā* commentary and elsewhere, he says that a person acting with true self-knowledge sets an example for others (3.20–1). This ethical theme is taken up in Chapter 3.

The *Gītā* is the most important text for the relation of knowledge and action—mystic "knowledge" and everyday action—in yogic traditions, in Vedic traditions of ascesis, that is to say. But Śaṅkara does seem right to point to Upaniṣadic passages that are earlier and, to his mind, possess greater authority, in the *Bṛhadāraṇyaka* especially, as well as the *Īśā*, as we shall see. And he can be read as taking to heart the *Gītā*'s excoriating "Veda-mongers." This is, I repeat, one key to his reading of the *Īśā*. However, my main contention is that we may presume that Śaṅkara is writing mainly with ritualists in mind, people who know Mīmāṃsā, or at least writing for contemporary high-caste colleagues, who would at least know *of* ritualist, Mīmāṃsaka teachings whether or not themselves practicing. I contend that Śaṅkara does not intend for his psychological metaphors such as *māyā*, commonly rendered "illusion," to be understood as having cosmological import, at least not as much as many, including Aurobindo, assume. In his *Īśā* commentary, in sum, Śaṅkara is a yoga guru using terms psychologically more than he is a theorist about the way the world is. His main task is to lay out the phenomenology of self-discovery and of the path. Pande writes (1994: 112) in support of what seems to be the misjudgment on the part of several scholars that Śaṅkara is the author of a commentary on the *Yoga-sūtra-bhāṣya* of Vyāsa: "It must also be remembered that Śaṅkara is invariably described in the traditional accounts as a great *Yogin* who had immense *vibhūti*s [psychic powers]." That commentary may not be by Ādi Śaṅkara, but the clearly yogic text, the *Upadeśa-sāhasrī*, "A Thousand Teachings," is, as has been convincingly shown by Mayeda.[11] And so we should not be surprised that he reads the *Īśā* as at least in part a yoga manual.

A word about Vedānta as an intellectual movement, as we shift our focus to Aurobindo. As a label "Vedānta" has fuzzy boundaries. Not simply referring to a philosophic school arising about 2,000 years ago in a context of rival intellectual systems, there is a "neo" version. *Classical* Vedānta is a system built on Upaniṣadic views abstracted into a web of interlocking positions mainly by the *Brahma-sūtra*. As indicated, it is a long-running school, with a literature running from the *Brahma-sūtra* (*c.* 200 CE) through hundreds of texts on into our own era. We may say that the classical trails off into the modern with the emergence of "neo-Vedānta" expressed in English and modern vernaculars as opposed to the Sanskrit of the classical school. The classical literature divides over time into seventeen or more sub-allegiances, the classical Vedāntic subschools, individuated principally over the issue of the nature of Brahman in precise relation to the individual. Neo-Vedānta arises under the influence of science and Western ideas as well as the fourteen or so earliest Upaniṣads and the *Gītā*. Neo-Vedāntins break with the classical school in several ways, but remain similarly focused on Upaniṣadic teachings. Along with Aurobindo (1872–1950), Swami Vivekananda (1863–1902), Mahatma Gandhi (1869–1948), K.C. Bhattacharya (1875–1949), Sarvepalli Radhakrishnan (1888–1975), and some other prominent authors are referred to as "neo-Vedāntins."

Sri Aurobindo, born "Aravinda Ghose"[12] in Kolkata (Calcutta) in 1872, has about thirty volumes of writing in a "Centenary Edition" (*SABCL* 1973) including translation and commentary on the *Īśā* (v. 12).[13] His principal works are *The Life Divine* (v. 18 and 19), *The Synthesis of Yoga* (v. 20 and 21), and the epic poem *Savitri* (v. 28 and 29). His work is in English, with a little in Bengali, and, as noted, he composed an *upaniṣat* in Sanskrit.

Aurobindo's Bengali family was wealthy and locally prominent. His anglophile father was one of the first native Indians to receive medical training in England. In 1879, Dr. Ghose took his family there, including his wife, that is, when Aurobindo was seven. Along with two brothers and under the guardianship in Manchester of a clergyman named Drewett and later Mrs. Drewett when the pastor left for Australia in 1884, Aurobindo remained in England until returning to India in 1893. This was after a stellar career as a scholarship student first at St. Paul's in London and then a couple of years at Cambridge University where he won a prize for Greek composition. Aurobindo is arguably the best-known Western-educated intellectual championing Upaniṣadic theses in the modern era. His audience at the time included educated Indians—most people could not read English—along with Westerners interested in yoga and meditation and Indian philosophies. Eventually his major works were translated into all the major Indian languages—and classical Chinese, French, German, and more. In his milieu, Aurobindo was not the only distinguished neo-Vedāntic author, and, in my judgment, Sarvepalli Radhakrishnan's translations of Upaniṣadic passages (1953) are often more elegant. But Aurobindo's, too, have fine poetic merit, generally speaking, although most were done in the earlier part of his career. Most importantly for us, he is able to weave ideas from the *Īśā* into interconnected positions in metaphysics and epistemology along with yoga and ethics.

Upon landing in Mumbai (Bombay) in 1893, Aurobindo, whose father had died, did not initially go back to Kolkata. After a short stint as a secretary and an academic in Vadodara (Baroda), he began practicing yoga and by his own account had in 1904 a "silent mind" experience during a three-day meditation session with a yogi named Lele. A little earlier, he had turned his attention to the nationalist politics of independence, and in 1906 settled in Kolkata where he became famous for apparently seditious articles in local English and Bengali newspapers. Arrested in 1908 for conspiring against the British Raj in the form of a plot to murder the chief justice (one Englishwoman was killed in an attempted bombing), Aurobindo, then among the most prominent of local leaders, was acquitted in 1910 in a spectacular trial (one of the judges was a Cambridge classmate). He nevertheless judiciously relocated to French India and the southern city of Pondicherry (the British police had issued another arrest warrant). There he announced in the Chennai (Madras) newspaper, *The Hindu*, retirement from politics with the intention to pursue yoga and "spiritual experience." A growing number of followers took residence in Pondicherry, but Aurobindo removed himself in 1926 from management of the "Sri Aurobindo Ashram" that had formed around him. Ironically given his emphasis on action in yoga practice, he did not emerge from a suite of three or four rooms from 1926 on until his death in 1950. His principal publications run from 1914, beginning in a serial journal of yoga and "synthetic studies of speculative Philosophy" (Heehs 2008: 270), *The Arya* (the word did not at the time have its current negative connotation), 1914 to 1920, leaving the epic *Savitri* unfinished (but only by a section or two). He revised his magnum opus of philosophy, *The Life Divine*, in the 1940s as well as a long expiation on karma yoga, "The Yoga of Divine Works," in *The Synthesis of Yoga*. Compared to his work on the *Īśā*, his other Upaniṣadic translations in the serial journal went largely unrevised.

Aurobindo worked on an *Īśā* translation over a long period. He appears to have read the Upaniṣad upon his return to India, having studied Sanskrit at Cambridge in the early 1890s. Most probably he did so *along with* the commentary of Śaṅkara, which in many cases can serve as a dictionary giving synonyms for unfamiliar words. Printing was well advanced in India as elsewhere by the end of the nineteenth century, and Sanskrit texts were available in book form. We do not know precisely what Aurobindo read, but it is easy to tell that he read the *Īśā* commentary of Śaṅkara. In his translation's first note, he disputes at length Śaṅkara's reading of verse 1 (*SABCL* v. 12: 63), the dialogue continuing in two more lengthy footnotes. In the best biography to date, Heehs (2008: 71) says that Aurobindo "read the texts [Upaniṣads] along with the commentaries of Gaudapada and Shankaracharya," and refers to an early manuscript (1902–4), unpublished during Aurobindo's lifetime, where the young writer says (*SABCL* v. 12: 427):

> To modern students there can no better introduction to Vedanta philosophy—after some brooding over the sense of the Upanishads—than a study of Gaudapada's Karikas and Shankara's commentary with Deussen's *System of the Vedanta* in one hand and any brief and popular exposition of the Six Darshans in the other.

(Deussen was a great admirer of Śaṅkara.) In the same passage, Aurobindo also mentions the Vedāntins, Ānandagiri (*c.* 1300) and Vijñānabhikṣu (*c.* 1575), who lived in the late classical age. My own opinion is that the two had little impact on Aurobindo's views as expressed in publications from his time in Pondicherry. But that is not the case with Śaṅkara.

At first blush, Śaṅkara and Aurobindo show sharp opposition on key topics, especially action and knowledge or, better, action and "self-awareness," or "Self"-awareness with a capital "s." But this is not, I think, correct. Despite Aurobindo's assault's on Śaṅkara's readings and despite, in his major work of philosophy, *The*

Life Divine, an extended attempt to refute what he takes to be Śaṅkara's "illusionism," *māyā-vāda*, the two, on close inspection, have very similar outlooks overall, surprisingly concordant in their understandings of the *Īśā Upaniṣad* and a great deal more. For a prime example, Aurobindo's positions on "knowledge" (*vidyā*) and action are easily misread as entirely world-affirmative, and Śaṅkara's are misread by many—including Aurobindo—as way too world-denying. The overall case I'll make softens the conflict one might presume just from reading Aurobindo and all the more from various scholarly treatments. To be sure, Śaṅkara finds a path to self-discovery that centers on a meditating, "witness" self to be superior to *karma-yoga*, the "yoga of action," which looks to be a path *championed* by Aurobindo following the *Gītā*. However, Śaṅkara's partiality should not be elevated to a metaphysical level, not thought to flow from a metaphysics of illusionism. The result of this study will be to bring Śaṅkara and Aurobindo closer together as Vedāntins and metaphysicians than is commonly supposed—two Vedāntic metaphysicians of meditation—and this despite the counterevidence in the form of explicit criticism of Śaṅkara's views, or what are taken to be Śaṅkara's views, by Aurobindo himself.

Such reconciliation is indicative of the overall unity of Vedānta as a worldview, is my sense, to take the widest overview. Informing this study is, notably, much of Radhakrishnan's work, especially the 900-page *The Principal Upaniṣads* (1953 in the Muirhead Library of Philosophy where eighteen Upaniṣads are translated along with copious notes), as well as commentaries by other Sanskrit authors, belonging to other Vedāntic subschools. However, differences among the readings, which are often subtle, cannot detain us lest the current effort be a series of volumes. It is nevertheless worth mentioning that many of the so-called "theistic" subschools of classical Vedānta precurse the views of Aurobindo and, also like him from time to time, unjustifiably criticize Śaṅkara, as though, for example, he was indeed a "crypto-Buddhist," as famously alleged (Potter 1981: 13). He is not. He is a theist, or, better, panentheist, like all Vedāntins (the pan*en*theism combining pantheism with a view of Brahman as in some way transcendent with respect to the world).

Aurobindo criticizes Śaṅkara on the purported incompatibility of knowledge and action, but has, I think, misread the Sanskrit author. Other schools of classical philosophy largely distort the issue, it seems to me; everyday agency provokes one position or another along with different theories of the "knowledge" (*vidyā*, *pramā*, *jñāna*, *buddhi*) required. The controversies loop over into the yogic in many instances. The school of Nyāya, for instance, finds critical reasoning crucial to a yogic endeavor. The goal of *samādhi*, "yogic trance," is thought to reveal a self as distinct from the body and mind. To help one maintain a sense of the distinction, one needs the philosophic knowledge that is established by argument (*Nyāya-sūtra* 4.2.46).

Then there is Sāṃkhya, which promotes disidentification from the body so that consciousness can know itself as it is in itself, separate from nature. This sounds a lot like Vedānta but there is an important difference. Briefly, it is that there can be—or, I should say, there is, according to both our two Vedāntins, not just Aurobindo—*divine* action, action inaugurated by the Lord (*īśvara*). Classical Yoga is a step closer to Vedānta, and both Śaṅkara and Aurobindo, though staunch advocates of yoga practices, reject the metaphysics of the *Yoga-sūtra* which is a form of Sāṃkhya. Nevertheless, as several have pointed out, Śaṅkara seems to embrace a Sāṃkhya-*like* dualism of consciousness and nature with regard to self-knowledge.[14] This is true but let us not fail to appreciate the *theistic* dimension of Śaṅkara's views, theism bringing together the two realms. Classical Sāṃkhya is famously atheistic. Like at least portions of the *Gītā*, Śaṅkara does indeed appear to embrace something very close to *seśvara-sāṃkhya*, "theistic Sāṃkhya," with equal stress on the two words. The Lord, the One, "looses forth" distinct emanations: *puruṣa*, "consciousness," and *prakṛti*, "nature." In this way Śaṅkara may maintain monism; there are at least two emanations from Brahman, one of consciousness, the other of nature. (Śaṅkara, Aurobindo as well, actually finds several emanations.)

The worldview of Patañjali's *Yoga-sūtra* is slightly different from the *seśvara-sāṃkhya* of the *Gītā*, and Patañjali is commonly read as *not* having a place for "divine" action. But the *Yoga-sūtra* seems incoherent on the issue, to consider (a) its embrace of "perfections," *siddhi*s, most of which are extraordinary capabilities of action, alongside (b) its dualist system that has action on the side of nature (*prakṛti*) while consciousness (*puruṣa*) as only a witness. But, to repeat, it is the Mīmāṃsā outlook that Śaṅkara seems usually to have in mind when he talks about action, and we shall look closely at the question of the generality of his remarks. Conceptual tensions in ideas about Brahman sometimes do indeed force him to make unintuitive claims. But when Śaṅkara denigrates action to a realm of "ignorance," we, to be fair, have to ask not only what sort of "knowledge" he has in mind but what sort of action, the rituals of the Mīmāṃsakas or another kind? All action? I think not. We have to keep in mind Śaṅkara's audience, namely, scholars trained in Sanskrit many of whom were also trained in rituals.

Both Aurobindo and Śaṅkara distinguish appearance and reality, and do so in both metaphysical and psychological terms, also in terms of value. The distinction is, we may say, fundamental in various ramifications in practically all Vedānta and Buddhism. Discovery of a supreme "Reality" is what is most valuable; contact with Brahman has supreme worth (*ānanda*) where its supreme existence (*sat*) and consciousness (*cit*) are also known. Everyday action where the agent acts out of personal, egoistic interests (*abhimāna*) falls on the side of appearance and is delusory—"delusory" in a deeper sense than having false or distorted beliefs, somehow an experiential deficiency as well as of identity, according to both Vedāntins. Both also say, however, that knowers of the self would still act "in order to set standards" (*Gītā* 3.21). And on the side of "delusory" appearance (*prapañca*), there is *karma yoga* available as a bridge between human and divine action, according to Aurobindo. Śaṅkara, too, sees right action as preparing one for self-discovery, though not, as mentioned, as necessary. But *for both* there is the Lord's own on-going creativity, including our "sunlit" paths, to use a locution of Aurobindo's, although only Aurobindo, and not Śankara, would count that as *action*, *kriyā*.

Like the process philosophy of A.N. Whitehead and its panentheism, the two Vedāntins view all instigations to action as "divine" in the broadest sense, animal desires emanating from Brahman as well as spiritually transformational energies, the ever-active "Grace" or "Shakti" of the Lord, according to Aurobindo and, so argues Malkovsky (2001) (among others), Śaṅkara. The Upaniṣads themselves are like this, says the Advaitin; an Upaniṣad is like a compassionate guru leading us to self-discovery (Halbfass 1983: 51–2). It is also worth noting that, in a conception of the *Yoga-sūtra* (*YS* 2.21), *prakṛti*, nature, is said to be *in the service* of *puruṣa*, the conscious individual, forcing, in time, a person to do yoga, that is, to do what's necessary for the highest *samādhi*, that is, for the supreme good of self-discovery. Both Śaṅkara and Aurobindo show traces of the Sāṃkhya idea: Aurobindo suggesting that nature eventually will provide the right desires (the desire to practice yoga), Śaṅkara viewing the path as having a natural inevitability. I repeat that although Śaṅkara sees the *Gītā*'s way of action, *karma-yoga*, as inferior to the yoga of "knowledge," he sees it as preparatory for the higher circuit. Aurobindo stresses that a *karma yogin* does not act to gain personally the fruit of the act—Śaṅkara entirely agrees—but acts with a mindset of "giving" and to maintain "harmony in the worlds" (*loka-saṅgraha*, *Gītā* 3.20), playing one's "righteous" part (*dharma*) according to the situation (*Gītā* 3.35, 18.47), all serving the even higher end of self-discovery. Aurobindo no less than Śaṅkara sees everyday action motivated by personal gain as delusory in a deep, existential way involving wrong identification, that is, action motivated by desire for wealth, sex, and/or power (cf., the *Bṛhadāraṇyaka*'s "threefold craving for children, wealth, and *loka*, 'worlds,'" *putra-vitta-loka*, *Bṛ* 3.5.1, often echoed by Śaṅkara including in his comments on the very first verse of the *Īśā*). Yet never is Aurobindo accused of being a Māyāvādin, an "Illusionist."

In sum, the teachings of Sri Aurobindo appropriate much of Ādi Śaṅkara's, and we know that Aurobindo studied Śaṅkara's commentary on the *Īśā*. Aurobindo's own commentary on the Upaniṣad may not have quite the same voice as that of the "mature" author of the 1940s, where Śaṅkara and "illusionism" appear practically as straw men for polemics in metaphysics. Nevertheless, the continuities in the two readings of the *Īśā* reveal much about Vedānta in general, and the metaphysics of meditation and self-identity in particular, as well as the perspectives of two great authors, and, presumably, something about the Upaniṣad. There appears to be continuity in the phenomenology of yogic endeavor and experience and perhaps in some metaphysical ramifications of "self-experience," despite lesser important differences.

2

"Blocked Out" by the Lord or "Integrated?"

Īśā 1, 2, and 3

Radhakrishnan (1953: 567–70) rendering *Īśā* 1–3:

1. (Know that) all this, whatever moves in this moving word, is enveloped by God. Therefore find your enjoyment in renunciation; do not covet what belongs to others.

2. Always performing works here one should wish to live a hundred years. If you live thus as a man, there is no other way than this by which karman (or deed) does not adhere to you.

3. Demoniac, verily, are those worlds enveloped in blinding darkness, and to them go after death, those people who are slayers of the self.

Thieme (1965: 89–92):

1. All this that moves on earth (= all living beings) is to be dwelled in by (= is the abode of) the LORD. Therefore you should nourish yourself with what is abandoned (voluntarily ceded to you); you should not covet anyone's property.

2. Do strive to live here (in this earthly world) a hundred years (that is: throughout your whole life) as one who is just (that is: without "attachment") doing his actions;/ Thus—not otherwise than this—your action actually does not smear off on you.

3. "Demoniac" are called those worlds, they are covered with blind darkness—to them those people go after death who are killers of souls (or: "a soul").

Śaṅkara (see Appendix B):

1. All this is to be blocked out by the "Lord," *īś*, whatever is moving in the moving world./ By that renounced, you should enjoy (the Lord, *īś*). You should not yearn for anyone's wealth.

> 2. Just in doing works here in this world, one may desire to live a hundred years./ Thus it is so—not otherwise than this—that karma sticks not to you as an individual.
>
> 3. "Ungodly" are those other worlds, with blinding darkness covered./ And it is to them, on deceasing, that self-slayers go.

Aurobindo (*SABCL* v. 12: 63–4):

> 1. All this is for habitation by the Lord, whatsoever is individual universe of movement in the universal motion. By that renounced thou shouldst enjoy; lust not after any man's possession.
>
> 2. Doing verily works in this world one should wish to live a hundred years. Thus it is in thee and not otherwise than this; action cleaves not to a man.
>
> 3. Sunless are those worlds and enveloped in blind gloom whereto all they in their passing hence resort who are slayers of their souls.

The most problematic word for understanding the first three verses of the Upaniṣad is *īśā* itself—"by God" (Radhakrishnan), "by the LORD" (Thieme), etc.—since each Vedāntic subschool—and translator!—seems to have an at least slightly different interpretation. But there are other words that are just about as difficult, in verse 1, "*tyaktena*," "by that renounced," which is tough for Aurobindo, and "*vāsyam*," right after "*īśā*," "to be blocked out," which prompts a brilliant, or at least dramatic, expansion of meaning by Śaṅkara.[1] Then in verse 3, "*ātman*" in "*ātma-hano janāḥ*," "people who are self-slayers," calls for ingenuity on the parts of both our subject commentators. How is it even possible, given the metaphysics of either Aurobindo or Śaṅkara, that there be "slayers of their souls" or a "slayer of self?" Thieme thinks this might refer to suicide, but both Śaṅkara and Aurobindo take the phrase to be metaphoric, and, perhaps surprisingly, they interpret it in much the same way. There is the difference, of course, that Śaṅkara is telling us how "scripture," *śruti*, would lead us to self-knowledge, whereas Aurobindo says he sees in the verse not necessarily his own view but one that, like his, flows from meditative experience. On the most important point, however, there is agreement: the world of the those who have self-knowledge is illumined, that is, is neither "sunless" nor "ungodly," neither negative applying. There is yet important difference, which, when made plain, will carry us deep into two versions of Vedāntic monistic theism.

First let me point out that *Īśā* verse 3 presents a telling example of disagreement that is prima facie only. Hume (1931: 362) renders it, apparently following Śaṅkara:

> *Devilish* are those worlds called,
> With blind darkness covered o'er!
> Unto them, on deceasing, go
> Whatever folk are slayers of the Self.

And Hume (1st ed. 1887/2nd ed. rev. 1931/1971: 362), who seems to have relied on the findings of the German sanskritist, Paul Deussen (1883), remarks that a variant of *asurya,* "devilish," is *asūrya,* "sunless," which is how Aurobindo takes it (with putative justification: *SABCL* v. 12: 64, note 1). My translation, trying to follow Śaṅkara, takes "*asurya*" to be correct:

> "Ungodly" are those other worlds, with blinding darkness covered.
> And it is to them, on deceasing, that self-slayers go.

Aurobindo:

> *Sunless* are those worlds and enveloped in blind gloom whereto all they in their passing resort who are slayers of their souls.

One might think that the different readings of "sunless" (Aurobindo) and "devilish/ungodly" (Śaṅkara) reflect a holistic difference in the attitudes of the two interpreters, Śaṅkara viewing action in general as meaningless, and worse, as distracting and preventing self-discovery, and Aurobindo seeing action as compatible with it, the sunless worlds being those, like ours, where many fumble in the darkness of "Self-ignorance." But I think the two understand the verse largely in the same way. Śaṅkara says that even the gods count as "ungodly" in the symbolism of the Upaniṣad if they do not know the self (*ātman*), and Aurobindo's "sunless" worlds are also peopled by those lacking "Self-knowledge." If the two are understanding this kind of "knowledge" concordantly, then the difference between "sunless" and "ungodly" is insignificant.

Yet there is significant difference concerning survival. Aurobindo explains verse 3 (*SABCL* v. 12: 77)[2]:

> By departing from the physical life one does not disappear out of the Movement, but only passes into some other general state of consciousness than the material universe.
>
> These states are either obscure or illumined, some dark or sunless.
>
> By persisting in gross forms of ignorance, by coercing perversely the soul in its self-fulfillment or by a wrong dissolution of its becoming in the movement, one enters into states of blind darkness, not into the worlds of light and of liberated and blissful being.

Śaṅkara (from Appendix B):

> The result of being spiritually aware is characterized by awareness of the self as not subject to old age and death. So for whom that awareness is, as it were, "slain," it is hidden. Thus those who are like that, who are "spiritually ignorant" as discussed, are called "self-slayers," "slaying" self-experience. For by fault of the self-slaying they are reborn in those worlds again and again.

Śaṅkara's view of survival is simpler than Aurobindo's in that the Advaitin talks about a "subtle body," *liṅga-śarīra*, as an entity which, like the physical body and mind, is separate from the self as is realized in "liberation," whereas Aurobindo makes central to "divine life" a *developing* subtle body or, as he says, "psychic being." A psychic being is an individual centered in a "psychic entity," a soul in a karmic process of forming bodies/dispositions/personality in several "worlds," physical, vital and emotional, mental, and more, simultaneously.[3] This is how, more precisely, Aurobindo would explain evil on panentheist premises, that is, as necessary to the development of "psychic beings." The developmental dimension of Aurobindo's theory is the most significant difference in the views of the two Vedāntins, in my opinion, although even there we have to be careful not to oversimplify Śaṅkara's stance. Śaṅkara insists, for example, that the development of character through yoga and the performance of good works can secure the circumstances needed for self-discovery, whether in this lifetime or the next.

Compared to Aurobindo, however, Śaṅkara is not much interested in character development—especially not across lives—except, again, as character is important to the attainment of self-knowledge. Thus, he has an *instrumentalist* theory of virtue, at least that's how it seems. Later, I want to explore the idea that Śaṅkara is simply and consistently silent about the possibility that certain character traits could *reflect* self-discovery, reflect the true "self," *ātman*. In any case, Aurobindo sees certain virtues as reflecting "psychecization" (a neologism of his invention) and yogic accomplishment. Indeed, building individual personality and skills is, according to him, just about as worthy a pursuit, depending on the person and circumstances, as self-discovery. The underlying assumption seems to be that the unitive nature of the self makes individuality fragile, difficult to forge, requiring many lives. Aurobindo lays out a theory of "spiritual evolution" of "sparks divine" where self-knowledge, as understood by Śaṅkara, is central but hardly the whole story of cosmic becoming.

Thus, for Aurobindo in commenting on verse 3—and apparently *reading in* his grand view, and offending the "non-eisegenic principle" touted by Maharaj (2020) to show the superiority of his reading to Śaṅkara's (a view addressed in

Chapter 4)—one "slays" the self *not only* by retarding discovery of an essential self or "God" (Brahman) *but also* by retarding the *psychecization* of the body, life, and mind. A subtle body that survives death is said to be shaped by enterprises and experiences, by one's "karma," on both accounts. But if it is possible to get a handle on the *Īśā* apart from how Vedāntins have understood it, then Aurobindo's reading of verse 3 does seem anachronistic compared to Śaṅkara's.[4] It is my view that in finding this "soul-making" expressed—the Upaniṣad foreshadowing John Keats and Romantic philosophy—in finding this chiseling out of spiritual individuals, "psychic beings," Aurobindo shows Western influence. However, he says he got the idea of progressive psychecization from the *Īśā*. And it is at least possible to read the verse Aurobindo's way. The difference between the two readings is not as great as it may now seem, since, as discussed, for Aurobindo "sunless" worlds would be those where, in Vedāntic terms, the inhabitants do not have the special knowledge, *vidyā*. Both commentators would agree about that, though their readings seem continents apart superficially.

Moreover, both stress the difference "self-knowledge" makes for an after-death journey. Actually, it is not so much death and rebirth but living in self-knowledge, or not, with which each is most concerned. The "Lord," *īśvara*, takes care of embodiment and re-embodiment, both assert. According to Śaṅkara, there is nothing you really need to do, except to stop doing those things that prevent self-discovery. But Aurobindo, interpreting Śaṅkara, and others, as promulgating a world-denying illusionism, sees the Upaniṣad targeting them too—and not only those thwarting what's needed for "self-experience"—when he says, "wrong dissolution of its [a soul's] becoming in the movement." In other words, he sees the Upaniṣad as warning against an extreme asceticism that would retard psychecization. Aurobindo reads Śaṅkara as promoting a world-denying asceticism that he railed against in his nationalist days as retarding India's *political* development. My sense is that Śaṅkara's reading is not so ascetic as Aurobindo thinks.

Now at the very end of *The Life Divine* Aurobindo leaves open the possibility that a psychic being dissolve back into the One from which it emanated.[5] But apparently the normal course—emphasized dozens of times in that treatise and in other works—of an individual, or incipient individual, in reincarnating is progressive development of "soul personality." That is, one develops more or less enduring and individual features on several planes or dimensions of Brahman's "manifestation," physical, vital, mental, and "supramental," to use his terms.

So, Aurobindo reads "self-slaying" in the *Īśā* as more than retarding knowledge of a true self, to include what he sees as false prophets preaching a world-denying enlightenment. This may be the source of his misreading of Śaṅkara, because a careful reading shows Śaṅkara hardly the ascetic traditionally pictured.[6] In any case, Aurobindo, echoing Mahāyāna Buddhists' condemnation of the selfishness of a saint becoming a *pratyeka-buddha*, a "solitary Buddha" (who is thought to dissolve individuality in the Void), presents his own version of the contrary Mahāyāna ideal of the "Bodhisattva." In becoming a Bodhisattva, a person continues to take form and birth for the good of everyone—an ideal Aurobindo praises explicitly in *The Life Divine* (1973, v. 18: 40). Here he also shows some influence of nineteenth-century progressivist and evolutionary ideas of European philosophy, though sensitivity to science as the major difference with Śaṅkara is easily overemphasized in my opinion.[7] Still, as might be expected given the nationalism of Aurobindo's earlier career, the yogic warrior Kṛṣṇa is the ideal touted much more than the quietest Buddha, also King Janaka as he takes him to be depicted in the *Bṛhadāraṇyaka Upaniṣad*.[8] Śaṅkara does not countenance such "soul-making" except as required for experience of the true self *along with*, as he says in his commentary on the *Gītā*, setting an example "to hold together the worlds," *loka-saṅgraha*.

Nevertheless, Śaṅkara's Vedānta is not as escapist as portrayed by Aurobindo. Śaṅkara has a different target in mind in reading verse 3. He finds a different warning: Don't put your hope in the "heavens" (*svarga*) touted by ritualists. Those worlds are just as lacking in value as this life without self-experience compared to life with self-experience. So don't put your trust in the heaven or fortunate reincarnation said to be secured by performing Vedic rites. For Śaṅkara, "self-slayer" is a metaphor indicating that not living in self-knowledge is so bad it's like hurting yourself (the Sanskrit root √*han* is elastic, not restricted to "(to) kill" but sometimes meaning simply "(to) harm"). Śaṅkara's message is that one should aim at self-knowledge. In that light, that is, in "enlivening through meditation the true self" (*satyâtma-bhāvanayā*)—which is the supreme value (*paramârtha*)—everything else is secondary, for that everything is "to be renounced" (*paramârtha-satyâtma-bhāvanayā tyaktaṃ syāt*).

Aurobindo does not disagree. He, too, claims that for a person nothing is more valuable than "self-discovery." He says as much in many, many places. For example, in the epic poem *Savitri*, the heroine, Savitri, at a crucial plot point experiences the cosmic self:

It was her self, it was the self of all,
It was the reality of existing things,
It was the consciousness of all that lived

And felt and saw; it was Timelessness and Time,
It was the Bliss of formlessness and form.
It was all Love and the one Beloved's arms,
It was sight and thought in one all-seeing Mind,
It was joy of Being on the peaks of God.

SABCL v. 29: 555.

For Aurobindo, it is not all a matter of self-discovery, however, and he takes the word *ātman* in verse 3 in a wider sense than Śaṅkara, to include psychic development. Yet he, too, holds out knowledge of a true self as the supreme goal of yoga. Of course, most of us do not attain any kind of mystical "enlightenment" or even try, and thus Aurobindo's seems a kinder interpretation than Śaṅkara's. For Aurobindo, "All life is yoga" (*The Synthesis of Yoga*, *SABCL* v. 20: 4), in the sense that all life is a psychic adventure while "yoga" is "living right," maximizing psychic influence, forging psychic individuality. This echoes tantric ideas such as everyone's being on the path of Śiva (whether knowing it or not).[9] Not initiated as a tantric and untrained in tantric practices, Aurobindo nevertheless speaks favorably of the tantric movement (for instance, *The Synthesis of Yoga*, *SABCL* v. 21: 37–8).[10] Although there is no evidence he studied Abhinava Gupta and cohorts, Arabinda Basu of the Sri Aurobindo International Centre for Education in Pondicherry advanced over a long career the proposition that of all classical views the closest affinity to Aurobindo's is Abhinava's tantric Śaivism. Be that as it may, it is Śaṅkara's Advaita that he seems to follow in promoting self-discovery as the best thing that can happen to anyone. It is the premier goal of the practice he advocated.[11]

Verse 2 draws upon the ancient psychological theory of "karma" (to use the anglicized word; *karman* in Sanskrit) understood to be mental dispositions with a dimension of "moral payback." Everything that one does creates, or reinforces, mental and bodily dispositions called in yogic texts "*saṃskāra*". Dispositions are properties that become evident only under certain conditions, like water's disposition to boil at 100°C.

Often thought of as memory impressions, including "muscle memories," *saṃskāra* firings are said to be tinged with pleasure, pain, or indifference, working, it seems, like a computer program to enable goal-directed action and the development of habits and skills. Repetition deepens the grooves, but a single evil act can seriously lessen overall merit: *saṃskāra* have axiological coefficients that work like magical vectors, and some acts, though not repeated in kind, can have such a large negative, or positive, score that a previous sum may be dramatically altered. (Don't murder your mother!) Some *saṃskāra* are said to shape personality and proclivities even in a future birth—these would seem to be those developed in crafts—and not only in the current lifetime (translife *saṃskāra* are called "*vāsanā*" in the fourth chapter of the *Yoga-sūtra*). This aspect of the common karma theory, the "skills" aspect, is underappreciated, it seems to me. Much more famously, karma affect one's future in rewards and punishments, not in making personality. The universe is justly arranged, particularly in reincarnation. This is a mainstream teaching, elaborated in practically all the schools. There is moral payback. The moral coefficients that attach to *saṃskāra* affect future behavior not only in the form of pleasures and pains but also in the very make-up of your body (including your intelligence) in your next birth along with personality traits.

Let me stress that such twofold influence of karma is not only a Vedāntic position but is promoted in other schools, notably Nyāya and the *Nyāya-sūtra* as well as the non-Vedic schools of Buddhism and Jainism. According to Buddhists who recognize no "Lord," *īśvara*, no arbiter of translife justice, the moral dimension of karma works like a magnet by attracting circumstances appropriate to the karma's ethical nature as well as in the patterns of activity that it—or they, the *saṃskāras*—provoke and guide. A murderer is prone to be reborn as a murderer, and a musician as a lover of music, and karma is not only a common assumption among classical philosophers of different stripes, it is discussed in a number of early Upaniṣads (dramatically at *Bṛhadāraṇyaka* 3.2.10 and 4.4.1–6).[12]

The "karma" conception is background for both Śaṅkara's and Aurobindo's readings of the second verse of the *Īśā*. But there is a striking divergence, not apparent at first. All four translations quoted above are similar concerning karma not having negative payback if there is the "right action" referred to at the end of verse 1 ("not coveting anyone's property," maybe also living on charity, as Thieme reads *tyaktena*, "by the renounced"). In particular:

Radhakrishnan:	karman (or deed) does not adhere to you
Thieme:	your action actually does not smear off on you
Śaṅkara:	karma sticks not to you as an individual
Aurobindo:	action cleaves not to a man

A hallmark of self-knowledge is commonly said to be "freedom from karma." For example, in the *Bhagavad Gītā*, Kṛṣṇa, apparently speaking from self-knowledge, says: "Works, karma, do not smear off on me; nor do I long for any result of action, for any result of karma. The person who realizes that I am thus is free from karma herself."[13]

Śaṅkara takes the way of meditative knowledge tied to self-discovery to be better than action of any sort, or, if meditation is itself a kind of action, of any other sort, including the *karma-yoga* extolled in the *Gītā* (and by Aurobindo). The goal is, after all, a special awareness, not something to be accomplished. And though character development seems on the whole secondary and instrumental for Śaṅkara, that's not the case when he speaks as a yoga guru in the *Upadeśa-sahasrī* and elsewhere or, for example, when he explains Kṛṣṇa's teaching in the *Gītā*. Furthermore, the *Gītā* itself indicates that self-knowledge transforms character, for example, at *Gītā* 4.36–9, where, in a figure of a boat on a choppy sea along with a person of the very worst character, self-discovery is said to wipe clean bad and even evil habits while good habits are provided somehow magically.[14] Still, Śaṅkara reads the "works" of *Īśā* verse 2 as rituals and distinguishes the audience targeted as those not seeking to know the self, an audience different from the audience targeted in verse 1 who are on the way of knowledge. Here Aurobindo's reading departs sharply from his. Maharaj 2020 argues pretty cogently that on verse 2 Aurobindo is right. However, Aurobindo may read in more of his meliorist metaphysics than is necessary. Let me explain.

Deep-set in the Vedāntic view why the Lord did not create the "best of all possible worlds"—to use the catchy phrase of Leibniz (mocked by Voltaire)[15]—is the karma concept; that is to say, the karma concept informs a "free-will theodicy" along with a consequent voluntarism. God allows a great range of choice but is also by nature *just*, such that virtue is rewarded, and sin gets its due (Śaṅkara's theodicy is presented in Appendix D in a translation from his *Brahma-sūtra Commentary*). Vedānta embraces a similar view where reincarnation has the soteriological function of the Christian "heaven and hell."

Freedom flows from the nature of Brahman, according to Aurobindo, who, however, does not think that self-determination through choices is the whole story or even the most important factor in psychic development. To an extent, he agrees with the modern existentialist mainstream that we make ourselves by making choices, but his emphasis is on self-shaping from the inside, and choice is only one ingredient. Here he joins a broad swathe of classical theory inherited by neo-Vedāntins, a view entirely in tune with Vedānta's emanationist cosmology which is "self-generative." The extreme view of modern existentialism is perhaps best pronounced in classical India in Kashmiri Shaivism. Śiva's last level of self-determination comprises the choices that you and I make along with the ensuing activities. Remarkably, much the same idea is expressed by Whitehead as the "consequent nature of God," each "actual entity" having at least some slight self-determinative freedom, with God "prehending" it all in an immediately subsequent act of comprehensive being and knowledge and allure for future choices. My sense is that Aurobindo would severely qualify such an emphasis on choice in tune with what we may call a "spiritual naturalism": it is Brahman who is responsible, largely, for what we are, not us.

The existentialist theme that we make ourselves through our choices if applied to the classical Indian doctrine of karma and reincarnation would have at least one momentous outcome: the chooser would have to survive and somehow, on some after-death "plane," learn from the choices made and their karmic outcome. Otherwise, no schema of karmic punishment and reward would make sense.[16]

Aurobindo, however, voices skepticism, even sarcasm, about popular teachings of karma and reincarnation, breaking from tradition, a departure marking his "world-affirmativism," to use again the common label. King Janaka in the *Bṛhadāraṇyaka Upaniṣad* is his example of an active person very much living in the world as opposed to an *āśrama* or hermitage, an active being who nevertheless lives in immediate awareness of the true self. As mentioned, what Aurobindo calls "psychecization" is championed both philosophically and as an ideal for life, a transformation of proclivities in the direction of Brahman's essential nature which is thought of by him as something like Plato's "Good." Not just ethical sainthood but creativity that turns things and events into delightful beauty and art are supposed to be the direction of the influence of inner divinity, a "psychic being," the presence of Brahman, one's "soul" that can feel intimately oneness with others and more. Aurobindo's cosmology of a developing "divine life" features the psychic being, said to be normally below the threshold of waking consciousness but turning us towards the "Light" and the "Good," coming to the "surface consciousness" in knowledge of the *ātman* whose delegate in the composite person it is. Or, more precisely, it is a "psychic entity" developing soul personality to become a "psychic being." Here there is somehow, according to Aurobindo, a sense both of universality and becoming an individual.

All this does indeed show a positive view of, especially, reincarnation (rebirth is something good since it allows possibilities of psychic development across lives), which is a view that does indeed contrast with the negative take on rebirth that we find in practically all classical Vedānta, at least as far as I am aware, including Śaṅkara. Nevertheless, with Śaṅkara—and much Buddhism as well as other Vedāntic subschools—too much emphasis can be given by interpreters to the idea of "freedom," *mukti*, it seems to me. All told, in the case of our two commentators and many other classical philosophers on point as well as modern neo-Vedāntic gurus, the contrast is not so sharp as to merit a "world-affirming, world-denying" distinction. That is, with all the details about practices recommended spread out, Aurobindo's position does not stand out. Sāṃkhya is commonly cited as a world-denying metaphysics, a trenchantly dualist philosophy putting all value on the side of consciousness, none in nature. But in the details Aurobindo's "psychecization" is on a continuum with Sāṃkhya "sattvacization" (to use the coinage of Sāṃkhya scholar Ian Whicher), in that both recommend generally what today is called "mindfulness" along with saintly ethical qualities such as *ahiṃsā*, "non-injury." However, Aurobindo does hold up *creativity* of various sorts as worth fostering, even for those following a yogic path, actually especially for *sādhaka*s, those filled with "aspiration" (his version of "desire for liberation," *mumukṣatva*). Thus, there is some truth to the opinion (e.g., Maharaj 2020) underlining opposition to the quietism of Advaita here, showing Aurobindo lining up with other Vedāntic subcamps, to consider the classical scene, along with Kashmiri Śaivism. In any case, lines of creative action are thought to flow up from Brahman, our true self, and our choices in small ways help to make an increasingly glorious, translife, progressively individual self. Aurobindo's is a philosophy of a "both/and," but his teaching of yoga practices is not dramatically different from Śaṅkara's.

Aurobindo's positive view of life resonates well with the end of *Īśā* verse 2, "Doing verily works in this world one should wish to live a hundred years" (his translation). But he does not take this is a license for much of anything (some may lament). Again, Aurobindo seems about as ascetic as any mountain meditator in the details of his prescriptions for yoga, which would be "right action," "dharmic yoga." It's that his ideal mountain meditator is also a poet or the like. Note that Aurobindo himself spent far the greater part of his literary life, particularly in the last decades, composing poetry, joining, by the way, a long and venerable tradition of poet/philosophers with Vedāntic sensibilities including the great Śrīharṣa and indeed Ādi Śaṅkara himself, granting with Mahadevan (1980), Pande (1994), and others that he authored even one of the poems and hymns to him ascribed. The idea of the yogi as a "seer/poet," a *ṛṣi*, emerges in Śaṅkara's comments on verse 15 and in Chapter 7 we'll give it a lot of attention.

In any case, we should now better be able to understand the different readings of verse 1 of the *Īśā*. According to Śaṅkara, the world is to be "blocked out" by self-realization, by "self-knowledge," where one's identity is no longer a desire-filled "I" of action. The self-knower may appear to act but transcends the world of ordinary action, whereas according to Aurobindo worldly activities and energies are to be "integrated" into psychic personalities being formed over lifetimes. The view of "liberation" extolled in classical Vedānta—and by Śaṅkara—is rejected by Aurobindo. *Mukti* is not, according to him, the goal most worthy of yogic pursuit, not as understood cosmologically.[17]

Thus, it turns out that background metaphysical assumptions do indeed make a difference here for reading the Upaniṣad. In Sanskrit, the optative, *jijīviṣet*, which is used in verse 2, in the phrase, *jijīviṣec chatāṃ samāḥ*, "desire to live a hundred years," could have the weak meaning of permissibility that Śaṅkara sees—in effect, "It's okay to live out the normal life span for a human being," that is, more literally, "one may wish to live a hundred years"—but, depending on context, it could also have the strong moral force of an injunctive, and if not strong *moral* force, then strong *prudential* force: "You should try to live a full hundred years." I admit that Aurobindo's "one should wish to live a hundred years" rings a little truer to my ear. In any case, there is nothing detrimental in karma, the *Īśā* seems to be saying, if one acts, "works," in the right ways.

3

The Whole in the Part

Īśā 4 and 5 and the *maṅgala-vācana*

Thieme (1965: 93):

> 4. The One (i.e., the *brahman*, the original principle that is identified with the "Self"), though not moving, is swifter than the mind: even the Gods did not reach it (catch it) when it was running in front. Though standing, it overtakes others, running ones. Wind puts water in it.
>
> 5. It moves: it does not move; it is far: yet it is near by. It is inside everything: yet it is outside everything.

Radhakrishnan (1953: 570, 571):

> 4. (The spirit) is unmoving, one swifter than the mind. The senses do not reach It as It is ever ahead of them. Though Itself standing still It outstrips those who run. In It the all-pervasive air supports the activities of beings.
>
> 5. It moves and It moves not; It is far and It is near; It is within all this and It is also outside all this.

Śaṅkara:

> Not moving the One is swifter than the mind. The gods do not catch it, which goes ever in front./ Standing still, it surpasses everything else though speeding along. It is that in which Mātariśvā puts the waters. || 4 ||
>
> That moves, that moves not. That's far, that's near./ That is on the inside of all this, of all this that is on the outside. || 5 ||

Aurobindo:

> 4. One unmoving that is swifter than Mind, That the Gods reach not, for It progresses ever in front. That, standing, passes beyond others as they run. In that the Master of Life establishes the Waters.

> 5. That moves and That moves not; That is far and the same is near; That is within all this and That also is outside all this.

There is a change of meter with verse 4 and a lengthening of lines from sixteen to twenty-two syllables. This supports a change of topic, from ethical/prudential advice to metaphysics. Verse 5 returns to the sixteen-syllable meter of verses 1 through 3, but the topic remains metaphysics, how *brahman* is to be conceived, if indeed that is possible.

Digging into our two Vedāntins' comments on verses 4 and 5, one might—at first blush, as with verse 3—take the readings to contrast sharply, with little agreement beyond understanding certain words in their regular ways. To be sure, there is an important difference in spin, one positive, the other negative. But both Vedāntins appear to appreciate the peculiar "logic" of the Brahman concept, which, to make a quick comparison, seems like the "Dao" concept in Daoism, which, like "Brahman," is suggested, if not expressed, to be a unification of contraries. Let us begin with Śaṅkara but bring in Aurobindo right away.

To itself, Brahman as self-illumining consciousness stands self-revealed. Brahman is the "self," *ātman*, in what is the self's essential and natural state, immediate, as with us, but "non-dual," *advaita*. This idea connects with the doctrine of *anirvacanīyatva*, "inexplicability," much promoted in later Advaita.[1] Śaṅkara does not deny that the self relates, beyond its character as immediately self-aware, somehow further to the body and the physical world. There may well be relations, but they are impossible to elaborate fully.[2] That is, self-illumining consciousness may be connected to material states; it is nevertheless not connected in a way that can be determined in thought. But guided by the traditional authority of the Upaniṣads augmented by rational argument, we form a conception to aid our yoga practice aimed at self-discovery.[3] Then, fundamentally, we think of Brahman as a unity, as our own immediate self-awareness but that of everything else too, that is to say, we think of Brahman as a pervasive conscious being, partly because of arguments for holism and the organic interconnectedness among beings and things—wholes are not reducible to their parts and everything seems related to everything else—but, according to Śaṅkara, primarily because unity is the message of "the wise" (defined as those who discovered the self as Brahman). We'll take all this up in the next chapter.

Whatever the epistemic foundations, Brahman, the "One," is conceived as indivisibly omnipresent and consequently does not "move." Here the broad-scope type of negation, *paryudāsa*, would appear to apply. As remarked, a horse is not a "non-*brāhmaṇa*, a "non-priest" (*a-brāhmaṇa* in Sanskrit); only a *kṣyatrīya* warrior or a person of another caste can be said to be "not a priest" in the narrow sense. A horse is neither a priest nor a non-priest, except in the broad sense. Brahman neither moves nor "moves not," since the Absolute does fulfill the preconditions for movement.

However, there is also an overlapping secondary sense. Śaṅkara suggests "moving" can be read as a metaphor for, as he says, "departure from the natural state," stating that Brahman eternally or, better, transcendently, remains Brahman. (This idea may be a source for the *vivarta* view of Padmapāda and Prakāśātman.)

The obvious question is then: How is our world of *nāma-rūpa*, of individual beings and material things, even possible? Given that Brahman does not depart from its natural state, what is the best answer to this question? The *Brahma-sūtra* opens with the thesis that Brahman is not just the world's original agential but also its on-going material cause, its very "stuff," *upādāna*. How then can Brahman both remain Brahman and include the world?

Aurobindo's answer centers on the "logic of the Infinite." He devotes about thirty-five pages to the notion in *The Life Divine* chapter, "Brahman, Purusha, Ishwara—Maya, Prakriti, Shakti" (*SABCL* 18: 322–64). There may appear to be incompatibility between (a) Brahman's being the One with an unchanging essential nature and (b) Brahman's being everything finite and delimitable. But according to Aurobindo, the central theme of the Upaniṣad is reconciliation of apparent opposites, and there are two "sides" to Brahman that, by the logic of the Infinite, are not really opposed conceptually in application to the "Infinite," although language, being normally about things finite, makes it *seem* like an irreconcilable opposition (*SABCL* 18: 324):

> Into the central fact of the two sides of the nature of the Absolute, the essential and the self-creative or dynamic, no real contradiction enters; it is only a pure infinite essence that can formulate itself in infinite ways. One statement is complementary to the other, there is no mutual cancellation, no incompatibility; it is only the dual statement of a single inescapable fact by human reason in human language.

According to Aurobindo, Śaṅkara goes wrong in viewing the dynamic side of Brahman as illusion and giving the word *māyā* the negative spin that implies trick or delusion, whereas, he says, the right way to undertand the *māyā* of the Upaniṣads (and the *Gītā*) is as a *power* of Brahman, Brahman's power of "self-delimitation" or "self-measurement": the Sanskrit root √*mā* can indeed mean "to measure," as Aurobindo points out, making a contrast with the negative connotation associated with Śaṅkara.[4] Our world of diversity is part of the dynamic side of Brahman, which is no illusion, despite what classical Advaitins claim, says Aurobindo.

But here is what Śaṅkara actually says in commenting on *Īśā* 4:

> It is certain that the One is motionless, and it is also certain that it is "swifter than the mind"—seemingly a contradiction—but no fault occurs in that what is without accidental attributes can appear to have them. In its native form, that which is beyond attributes is said to be "not moving," the "One."

That is, Brahman *can appear* to have "accidental attributes" whereas in its "essential nature," *sva-rūpa*, it transcends them. Is this so different from Aurobindo's idea of the *Infinite*? We should remember that Aurobindo, too, accepts that we live in "spiritual ignorance," *avidyā*, unless we know ourselves as Brahman as Brahman is *in its essential nature*, an enlightened state termed "(self-)knowledge," *vidyā*.

It is core Vedāntic teaching that Brahman has become each one of us, and Śaṅkara does not shy away from asserting that Brahman, as each one of us, has, as we have, our experience.[5] The deep meaning of the *Īśā*'s idea of the whole in the part is that, while there may be other emanations, each of us as a self is Brahman in a special way, as our very self-awareness and the immediacy of our consciousness (a yantra could be a good model). And we can know this ("Thou art That") existentially right here in this life, in this world, *jīvan-mukti*, through yoga practice. The living individual loses any sense of individual identity in breaking through to what Aurobindo would call "cosmic consciousness" and Śaṅkara "knowledge," *vidyā*, along with the familiar cosmological terms used for the cessation of transmigration (*mukti*, etc.).[6] This is the right way to read Śaṅkara, in my opinion. There is a tendency to make him too insistent on transcendence, among both classical and modern scholars, too insistent on transcendence at the expense of immanence.

Śaṅkara is not much interested in the metaphysics of individuation. There is no ever-lasting individuation, a view, to which Aurobindo as also a monist, would agree. But in contrast with Śaṅkara he does see it as a power of Brahman to self-individuate and become seemingly separate consciousness centers, accomplished by something similar to the yogic ability of "exclusive concentration" (*ekāgratā*, "one-pointedness of mind"). Brahman has nothing to work with except itself, but the power to self-limit, to "exclusively concentrate," is inherent.[7] Aurobindo sees "cosmic consciousness" as the divine power of "exclusive concentration" put in reverse.

Śaṅkara, like Aurobindo, finds two sides to Brahman. Despite some scholarly complaints to the contrary, Śaṅkara accepts that Brahman includes us and everything finite and limited, though not, as we are, as subject to "spiritual ignorance," *avidyā*.[8] Of course, this is only in Brahman's non-essential nature, on that "side," and, furthermore, for an individual, *avidyā* can be overcome. In his comments on verse 4:

> The nature of this all-pervasive self is that it is without accidental attributes. It excludes, in its proper form, all characteristics native to transmigratory existence. Although its nature is absolutely unchanging, the One experiences, as it were, all sorts of changes in the transmigratory realm, changes formed as accidental attributes.

Thus, here the central difference between Aurobindo and Śaṅkara is whether the power so to appear is something positive or negative *from our perspective*. And since all negativity is bound up with our perspective as "spiritually ignorant," according to both Vedāntins, even that difference can be overstressed. Our failure to "realize" our essential self, to know it immediately, experientially, is a negative according to the modern yogi as well as to Ādi Śaṅkara. Moreover, for Śaṅkara everything about Brahman is positive, and thus so too its power to appear limited, to take "the view from nowhere," so to say. Admittedly, this is not stressed by the classical Advaitin who is, as I have now many times maintained, mainly concerned to teach us a way to self-discovery.

So, despite complaints that the "Māyāvādins" over-intellectualize, building castles in air (a common disparagement among Aurobindo's followers), it is more Aurobindo who dares pronounce on the metaphysics of Brahman, cashing out what he calls the "logic of the Infinite," to include the material world. Advaita's "transmigratory realm," *saṃsāra*, he sees as something positive, while also maintaining the Vedāntic premise of Brahman's unity and transcendence. He sees all this as the message of verses 4 and 5 of the *Īśā*. He writes in *The Life Divine* (*SABCL* 18: 335–6):

> Whatever astronomic or more than astronomic figures you heap and multiply, they cannot overpass or exceed that Oneness; for, in the language of the Upanishad, it moves not, yet is always far in front when you would pursue and seize it.

Yet again we find Śaṅkara saying pretty much the same thing. For instance, in the midst of defending the causal thesis which stands at the very heart of his *Brahma-sūtra-bhāṣya* (a thesis to be taken up by us rigorously in Chapter 5), Śaṅkara reads sūtra 2.1.24 as first entertaining an objection based on the idea of Brahman's essential unity ("*[Your causal thesis is] false, because common experience shows causality to require a collection of factors*") and then rejecting it ("*Wrong. For, it is like milk*") by bringing out a "logic" that surely resonates with what Aurobindo calls the "logic of the Infinite." The passage is worth quoting at length:

> (Śaṅkara, *Brahma-sūtra-bhāṣya* 2.1.24:) Brahman, who is a conscious being, "one without a second," is the cause of the world. This (our central) thesis is not possible according to the objection voiced in the sūtra. Why? Well, as the sūtra says, *because common experience shows causality to require a collection of factors* (and Brahman is supposed to be a unity). For here in this world potters and other agents producing pots, cloth, and the like bring together several factors such as clay, a stick, threads and the like, and once all the factors are in place, the intended effect comes about—this is the common experience. And according to your idea Brahman has no helpers. There being no other causal factor, according to you, how could Brahman be the agent of creation, of "emanation" (*sraṣṭṛtva*), how could that come about? Therefore, Brahman is not the cause of the world.
>
> This objection is voiced in the sūtra. But it does not show our view to be flawed, because, as the sūtra also says, *like milk*, causality can occur because of the unique nature of a thing. For, as here in this world milk or, in another example, water, just on its own changes into curd, or snow, as the case may be, without depending on means external to itself, so too in the case of Brahman's causality.
>
> Objection: Things like milk in changing into curd or whatever also depend on external factors such as heat. So how can you think it an adequate response to the causal objection to say *For, it is like milk*?
>
> Response: This is not a problem. For, milk, too, by itself along with whatever and however extensive is its change as commonly experienced, just that is what happens immediately through, admittedly, in the case of turning into curd, the presence of heat, for example. And if the curd had the nature not to have been produced out of milk by itself, no factor such as heat would be able to make it turn into curd. For neither the wind nor the sky could turn into curd by force of heat as a causal factor, for instance.
>
> Furthermore, it is by causal *sufficiency* (*sāmagrī*, as opposed to the causal necessity of each of several factors, *karaṇa*, such as a stick needed to make a pot), that the fullness of anything comes about in a complete way. Brahman, let us emphasize, has powers in the most full fashion. No further completeness by anything else is imaginable.
>
> And this view finds support in *śruti* (*Śvetāśvatara Upaniṣad* 6.8): "There is nothing Brahman needs in order to create, no instrument. And no equal or superior is to be found. We have learned that Brahman's supreme power (*śakti*) is as various as it needs to be. As intrinsic to Brahman's nature come the knowledge, force, and action (necessary to manifest finite things)."

> Therefore, it is possible that Brahman, although unitary, change, *like milk*, for example, since Brahman is endowed by nature with power for diversity (alternatively, "is endowed with diverse powers").[9]

By nature, Saṅkara says, Brahman manifests the world. This is a central Vedāntic thesis, or at least Advaita thesis, accepted by Śaṅkara though maybe not by more "voluntarist" theists in the Vedānta camp who see manifestation as the result of the Lord's "choice."[10]

The question *why* Brahman manifests is addressed by both commentators at length, whether successfully or not we'll consider in a later chapter. For the present, let us focus on this notion of "fullness" (*pūrṇatā*, "completeness") as expressed here by Śaṅkara, echoing the *maṅgala-vācana*, "auspicious statement," of the *Īśā*.

In manuscripts and now printed editions, though not in every translation out there, the text of an Upaniṣad is preceded by a kind of prayer, an "auspicious performance," *maṅgala*, thought to bring an air of gravity to an enterprise such as studying an Upaniṣad. Consonantly there is with the *Īśā* a "statement that is an auspicious performance," *maṅgala-vācana*, which in this case is a famous mantra called a *śānti-mantra*, a "peace mantra." The mantra also appears as verse 5.1.1 of the *Bṛhadāraṇyaka*, which scholars tend to think is the oldest Upaniṣad. The mantra was probably prefixed to the *Īśā* early after Upaniṣads began to be collected across the Vedic recensions (*śākhā*) since it seems to fit the *Īśā*'s themes quite well, connecting especially well with verses 4 and 5.

In the translation by Radhakrishnan (1953: 289):

> OM. That is full; this full. From fullness fullness proceeds.
> If we take away the fullness of fullness, even fullness then remains.[11]

Here we find the seed ideas for the metaphysical reasoning drawn out by Śaṅkara and Aurobindo in their comments on verses 4 and 5 and elsewhere.

In glossing the mantra in writing on the *Bṛhadāraṇyaka*, Śaṅkara provides a yogic, experiential twist. The Full remains when in meditation one transcends everything limited, to include, of course, all individual identity; one transcends everything else but there is no transcending of It. The Full emanates our world, all worlds, all finite bodies and things, but does not change in essence, being in itself something like a "block of consciousness," Śaṅkara says, using practically the same words as the Upaniṣad. And the recovering of this our truest "self" *as it is in its essence* is the point of the verse (*the Full remains*), Śaṅkara says. Though he does not take up the mantra in his *Īśā* commentary, there is concurrent emphasis on practice, as there is some unpacking of the Brahman concept in the *Bṛhadāraṇyaka-bhāṣya* passage.

Here are excerpts from that, along the latter line, complete with a translation following Śaṅkara's reading of the mantra:

> *That is the Full. This is the Full. From the Full, the Full proceeds.*
> *Taking the Full of the Full, it is just the Full that remains.*
>
> *That is the Full* means that nothing is excluded from Brahman, that is to say, Brahman is pervasive.... It is perfectly full, pervasive like ether (*ākāśa*), partless, free from finite attributes. And just that is this world of things individual about which we converse everyday. It is the Full in that it is pervaded, as it were, by the Supreme Self in its native form, by the Self as it is in itself; that which is finite, limited, is not pervaded by any self that is finite and limited. Brahman (as this world) endowed with finite particularities is an effect proceeding out of, so to say, the Full as cause. The verse says "*proceeds*" which means the world emanates *from the Full*, from Brahman as cause. Although it is as a self that it is an emanated effect, still it remains as it is in itself—this is the meaning of the emphasis in "*it is just the Full*," that is, the Full emanates. "*Taking the Full of the Full*," that is, realizing the Fullness of Brahman in the self that is an effect, one attains to the native state of the self in its essence, through spiritual knowledge (*vidyā*), crossing beyond appearance of division generated by spiritual ignorance (*avidyā*), appearance where only accidental combinations seem real. The final phrase "it is just the Full" means that it is Brahman as a block of consciousness, without divisions, without an exterior, *that remains*.[12]

In *The Life Divine*, Aurobindo quotes the mantra, interpreting it as capturing a "mathematics" of the Infinite:

> This incoercible unity in all divisions and diversities is the mathematics of the Infinite, indicated in a verse of the Upanishads—"This is the complete and That is the complete; subtract the complete from the complete, the complete is the remainder." For so too it may be said of the infinite self-multiplication of the Reality that all things are that self-multiplication; the One becomes the Many, but all these Many are That which was already and is always itself and in becoming the Many remains the One.
>
> *SABCL* v. 18: 339

I remember a lecture by Robert Nozick where, coming across this idea, probably from Aurobindo, he elaborated that whereas members of a finite set {dog, cat, pot} *cannot* be put in a one-to-one relationship with a proper subset of itself {pot}, the members of an infinite set {whole numbers greater than zero: 1, 2, 3, . . . ∞} *can be* {2, 4, 6, . . . ∞}. In other words, in set theory a set with an infinite number of members obeys a different logic than a set with a finite number. Accordingly, anything infinite would have a different nature from anything finite, such that, Aurobindo reasons, attributes that would be "contradictory," that is, in impossible opposition if the bearer of the properties were something finite, need not be in opposition when the bearer (to wit, Brahman) is something infinite. When Śaṅkara says Brahman is "pervasive," I think he means about the same thing.

The next chapter takes up the epistemology of mystical experience, in particular the question whether there could be mystically experiential evidence for Brahman as conceived by Śaṅkara or as conceived by Aurobindo. Here and now, we should note how august the conception on both their parts. How could anything like that be *experienced*? However, I shall argue that it is not the principle of experience of Brahman as putatively foundational for views about Brahman so conceived that makes Vedāntic mystic testimony dubious, but rather, in wide overview, conflicting testimony, testimony originating in, especially, Western traditions. Brahman as putatively evident in "self-discovery," is not the only candidate proffered as a "mystic object" in traditions viewed worldwide. This difficulty faces all Vedānta, it seems to me. But it seems worth remarking now in the current context that the idea of the "logic of the Infinite"—to use Aurobindo's phrase—surely helps the Vedāntic position as is brought out in a Purāṇic parable of blind persons and an elephant recounted by Aurobindo in the midst of a long exposition of the Brahman concept in *The Life Divine* (*SABCL* 18: 325–41). As a problem for Vedānta my sense is that conflicting mystic testimony viewed worldwide is outpaced only by the theistic problem of evil. Both difficulties will be addressed in subsequent chapters.[13] But let us look first at Aurobindo's attempted solution of the diversity problem which involves the peculiar "logic of the Infinite."

Consideration of the nature of the "Infinite" should lead us, he says, to *expect* different experiences of it, personal and impersonal, transcendent and immanent, self and no-self, and so on. Brahman is like the elephant in the parable only partially perceived from different perspectives.

> If we concentrate only on one aspect and treat it as the whole, we illustrate the story of the blind men and the elephant; each of the blind inquirers touched a different part and concluded the whole animal was some object resembling the part of which he had the touch. An experience of some one aspect of the Infinite

> is valid in itself; but we cannot generalise from it that the Infinite is that alone, nor would it be safe to view the rest of the Infinite in the terms of that aspect and exclude all other viewpoints of spiritual experience.
>
> *SABCL* v. 18: 331.

Aurobindo argues that the concept of Brahman is broad enough to handle many varieties of mystical experience. He would in this way turn into an asset what seems to be a liability.[14] And he claims that the manysidedness of his own yogic experience supports the idea of Brahman as, as he says, "Infinite."

To wrap up our discussion of verses 4 and 5, we need to note that there is an obscure subject word in verse 4, *mātariśvā*, the nominative singular of *mātariśvan*. This is rendered in the Monier-Williams Sanskrit dictionary as "growing in the mother," and said there to be specifically the fire in the fire-stick in a Vedic sacrifice. Aurobindo, however, has it as "Master of Life" and provides an explanation in a footnote:

> *Mātariśvan* seems to mean "he who extends himself in the Mother or the container" whether that be the containing mother element, Ether, or the material energy called Earth in the Veda and spoken of there as the Mother. It is a Vedic epithet of the god Vayu, who, representing the divine principle in the Life-energy, Prana, extends himself in Matter and vivifies its forms. Here it signifies the divine Life-power that presides in all forms of cosmic activity.
>
> *SABCL* v. 12: 64.

The conception is filled out in a footnote to verse 17, where Aurobindo identifies Mātariśvan with Vāyu, "Air":

> Vayu, called elsewhere Matarishwan, is the Life-Energy in the universe. In the light of Surya he reveals himself as an immortal principle of existence of which birth and death and life in the body are only particular and external processes.
>
> *SABCL* 12: 67.

"Surya" (*sūrya*) is the "Sun" which as a Vedic symbol is used in the *Īśā*'s last four verses to be discussed by us in Chapters 7 and 8. For the present, contrast Aurobindo's understanding of *mātariśvā* with what Śaṅkara says (from Appendix B):

> "It is that in which," meaning the self in its true nature as constant, conscious, self-existent, in that reality Mātariśvā—things breathe, move, in the "mother," *mātṛ*, thus "Mātariśvā," in the intermediate space, that is, the "Air" that supports all life, itself active—"puts" things supported by it, things, that is, whose origins are causal, things that are woven warp and weft in it, which may be called the

> thread of everything, well, that is "Mātariśvā," the supporter of everything in the world.

Aurobindo's "god Vayu" is by Śaṅkara rendered "the 'Air' that supports all life," and, since *vāyu* is a common word for "air" in Sanskrit, both seem to conceive of an *īśvara*, the "Lord," or *īśvarī*, feminine, as having a status in the emanation of "life," *prāṇa*: all finite creatures breathe. Thus, both see an occult twist here which we'll take up in a general way in the next chapter in addressing, following *Īśā* 6, purported personal consequences of self-discovery.

In marked contrast to the Vedāntic readings, the great sanskritist Thieme (1965: 93–5) finds a discourse break between the two verses, 4 and 5 together, in relation to the next verse, 6: the pair being a *pūrva-pakṣa* in relation to 6 as *siddhānta*, that is to say, a wrong but prima facie correct view in relation to the right view which in some way can be seen to be better. Thieme (1965: 93):

> 6. Who however sees all beings in his own self, and his self in all beings—from him it (the One) does not strive to protect (hide) itself (= to him it reveals itself readily).

In the classical Sanskrit texts of the philosophic schools, *pūrva-pakṣa/siddhānta* constructions highlight argument, and argumentation is a hallmark of philosophy in India as elsewhere. Thus, Thieme projects a genre mark on a preclassical composition that on the face of it does not belong to the self-consciously argumentative genre of philosophy, which, please note, is normally taken by scholars to begin much later than the epoch of the *Īśā Upaniṣad*. Both Śaṅkara and Aurobindo find continuity between this verse pair, with a second, 6 and 7, which are, in their view, epistemic, while verses 4 and 5 are about the metaphysics of Brahman.

Finally, Aurobindo expands, in the context of verses 4 and 5, a Vedāntic causal argument for Brahman beyond the reasoning of Śaṅkara (to be reviewed by us in Chapter 5) by citing worldly instances of interconnectedness taken as evidence for metaphysical unity, for Brahman as "One." To preview the later discussion, let me say that Śaṅkara puts forth a theistic argument that includes as evidence: (a) the artistry of "manifestation" as well as (b) the fact of creaturely consciousness coupled with (c) progressive delimitation (pot-clay-earth-*pradhāna*) in a Sāṁkhya-like argument for a universal, primordial stuff, all as supporting the thesis that Brahman is the original cause of the universe, both materially and instrumentally. But, unlike Aurobindo, who sounds like a Mahāyāna Buddhist in finding "interconnectedness" practically everywhere, *pratītya-samutpāda*, Śaṅkara does not much focus on worldly indications of Brahman's unity (I have found a few stray remarks only).[15] And he says nothing in favor of oneness in his commentary here. In contrast, Aurobindo's preoccupation with interconnectedness in various realms of life and culture makes one think that the idea of Brahman's unity is not, according to him, experiential but a conclusion of natural theology. The Upaniṣadic thesis of an original "One" would then, according to him, not be based on an "experience," *anubhava*, but rather would be established by argument, whether cogent or not would be the question. And various "holisms" in common experience—in the life world, in language, in the several sciences—do indeed appear to indicate a unitive metaphysical ground.[16] However, it is not an argument in this vein but rather a kind of mystic empiricism that the next verse seems to state in favor of the monism in the concept of Brahman, *Īśā* verse 6—which is, by the way, distinctly echoed in the *Gītā* (*Gītā* 13.30: "When one comes to 'see' the whole range of individual beings as resting in the One, then and then alone Brahman can be realized in its breadth"). And our two commentators both read it that way.

4

Mystical Knowledge of Unity

Īśā 6 and 7

Śaṅkara:

> Whoso sees all beings in nothing but the self,
> And the self in all beings, shrinks therefore from nothing. || 6 ||
>
> When "Nothing but myself has come to be," when in this way one knows all beings,
> How then can there be delusion? What grief can there be? For a person realizing oneness? || 7 ||

Aurobindo:

> 6. But he who sees everywhere the Self in all existences and all existences in the Self, shrinks not thereafter from aught.
>
> 7. He in whom it is the Self-Being that has become all existences that are Becomings, for he has the perfect knowledge, how shall he be deluded, whence shall he have grief who sees everywhere oneness?

The key word in verse 6 is *anupaśyati*, translated "sees" in both renderings. Similarly, in verse 7 *vijānataḥ*, "knows" (Aurobindo: "has perfect knowledge") in the first line and *anupaśyataḥ*, "realizing," in the second. All three verbal forms have prefixes, *anu-* or *vi-*, which alter—deepen in context—the meaning of the roots, "to see" and "to know": thus *anudṛś* (an irregular conjugation) = "to realize" and *vijñā* = "to know profoundly," that is, not in an ordinary way, not intellectually—according to both commentators—but rather in extraordinary, meditational experience. This is an important point as it contradicts the scholar Thieme (1965: 93–4) for one, who splits the two verses as belonging to two distinct philosophic arguments with a conclusion in verse 6, answering verses 4 and 5, and a new *pūrva-pakṣa* in verse 7, all the ideas squarely in the realm of philosophic hypotheses. Furthermore, it is easy to misunderstand English "sees," since it is common to say that a person S "sees *x* as *F*" meaning S "believes *x* is *F*," using the locution to express S's opinion ("Jack *sees* the monument as patriotic.") In any case, our mandate is to take up the epistemology of mystical experience, since both Aurobindo and Śaṅkara interpret in a mystically experiential way the verbs rendered here "sees" and "knows."

In support of the mystical reading we may recall that Śaṅkara in commenting on *Īśā* 4 and the phrase "swifter than the mind" anticipated Thieme's position.[1] Śaṅkara has the "self" as still wider, stressing the yogic and experiential throughout his Upaniṣadic commentaries. That drumbeat is sounded at the expense sometimes, it seems to me, of what *is* a matter of metaphysics and the "mind." But no matter, Śaṅkara's main aim is to promote a path to what he calls "(self-)knowledge," *vidyā*.

Aurobindo writes in much the same vein, occasionally overgeneralizing Vedānta's mysticism, or exaggerating it, I should say, in any case apparently degrading Vedāntic metaphysical reasoning (including his own!). He says implausibly for instance:

> The sages of the Veda and Vedanta relied entirely upon intuition and spiritual experience. It is by an error that scholars sometimes speak of great debates or discussions in the Upanishad. Wherever there is the appearance of a controversy, it is not by discussion, by dialectics or the use of logical reasoning that it proceeds, but by a comparison of intuitions and experiences in which the less luminous gives place to the more luminous, the narrower, faultier or less essential to the more comprehensive, more perfect, more essential.
>
> *The Life Divine*, *SABCL* v. 18: 69.

Aurobindo's exaggeration ("*entirely* . . .") underscores the importance for us of the epistemology of mysticism and, specifically, experiential sublation, since that serves for both commentators as a model for self-discovery. An example of this kind of error-correction is someone seeing a rope as a snake then suddenly noticing that the thing is the rope it really is, a possibility terminating, argues Śaṅkara, echoed by Aurobindo, in what Aurobindo calls "knowledge by identity," which is said to be unsublatable. These are the main topics of this chapter.

Maharaj (2020) touts a special methodology on Aurobindo's part in interpreting the *Īśā* and other Upaniṣads, a methodology that, Maharaj argues, shows his reading to be superior to Śaṅkara's. He identifies five hermeneutic principles in Aurobindo's approach, five principles practiced although not stated in Maharaj's words: (1) the Anti-Eisegesis Principle, (2) the Mystical Receptivity

Principle, (3) the Vedic Context Principle, (4) the Etymological Meaning Principle, and (5) the Internal Consistency Principle. Let me say a word on each, though only the second connects directly with our current concerns.

On (1), Aurobindo does indeed try to be objective and not project preconceived notions, and Śaṅkara does indeed think—he says explicitly—the main message of the dozen or so Upaniṣads he recognizes as "scripture," *śruti*, is one and the same, namely, the nature and value of self-discovery. Maharaj is correct that Śaṅkara does read in this message in some places in his commentaries, and we do indeed need to be sensitive to the tendency. But as explained in the introduction, Śaṅkara hardly gives all Upaniṣadic passages the same weight, seeing many as targeting audiences preparing for the path to *vidyā* but not yet ready. Furthermore, "reading in" would appear to be a pitfall for any commentator, including Aurobindo, who, as we have seen, appears to read his cosmological theory into verse 3. In any case, the real nub has to do rather with the special knowledge, the nature of the "self-discovery," as in connection with our current verses, *Īśā* 6 and 7. The other principles—bracketing (2)—can be dispensed with with just a few more words.

To his credit, Aurobindo tries to integrate Upaniṣadic symbolism with Vedic, having spent much time working on the *Ṛg Veda*. On this score (3), he does a better job overall, in my estimation as well as Maharaj's, than Śaṅkara, who is not nearly as sensitive to reverberations from other parts of *śruti*. Possibly this is because Śaṅkara wants to make a sharp break with Mīmāṃsā. In any case, the relevance of Vedic echoes is limited to certain verses in the case of the *Īśā*, it seems to me, coming into play with mentions of "the waters," "Mātariśvan," and the like in previous verses and most prominently with epithets for the "Sun" and so on in the *Īśā*'s last eight lines where one *does* have to try to crack a code (and, fortunately, Śaṅkara and Aurobindo are there pretty much in agreement, as we'll see). But here with verses 6 and 7, which are about a special experience, there seems to be nothing Vedic except perhaps shamanic precursing of yoga.

About (4), both make use of etymological analysis, on which some of the targeted texts do indeed depend, punning in the *Bṛhadāraṇyaka* in particular. Śaṅkara is sensitive to core meanings of verbal roots, and also Aurobindo who thought of himself as more a poet than a philosopher or exegete.

Both Aurobindo and Śaṅkara may be faulted for misuse of (5), "Internal Consistency," since Śaṅkara finds, as mentioned, a single, unified message running across distinct Upaniṣads, and Aurobindo, too, fails to bring out inconsistencies in his zeal to find mystical meaning throughout the early corpus—to include the *Bṛhadāraṇyaka* and *Chāndogya*, which seem the most divergent concerning the nature of Brahman. But of course, to prize consistency within an Upaniṣad is no deficiency, even with a composite text such as the *Īśā* since it was edited to be a unit and read that way by the two Vedāntins as well as countless others over the centuries, as was brought out in the introduction here. And Maharaj is right that Śaṅkara is at least prima facie to be faulted for a sharply distinct rendering of the word *vidyā* in *Īśā* verses 9 through 14, as will be detailed in Chapter 6. Let us turn now to (2) and the logic of experiential sublation along with what Aurobindo calls "knowledge by identity," which is, I think, the same as Śaṅkara's concept of "self-illumination," *svayam-prakāśa*, belonging to the self by nature.

Actually, several terms and phrases are employed to express the idea of non-dual self-consciousness in the early Upaniṣads, passages consistently interpreted by Śaṅkara as saying that the native consciousness of the "self," *ātman*, is "self-illumining," *svayam-prakāśamāna*. And Aurobindo seems entirely on board with a "non-duality of consciousness" as essential to Brahman and to our own truest awareness. There is little disagreement here. However, it is hardly a stretch to say that right now each of us does—or easily can—know ourselves in a self-illumining fashion, that is, experientially but non-dualistically, unlike with sense experience, as indeed is claimed by both Śaṅkara and Aurobindo (as well as a host of modern philosophers).[2] Decidedly, that is *not* the state meant (it requires no yogic practice, etc.), although focusing on one's own immediate awareness is key, they say, to opening into the mystical "self-discovery" so highly prized.

The broad question is, then, whether this or any mystical experience has epistemic value—to which I shall argue, in line with classical Nyāya, "Yes, why not!" The particular question, coming from our current verses, concerns Brahman and "oneness," *ekatva*, whether there could be an "all-encompassing self" known so intimately as by identity. Aurobindo's notion of the "logic of the Infinite" seems wispy and intellectual whereas mystics' accounts of special experiences, including, especially, Aurobindo's, are full of spice, expressing "bliss," *ānanda*, which is a description wider than what's found in Vedānta and even the whole of indic traditions. However, the current verses force us to focus on unity to include other selves if not everything in the universe. So could a yogi "see" in any special way others as self, indeed as "the One?" And does yogic/mystic testimony to the effect that there is an inclusive, cosmic self—Brahman—as in verses 6 and 7, mean that a "non-mystic," a person who has not had the realization, would have a reason, or not, to accept two central propositions: (a) that there is a "self" that is somehow everyone or veiled in everyone and (b) that that can be unveiled and known as a matter of self-experience, like the way we know ourselves without any special experience. I think not. The mystic testimony of the verses is reinforced, to be sure, by similar testimony in the *Gītā* as well as other Upaniṣadic passages.[3] And it is admittedly bolstered by hundreds of Vedāntic and neo-Vedāntic voices over the centuries, including the work of Śaṅkara and Aurobindo, as well as, arguably, the somewhat contrary testimony from practice allies such as Buddhists, Sufis, Christians, and others. However, I do not think it provides warrant for a non-mystic to believe these two propositions (a) and (b). It may well do so for people like Śaṅkara and Aurobindo and even novitiate meditators in their tradition (compare Maharaj's "Principle of Mystic Receptivity"), but not for the mere student of mystic accounts.

Similar issues are addressed in classical Indian philosophy, in Nyāya as well as Vedānta and, assiduously, Mīmāṃsā and Buddhist Yogācāra. Despite broad differences in overall outlook, several schools accept the "knowledge-source status," *pramāṇatva*, of "yogic perception," *yaugika-pratyakṣa*, along with a parallelism thesis for the epistemic value of certain extraordinary experiences. That thesis runs: whatever value perception has for justified belief and knowledge, so, too, has yogic perception, *yaugika-pratyakṣa*, such a parallelism thesis being implicit in the Sanskrit expression. Furthermore, Nyāya holds that yogic perception includes self-perception, using a yogic term, *samādhi*, for self-awareness as a goal of both intellectual and physical practice (*Nyāya-sūtra* 4.2.38, introducing a long discussion of yoga including practices explicitly mentioned in the *Yoga-sūtra*, such as "constraints" personal and social, *yama* and *niyama*).

So far so good, but there is little agreement about *what* is shown—*a fortiori* considered worldwide, not just in indic traditions—such that anyone at a distance cannot help but worry about the truth of the epistemic claim. The five blind men in the Purāṇic parable about the elephant could, with further investigation, come to agree. But if five "eye-witnesses" were to disagree about an event, a neutral judge would rightly wonder which, if any, really *saw* what happened (if anything). Classical epistemologists who acknowledge the epistemic value of sense perception ("Yes, that's Devadatta, because I *see* him") urge that there is no reason not to accept yogic perception, *yaugika-pratyakṣa*, as also having epistemic value ("The self is real because I perceive it yogically"). But that is all very abstract. What kind of self? And there is a coven of modern philosophers considering mystic claims who worry that there is too much disagreement about what is learned to support any mystic testimony. Is it really like sensory testimony which is sometimes wrong but reliable generally? Can an outsider check the claims? Why don't other traditions concur? Buddhist

Yogâcārins, for example, practice meditational disciplines (the word *yogâcāra* means etymologically "one who practices yoga") and uphold the epistemic value of meditational experience. But Yogācārins hardly preach that there is a cosmic "self." Abstractly, the parallelism thesis implicit in notion of "yogic perception," *yaugika-pratyakṣa*, may seem reasonable, but *what* there is perception *of* is, in overview, unclear.[4]

Classically in India, Nyāya philosophers take the lead in epistemology. In Nyāya, perceptual illusions are called *pratyakṣâbhāsa*, "perception-semblance." In Nyāya, "perception," *pratyakṣa*, is a knowledge-generating process such that an embedded sensory proposition would be true. A factive logic is imputed, like English "knowledge" as understood in analytic epistemology. (There is no "false knowledge" but only false belief, and no false belief counts as knowledge.) But the English word "perception" is not like this; there can be non-veridical perception and false sensory beliefs. For Nyāya, in contrast, veritable *pratyakṣa* is veridical by definition; false sensory claims are generated by perception-imitators. Of course, classical Indian theorists were well aware that what we take to be true by way of experience that seems to be perceptual could prove to be false. Any instance of "perceptual" experience could be the result of a process where there is some flaw or abnormality in relation to the true nature of the knowledge-generator: awarenesses can be sublated and in other ways shown to be non-veridical and their generation defective. This is assumed by Śaṅkara (introduction to *Brahma-sūtra* 1.1.1) as precursed by Naiyāyikas in debate with Mīmāṃsakas, who defend a view of intrinsic veridicality for awareness in general.

The Mīmāṃsaka position would let too much into the charmed circle of warranted belief.[5] (One suspects an unacknowledged motivation for Mīmāṃsā here, namely, defending Vedic authority for ritual practice.) But the rub with the Nyāya stance is, again, that whereas the truth of a simple sensory claim, "That's a pot," for instance, can pretty easily be supported by a certain intersubjectivity, the same is at the least not obvious for yogic/mystic claims.

However, *within* Vedāntic traditions that views about Brahman and the self are experientially founded is commonly held. Is this wrong? No, not necessarily, and there is a lesson here that is, I think, underappreciated. William James, the leader of modern philosophers in this area, would say that mystic views such as Śaṅkara's and Aurobindo's about Brahman are a matter of "overbelief": overbeliefs are key to a spiritual life, according to the American philosopher, but are not, James reasons, assertible *across* traditions or cultures. A "piecemeal supernaturalism" is James' conclusion voiced at the end of his study of mysticism now well over a hundred years old. And minor variations on James seem to me to be the only advances in the small corner of philosophy where this is found interesting.[6] But beyond James, there is the following consideration: mystics and their followers (by way of their testimony) are *committed* to some kind of cross-cultural convergence *because* they are committed to the *reality* of what is taken to be revealed. This is not, from their perspectives, a matter of overbelief. In sum, while the going wisdom is that to follow a yogic or any mystic path would mean accepting a measure of provincialism—the Jamesian stance—mystics themselves take a much more robust position, claiming connection with a "Reality" that has to be intersubjective. Are they simply wrong?

Yogically we have to trust our teachers.[7] Without presumptively taking what we are told to be correct, how could we learn whatever discipline? Maharaj goes too far, almost seeming to suppose a secret Upaniṣadic language discerned by Aurobindo and other yoga masters but impenetrable even linguistically to the uninitiate. But he is on the right track with his "Principle of Mystic Receptivity" (Maharaj 2020: 314–15) in that, as indeed is stressed by Aurobindo, we have to be open to descriptions of states of consciousness not belonging to us, at least not yet, if a mystic teaching is to be instructive, whether just intellectually or as a matter of practice.

Granting, then, that mystic testimony is rightly understood to be presumptively but defeasibly veridical, the philosophic problem is, again, that discordant testimony rears its head as a defeater. Is it then that the novitiate who would follow Śaṅkara's or any path would have to reject philosophy? Maybe not. Is a *defeater-defeater* available? William Alston in *Perceiving God* (1991: esp. 79) musters a defense for Christian mysticism in the phenomena of partial intersubjectivity. Wine-tasting, knowing the sounds of letters, jewel-assessment, and so on are sensory practices requiring training but practices where, nonetheless, experts make objective, certifiable judgments. This, as with James, would leave cross-cultural exchanges problematic, and so cannot be the last word.

Let us sharpen our focus, following Alston's suggestion. Perceptually, there are special requirements governing how various objects are known. Let us assume the same to hold for the mystic object or objects. In this way the peculiar nature of the mystic "path" would be revealing in the way that training in jewel-assessment, learning an alphabet, etc., are crucial to the specific areas of sensory expertise. Now a line of criticism of the claims of meditation and yoga is that the training is distortional, like seeing two lamps, when in reality there is just one, by pushing an eyeball a certain way. But if there are clues to the nature of the mystic object in "calm, control, and compassion," *śama-dama-dayā*, as Śaṅkara insists should be practiced, *and* such qualities are fine in themselves, then the luminous, non-distortional sense of the reality of the mystic object as reported blunts, it seems to me, this "training as distortional" worry. In all Vedānta and yoga, training is clearly crucial. Few spontaneously have self-discovery or any kind of "yogic trance," *samādhi*. Moreover, the goal of yoga is typically viewed as ecstatic, "bliss," *ānanda*, and it would surely lose that lustre if considered distortional, like a drug experience.[8] In an example from the classical discussion, something in the distance may be a post or a person—we can't tell from far away, we have to get closer to know. So, in parallel fashion we need to follow a path of "knowledge" (à la Śaṅkara) or the like to know the self and Brahman. As looking for a gnat in the room is different from looking for an elephant, seeking the "supreme personal good," *parama-puruṣârtha*, requires, our yoga masters teach, special training, in particular *imitating* the self's intrinsic qualities, which are to be known in the end as a matter of immediate experience: blissful wide consciousness that is independent of external circumstance, calm and secure. That these qualities appear good in themselves supports the mystics' appeal.

So, it seems a philosophic critic *can* get an idea of what would be mystically known by focusing on the requirements for the *summum bonum* experience and making judgments about how they might or might not hook up with the nature of what is putatively revealed, like up-close, improved discernment, and like learning a script. Then, specifically for us the question is then how all this would work with the two verses from the *Īśā*, where what's claimed is that there is knowledge of "the One" as oneself and all beings? On the face of it, that seems quite far-fetched. Maybe we *are* presented with metaphysical speculation and presumed consequences of espousing a theory. But I think not.

How could mere belief bring about the results claimed in these verses of the *Īśā*? The results: (i) not shrinking from anything, interpreted by Śaṅkara as freedom from all negative feeling, and (ii) freedom from grief. Surely these are two great goods. And so how are they to come about? Not, I think, from mere belief, however broad. It would be all too easy to consider, to "see," like Spinoza or Parmenides, all things as the One.[9] In contrast, the yogic practice of "calm, control, and compassion," or the similar teaching of Aurobindo, is life-consuming, involving a lot more than taking an intellectual position. Furthermore, such a path also connects with "knowledge by identity" since basic to the phenomenology of meditation is stillness, not being moved by desire into action but calmly to attend to one's own consciousness. And there is arguably an extension of identity in "compassion," *dayā*, and, at the very least, natural practice of "non-injury," *ahiṃsā*, which, by the way, leads off the list of practices in the "Eight-limbed Yoga," *aṣṭâṅga-yoga*, made famous by the *Yoga-sūtra*.

The sixth chapter of the *Gītā*—traditionally labelled *dhyāna-yoga*, the "Yoga of Meditation" (excerpted in Appendix C)—is all about coming to know "self" experientially as all-encompassing through a process of quietening the mind. In his *Gītā* commentary (on *Gītā* 6.32), Śaṅkara writes that yoga involves trying to see "the same everywhere" such that by equality of selfhood one practices *ahiṃsā* simply because no one wishes harm for oneself.[10] If there are candidate traits continuous with "freedom from all negative feeling" and "freedom from grief," to cite the translation of Aurobindo, then "non-injury," *ahiṃsā*, and "calm, control, and compassion," *śama-dama-dayā*, have to be top candidates, to say the least. Furthermore, knowledge by identity does appear to be native to self-awareness understood as neither mental nor sensory but as consciousness attending to itself—such attending being the hallmark of meditation in the tradition of the *Śvetāśvatara*, the *Gītā*, Śaṅkara, and other Vedāntins (not to mention the *Yoga-sūtra* or Buddhist meditation manuals or the Jaina).[11]

Now, Nyāya takes "attending" to self to have a subject-object structure. Apperception ("after-cognition," *anuvyavasāya*) is required to be aware of a self in the process of, for example, seeing ("I see my seeing a pot"). But Vedānta insists that phenomenologically consciousness is, or can be, non-dual, being and awareness converging, like a lamp that does not require another to be visible.[12] Mīmāṃsā famously attacks the Nyāya position by alleging an impossible infinite regress in the notion of a distinct moment of awareness required for awareness of awareness. Vedānta in general concurs: self-awareness is intrinsically non-dual. Over the centuries, dialectics by the poet Śrīharṣa and other great masters of Sanskrit advance the Advaita cause—the main trick seems to be the "Bradley problem" of relations (if *a* is related to *b* by relation R, *a*R*b*, then what relates R to *a* and R to *b*? an answer threatening multiple infinite series).[13] Possibly, "non-distinctness"—metaphysical unity—can be proved in this way: no two things can be entirely distinct since otherwise they could not be related. Necessary interconnectedness is supposed to be a ramification of Brahman's unity. But that is not the main message of the early Upaniṣads, it seems to me, which is, rather, like these two verses of the *Īśā*, phenomenological. And some of the dialectics seem motivated by a conflation between the psychological process of thinking—which is to be quieted in meditation—and conceptualization considered impersonally. Surely, meditation masters utilize concepts in teaching, "self-illumination," for instance.

Of course, in the Advaita understanding the "self" in "self-awareness" does not refer to a concept or to the body or to the person but only to the consciousness that is self-aware. It is admitted that we often forget ourselves as we concentrate on a particular line of action and its goal. But the call is not to act but to meditate, to tune into a kind of self-awareness that is not looking at oneself as in a mirror but being directly self-aware. Immediacy is the gateway to self-discovery.

This, Śaṅkara's great theme, is taken up by scores of followers and sustained by Aurobindo, too, with his notion of "knowledge by identity." He writes, for example, in a chapter of *The Life Divine* entitled, "Knowledge by Identity and Separative Knowledge":

> The first way of knowing [knowledge by identity] in its purest form is illustrated in the surface mind only by our direct awareness of our own essential existence: it is a knowing empty of any other content than the pure fact of self and being; of nothing else in the world has our surface mind the same kind of awareness.
>
> *SABCL* v. 18: 525

In that chapter, Aurobindo takes his task to show how "separative knowledge" derives from this premier way of knowing, which, like Śaṅkara, he takes to be native to Brahman as well as key to yogic expansion of consciousness.[14] Yogic, meditative experience is the ultimate court of appeal for both authors, or a *shared* ultimate court of appeal for Śaṅkara, if one insists that the message of "scripture," *śruti*, is for him distinct from his understanding of self-knowledge, *vidyā* (a thesis I think is false).

Vedānta's resources for its self-illumination view of "self" include a sublatability argument, an Upaniṣadic (and Buddhist) argument popularized by Śaṅkara and extended, with a twist, by Aurobindo. Knowledge by identity is claimed to be "unsublatable"—not possibly shown to be wrong by subsequent experience—as it is viewed as the ground of all subjectivity, making possible all modes of ordinary, "separative" experience.

First, the classical argument.[15] An awareness presenting an object as distinct from the subject is subject to sublation, on analogy to a snake appearance turning out to be of a rope as shown by subsequent rope experience. Knowledge by identity, in contrast, is always there, for most in the background usually but as always there to be enlivened, as in self-absorptive trance. And it cannot be sublated; there can be no further, correcting experience that could replace it. As Śaṅkara argues, "No one says, 'I am not.'" Any awareness with content directing one to something outside of itself could prove to be non-veridical—so goes the classical argument—not actually to hit what it seems to. But this is not true for self-illumining consciousness. In all subjectivity, there is nothing behind it; it presents nothing but itself. It is the subject, but it is the object, too. A perceptual illusion can be sublated because an object is presented as qualified by a property. And a property presented may not qualify the perceived object in fact, as with snakehood falsely presented as qualifying what is in fact a rope. Self-illumining consciousness is not, however, in this way "qualificative," to render the Sanskrit expression, *vaiśiṣṭya*. Its non-dual presentation precludes sublation, in sum. It cannot be shown non-veridical—unlike all perception and indeed all thinking (remembering, inferring, understanding what someone has said, et cetera), all normal cognition which is invariably "consciousness-of" of a transitive type.

This means that self-illumining consciousness is self-authenticating (*sva-prakāśa* = *svataḥ prāmāṇya*) since nothing has access to it except itself. Any attempt at a "third-person" explanation would be like trespassing. Advaitins say also that there is no real point to the question about authentication. To itself, self-illumining consciousness stands self-revealed.

Now Advaitins—including Śaṅkara but especially Padmapāda and the Vivaraṇa subschool—equate self-discovery with "liberation," *mukti*, and claim that when it happens there is no further experience conditioned by *avidyā*. But that last part seems at least subject to debate by outsiders, surely not a "self-authenticating" claim. Furthermore, given what we know about the lives of yogis and saints, self-discovery, understood as "immediate experience of Brahman," *brahma-sākṣātkāra*, is not final in the way Padmapāda and company appear to hold. As I argued long ago in a paper about Padmapāda's version of Advaita (1987), the evidence is that yogis return to sensory awareness, or include it in their overall state of consciousness, to eat lunch, for instance. Does the lunch experience *sublate* the experience of a unitary self? This is a tricky question, since according to Mahāyāna Buddhist philosophies as well as Vedānta (including Aurobindo's position), once one has a thorough-going non-dual experience it remains—though, according to some, perhaps not as entirely "stable"—when the yogi returns to everyday activity. The reason why inclusion of sensory experience does not count as further sublation should be explained, and so far as I can tell it is not, at least not by Śaṅkara.[16] Why cannot the non-dual experience be sublated? There has to be more to the story than "No one says, 'I am not.'"

Note that in the snake illusion there is something there, the object of attribution, that remains the property-bearer after the sublating rope experience. This is how Aurobindo appears to understand sublation: the self-as-object side of self-awareness, when revealed, he says, cannot be sublated, not only the self-as-subject side. Yet he also claims, well, not just that someone "liberated" could later have ordinary perception, but that there can be, and is, "spiritual experience" of a unitary self *simultaneous with* a new kind of world-directed experience, a convergence or harmony of the higher knowledge with objects, and action, in the world. He agrees with Śaṅkara that the awakening that is *vidyā* provides something that cannot be sublated (see the quote below). But personal transformation, post self-discovery, and worldy action are not only possible, according to him, but built right into a telos of nature.[17] Śaṅkara is commonly interpreted as holding that self-knowledge and action are incompatible. According to Aurobindo, however, post self-discovery all life appears beautiful to transformed sensibilities, all its lines of action are seen and felt as the *ānanda* of "the Divine" expressed in finite forms and circumstances. Thus for Aurobindo, the aesthetic concept of *rasa*—"juice," "relish," "aesthetic delight"—looms as crucial to a revised idea of the "supreme personal good," which would be, in his terms, "divine life," not *mukti*.[18]

Yet in explaining the Lord's creative activity, Śaṅkara presents a view that, at a distance, seems not far from Aurobindo's: the world is the Lord's "play," *līlā*. From his *Brahma-sūtra-bhāṣya*:

> Like activities on the part of a prince or minister who has no compelling desire, activities undertaken in playgrounds just for sport (*līlā*) without a particular motive, and like inhalation and exhalation of breath as activities that can occur on their own just from their own nature without regard to any exterior motive, so the creative activity of the Lord we may suppose to come about as nothing but play, sport (*līlā*), just naturally without depending upon any exterior motive whatsoever. For it is false that the Lord has some motive or purpose that is to be discerned by either reason or revelation. Nor is it implausible that the Lord's creative activity is simply a matter of the Lord's nature. Although the universe appears to us to be so intelligently arranged as to require prodigious effort of a very weighty sort, to the Supreme Lord it would all be like mere play, because the Lord's power is immeasurable. Admittedly, in our experience a subtle motive might be detected even in play. Still, no motive whatsoever can be discerned with regard to the Lord's creative action; we know as much from Upaniṣadic statements about those whose "desires are all satisfied."[19]

Furthermore, as mentioned, Aurobindo agrees that self-discovery does leave even the lunch-eating yogi with something that does not go away, though it gets modified or expanded and progressively, according to him, spills into everyday life. It is false, he says, that one could fall back into ordinary consciousness, but self-discovery is not the whole story, he attests.

Śaṅkara and followers extol the value of self-illumining consciousness to which they too tie a supernal bliss (*ānanda*). That is, they attribute imperishable bliss to self-discovery as the supreme personal good, the ultimate goal of yoga practice and the full realization of self-illumining consciousness. Aurobindo would say that that is correct, largely because, he states, self-discovery is the decisive step in a progressive series. The idea is absent with Śaṅkara, who is, nevertheless, a theist, as we have seen, viewing action, *post* self-discovery, as in a special way directed by the "Lord," the *īśvara*, presumably as the most exalted of Brahman's on-going creative activity—through persons, self-realized yogis, "delighted in the welfare of all" (*Gītā* 5.25: *sarva-bhūta-hite ratāḥ*). Although these two verses from the *Īśā* do indeed make us think about what life would be like afterwards, this is not stressed, I think, by Śaṅkara because for him our business is self-discovery, not action after the dawning of *vidyā*. But he is yet a theist, in a dimension of his thought that is commonly missed.

Aurobindo tells us that a "Nirvana" experience he had was never for him negated but did "heighten and widen," as happened, he says, in the progress of his yoga, in developments of the greatest import. There was no series of sublations by his account, but an expanding out from a core that I believe he took to be the experience Śaṅkara calls "knowledge," *vidyā*, and, notably, sometimes *nirvāṇa* (like Buddhists but also the *Gītā*), which, Śaṅkara says, is forever constant.[20] Aurobindo reports that sensory experience became "fused" for him to a core self-discovery, becoming transformed, not sublated. He writes in a letter about himself:

> Now to reach Nirvana was the first radical result of my own Yoga. It threw me suddenly into a condition above and without thought, unstained by any mental or vital movement; there was no ego, no real world—only when one looked through the immobile senses, something perceived or bore upon its sheer silence a world of empty forms, materialized shadows without true substance. There was no One or many even, only just absolutely That, featureless, relationless, sheer, indescribable, unthinkable, absolute, yet supremely real and solely real. This was no mental realisation nor something glimpsed somewhere above—no abstraction—it was positive, the only positive reality—although not a spatial physical world, pervading, occupying or rather flooding and drowning this semblance of a physical world, leaving no room or space for any reality but itself, allowing nothing else to seem at all actual, positive or substantial.... I lived in that Nirvana day and night before it began to ... modify itself ... into a greater Superconsciousness from above. But meanwhile realisation added itself to realisation and fused itself with this original experience.... [It gave place to a sense of] an intense Divine Reality in the heart of everything that had seemed at first only a cinematic shape or shadow. And this was no reimprisonment in the senses, no diminution or fall from supreme experience, it came rather as a

> constant heightening and widening of the Truth; it was the spirit that saw objects, not the senses, and the Peace, the Silence, the freedom in Infinity remained always with the world or all worlds only as a continuous incident in the timeless eternity of the Divine.
>
> *On Himself*, *SABCL* v. 26: 101–2

So, for Aurobindo self-discovery is a quantum leap out of everyday consciousness but also pivotal for a new kind of being in the world. And it is here that he finds the significance of the ideas of *Īśā* 6 and 7 about unity. One has to wonder, however, whether he had the unity idea followed by the *abhimāna*—the "self-regard," the "self-concept"—before he had his yogic realizations or whether the realizations came first, providing for him the key to these verses of the Upaniṣad. Since altering how one looks upon oneself (*abhimāna*) is taught throughout Vedānta as part of practice, the answer may be "both," as he says about other apparent antinomies. Thus, for example, encouraged is both "mental silence" as taught in the *Yoga-sūtra* and intellectual development including, to be sure, philosophy. In this way, Aurobindo sets himself apart from the anti-theoretical dialecticians, though not necessarily from other Advaita subschools (for example, the tantric).

A final note on Aurobindo's reading of verse 7 and the Sanskrit *sarvāṇi bhūtāni*, which would be translated straightforwardly as "all beings." Aurobindo has a footnote to his rendering, "all existences that are Becomings," which, on the face of it, is forced and awkward but also telling about the whole flavor of, if not his cosmology, his reading of the *Īśā*:

> The words *sarvāṇi bhūtāni* literally, "all things that have become," is opposed to Atman, self-existent and immutable being. The phrase means ordinarily "all creatures," but its literal sense is evidently insisted on in the expression *bhūtāni abhūt* "became the Becomings" ["the Self," *ātman*, "became," *abhūt*, "the Becomings," *bhūtāni*"]. The idea is the acquisition in man of the supreme consciousness by which the one Self in him extends itself to embrace all creatures and realises the eternal act by which the One manifests itself in the multiple forms of the universal motion.
>
> *SABCL* v. 12: 65.n1

5

(K)nots of Metaphysics: The Causal Argument for the "Self-Existent," *svayam-bhū*

Īśā 8

Śaṅkara's reading of *Īśā* 8:

> That one has become all-encompassing, the bright, the bodiless, the flawless, not sectioned, pure, not pierced by evil or sin;
> The poet, the seer, the thinker, who is everywhere, the self-created (*svayam-bhū*) has set things in order, as they should be, for years immemorial. || 8 ||

Aurobindo:

> 8. It is He that has gone abroad—That which is the bright, bodiless, without scar of imperfection, without sinews, pure, unpierced by evil. The Seer, the Thinker, the One who becomes everywhere, the Self-existent (*svayam-bhū*) has ordered objects perfectly according to their natures from years sempiternal.

Continuity from Śaṅkara to Aurobindo is dramatic in a shared monistic theism, not just in meditational practices and experiences. But as may be inevitable in metaphysics, both philosophers face conceptual problems, many of which arise in Western attempts to combine theism and monism, such as Plato's, neo-platonism, and others. There are also difficulties that attach to any monism as evidently a "revisionist" metaphysics difficult to square with the pluralism of everyday objects (to use P.F. Strawson's adjective). A multi-dimensional causal argument for Brahman is this chapter's main topic, and so let us focus first on the premise of Brahman itself as uncaused, *svayam-bhū*, and then try to unpack Vedāntic natural theology in the face of difficulties.

Here is Śaṅkara's gloss of "*svayam-bhū*," which is a compound word:

> "The self-created" (*svayam-bhūḥ*) is said because just by itself (*svayam*) it comes to be (*bhavati*). Coming to be beyond those (created things) and coming to be as beyond, that is the "all" who comes to be just by itself, thus "the self-created."[1]

Śaṅkara's view is that there is an origin of things that itself has no cause other than itself, in effect halting a series of causal questions.[2] Aurobindo understands Brahman similarly as halting an explanatory regress, but the idea, which is expressed many times in *The Life Divine*, is not emphasized in his comments on verse 8 of the Upaniṣad. Rather, harmonization of dualities is stressed. The main idea he finds is the "logic of the Infinite." As we learned in Chapter 3, this, he reasons, is different from the logic of the finite: the Infinite permits what to something finite would be opposed attributes. The *svayam-bhū* idea is the conception of a necessary being from which opposed contingencies can originate. Aurobindo, unfortunately, appears to lose the term's causal sense by capitalization, the "Self-existent," as though this type of existence is qualified by being the universal *ātman*, the "Self." The Self would be that which exists primordially. Of course, according to Śaṅkara (and many other Vedāntins), that is correct: Brahman is "Self," as known in the experience of self-discovery. But this does not seem to be the meaning of the word in the Upaniṣad. Aurobindo nevertheless extracts cosmological argumentation, as we shall see.

The *Bṛhadāraṇyaka Upaniṣad* opens with the idea, symbolically expressed, of integration of nature in all her forces with psychology and culture, all celebrating "the One." And early on, there is an emanationist creation story. The mythology seems playful but also to presuppose Brahman. Cosmic interconnectedness along with causal unity seems to be the main theme. Then after a second emanationist story, there is a shift in tone in the form of a question. What is the nature of this One *in itself*, apart from all its manifestations? What is its *rasa* (*Bṛ U* 2.3.2–4), its "essence," its *self*, *ātman*? The remarkable passage, which occurs in the second of six long chapters, continues by providing an answer, or quasi-answer, about Brahman's essence apart from all its expressions, its emanations in subtle and gross forms. The answer is *nêti nêti*, "Not this, not that" (*Bṛ U* 2.3.6). Brahman is transcendent of "name and form" (*nāma-rūpa*).[3]

No characterization of Brahman as it is in itself could be adequate, including how the world looks from Brahman's perspective *and* to a Brahman-knower as well. Śaṅkara's view, in the face of this, is that the best conception among several candidates listed (*Brahma-sūtra-bhāṣya* 1.1.2) is that Brahman is the *source* of everything (including itself, *svayam-bhū*). Later, with Vācaspati (*c.* 900), who here apparently follows Maṇḍana (Śaṅkara's older contemporary), "inexplicability," *anirvacanīyatva*, is said to be the result of an analysis of illusory perceptual content: in the case of shell taken to be silver, the "silver" is neither real (*sat*)—it won't buy anything in the market—nor unreal (*asat*)—it is phenomenal—a case that is supposed to be parallel to Brahman's relation to "lack of knowledge of the true self," *avidyā*. Śaṅkara is not so specific as Vācaspati but for him, too, Brahman's transcendence of "name and form" blocks expectations about what the world should be like given that Brahman is its source (at least some expectations). Nevertheless, there is a lot to be said about Brahman in relation to us. We need a worldview to guide our yoga practice, and though the transcendence of that which is revealed in the experience (*anubhava*) that is a person's supreme good (*parama-puruṣârtha*) blocks comparisons with anything with which we are familiar ("Not this, not that") and to which words commonly refer (*Kena* 1.3: "That which is by speech *un*expressed"), Upaniṣads, supported by reasoning, tell us that Brahman is the *causal* ground of the world, in particular the underlying self of selves, everything depending upon it and it depending on nothing except itself (*svayam-bhū*), according to Śaṅkara following especially the *Bṛhadāraṇyaka* along with the sūtras of Bādarāyaṇa.

There is thus broad convergence with a line of argument for the existence of God in the Western tradition of natural theology that stretches from Plato, Aristotle, and Proclus through Avicenna and Thomas. This argument-wise convergence is just as striking, it seems to me, as the conceptions of God, or Brahman, gleaned from whatever "scripture," indeed more pronounced (as might be expected for "*natural* theology").[4]

Only a few passages in the early Upaniṣads explicitly express an argument for Brahman. There is *Chāndogya* 6.2 ("In the beginning everything was just this Being, since nothing comes from nothing"), a passage discussed at length below. But in the *Brahma-sūtra* and Śaṅkara's *Commentary*, the reasoning is right out front. The second sūtra of the *Brahma-sūtra* defines *brahman* as "That from which the world's creation and the rest proceed" (*janmâdy asya yataḥ*). Śaṅkara tells us that the point of the words "and the rest" is to include maintenance and destruction (*BSB*, Shastri edition: 46–7). Brahman is that from which all things arise. Dialectically, it is crucial that the causal thesis is coupled with the notion that Brahman is uncaused as "self-existent," *svayam-bhū*, *causa sui*. This is said in the same section of the *Bṛhadāraṇyaka* as the *nêti nêti* passage, *BṛU* 2.6.3, indeed in the very last words of the chapter, thus given emphasis.[5]

Now a common device in poetry is oxymoron, where *apparent* oppositions are expressed. This occurs in *Īśā* verse 8, also in other Upaniṣads, and in other verses of the *Īśā*, in particular 4 and 5, as we have seen. To me, the message is that somehow paradox is appropriate in reference to the ultimate origin. This is how Śrīharṣa, the premier Advaita dialectician of the eleventh century, who was also a world-class poet, would see the matter, and of course others as well.[6] Aurobindo, however, argues that the central purpose of the Upaniṣad is to capture an underlying harmony between oppositions and discords. Let me quote his list of nine (*SABCL* v. 12: 135-6; the capitalizations are his):

1. The Conscious Lord and phenomenal Nature
2. Renunciation and Enjoyment
3. Action in Nature and Freedom in the Soul
4. The One stable Brahman and the multiple Movement
5. Being and Becoming
6. The Active Lord and the indifferent Akshara Brahman
7. Vidya and Avidya
8. Birth and Non-Birth
9. Works and Knowledge

Thus, an important difference between the two readings is that reference to Brahman and spelling out Brahman's nature are by Śaṅkara thought to be far more problematic than by Aurobindo who seems sanguine about philosophic theory and Brahman conceived not just coherently but compellingly: following the Upaniṣad, he sees the goal to articulate a harmonization of monism and theism and indeed everyday knowledge. Taking cues from the *Īśā*, he alleges—in his commentary and all the more in *The Life* Divine—to untie the metaphysical knots in Vedānta. But does he?

There are two knots in the Vedāntic understanding of Brahman that seem to me intractable, plaguing both theorists, (a) mutability and (b) evil. There is also (c) a problem of how reference to Brahman is a possible and positive description, but that seems minor in comparison to the other two.[7] And there are (d) problems attaching to attributes of Brahman, especially Brahman's all-inclusiveness and causal power, which should not be ignored but will not be our main focus. Historically, efforts to unravel knots form as much a part of the Vedāntic literature in metaphysics as the causal argument. Furthermore, Śaṅkara often invents interlocutors who give them voice. He is not shy about posing difficulties for Vedāntic theory.

Historically, the most burning of questions is whether Brahman changes in manifesting, in becoming the world, as is reflected in the conflict over "transformation" versus "transmogrification," *pariṇāma* versus *vivarta*, and in the Bhāmatī versus Vivaraṇa subschools of Advaita. To almost all classical

Vedāntins, this seems to be the most worrisome knot. Brahman would appear to lose its essence if transforming, and transmogrification jettisons realism, spawning a world-illusionism objectionable on many counts, as brought out by critiques both classical and modern (including Aurobindo's). Aurobindo's attempt to solve this will occupy us in the next essay, Chapter 6. In a nutshell, the problem is that if Brahman changes to be aware of Hitler as Hitler was aware of Hitler with his limited (and twisted) perspective, then Brahman ceases to be so wonderful. And if Brahman is not aware of Hitler as Hitler was aware of Hitler (granted that Brahman is aware of Hitler's phenomenology save the absence of Brahman awareness), then Brahman is not all-inclusive, *vibhu*, and not all-knowing, *sarvajña*.

Deep-set though this difficulty may be, to my mind the toughest problem for Śaṅkara's monistic theism—Aurobindo's as well—is evil. For the moment putting aside qualms about Brahman being beyond "name and form," we find Brahman characterized by Śaṅkara—in line with a mainstream conception found in later, non-Vedic Upaniṣads such as the *Mukti*, *Vāsudeva*, and others—as essentially "being-consciousness-bliss," *sac-cid-ānanda*, as well as "omnipresent," *vibhu*, as he often says. How, then, are pain and suffering possible? Aurobindo does not much disagree with the characterization of, as he puts it, an "essential Divine," and this seems to compel his theory of inevitable "divine life." Otherwise, our world would not be possible as incompatible with Brahman essential nature as consciousness and bliss.

Excepting unity and all-inclusiveness, problems concerning Brahman's attributes of "omniscience," *sarvajñatva*, and others need not detain us. Analytic philosophy of religion—going at least as far back as David Hume (*Dialogues Concerning Natural Religion*: 1776)—has shown the fallaciousness of many theistic arguments. Process philosophers such as Charles Hartshorne (*Omnipotence and Other Theological Mistakes*: 1984) inherited plenty of ammunition with which to attack the "classical" idea of God in support of a Whiteheadean all-encompassing, "prehending actual entity," both "primordial" and "consequent" to all choices. It seems to me that the Process "God" is not so different from Vedānta's "Brahman," especially as explained by Aurobindo: whatever the precise relation to the world, Brahman changes as the world changes; an "essential Divine" contrasts with a part that changes, much as the Process theologians hold. But it also seems to me that the inexplicability doctrine of *nêti nêti* can blunt puzzlement arising from atheistic arguments targeting the classical idea of God. Nevertheless, the idea of Brahman, however vexed, is what is confirmed in the Vedāntic reasoning, like the idea of God in the cosmological arguments constructed outside of India. Brahman is transcendent, but also everything that exists comes out of Brahman and is instrumentally dependent on Brahman, too.

It is easy, therefore, to reconstruct a Vedāntic argument akin to Aristotle "first-cause" argument famous in natural theology. The argument is implicit, says Śaṅkara in his *Brahma-sūtra Commentary*, in the meaning of sūtra number two: (*BSB* 1.1.2) "[Brahman is] That from which the world's creation and the rest proceed." Because creation, maintenance, and destruction are caused, we have to imagine an original cause, called "Brahman" in the Upaniṣads, which has to be self-caused, or uncaused, "self-existent," *svayam-bhū*, literally, "by and of itself coming to be," *causa sui*. The causality works in more than one way: Brahman is both the ultimate *material* of everything, the widest kind ("being": e.g., *Chāndogya* 6.8.4: "All these creatures, my dear, have their root in Being. They all have Being as their abode, Being as their support"; Radhakrishnan 1953: 457)—as the original material cause of everything Brahman's all-inclusiveness is accounted for—as well as the original *instrumental* cause, to use the terminology of the later philosophers, specifically the original *agential* cause: Brahman is the "Lord," *īśvara*. Aristotle's "formal cause" is not so well articulated in Vedānta, but Śaṅkara and others reason that the Lord has to be "omniscient," *sarvajña*, in order to perform the creational/emanational task. And Aristotle's fourth of his causal quatrad, the final cause or *telos*, is captured in the notion of experience of Brahman (*vidyā*) as the "supreme personal good," *parama-puruṣârtha*.[8]

In brief (from *Brahma-sūtra-bhāṣya* 2.2.1–10, in the context of Śaṅkara refuting Sāṃkhya):

1. All things finite, that is to say, delimited, have a material cause that is less delimited, like a pot made of clay.
2. The universe as a whole is delimited, having a material cause.
3. The world (a) originates out of an inconscient *pradhāna*, "primordial matter," or (b) originates *out of* Brahman *because of* Brahman as *īśvara*, the "Lord," who has the consciousness capable of creation/emanation.
4. No non-sentient *pradhāna* could have brought about our world of wondrous arrangement.
5. Therefore, Brahman is *īśvara*, the world's original material and agential cause.

The most famous passage in the Upaniṣads themselves connected to this reasoning comes from the *Chāndogya*. Without Brahman—termed "being" (*sat*)—there would be nothing. The metaphysical principle is: "From nothing comes nothing" (*ex nihilo nihil fit*):

> *Chāndogya* 6.2.1–2. In the beginning, my dear, this was being alone, one only without a second. Some people say, "In the beginning this was non-being alone, one only, without a second. From that non-being, being was produced." But how, indeed, my dear, could it be thus? said he [a father teaching a son], how could being be produced from non-being? On the contrary, my dear, in the beginning this was being alone, one only without a second.
>
> Radhakrishnan 1953: 447–9

Radical emergence seems intuitively impossible. This is a mainstay of Vedāntic monism and any "top-down" metaphysics, against atomism which is well represented on the classical Indian scene in the schools of Nyāya and Vaiśeṣika. And what could be more radical than the emergence of things from a generic "non-existence?" Big-bang cosmogony seems to me to be no exception. There *is* something rather than nothing, and it is unimaginable that there could have been nothing at all.

That Brahman cannot be adequately conceptualized is an important theme with Śaṅkara, but apparently mindful of potential ambiguity in the *nêti nêti* doctrine, Śaṅkara points out in commenting on the first sūtra of the *Brahma-sūtra* that if Brahman were entirely and in every way unknowable, there would be no point to the inquiry. But we do know something about Brahman, says the Advaitin in commenting on the very first sūtra, expressing a worry similar to Plato's "Meno's paradox," and a solution. To be precise, Śaṅkara presents the objection that if Brahman were unknown, then the current endeavor as conceived at *Brahma-sūtra* 1.1.1 would make no sense. Brahman is known at least vaguely by extension of ordinary meanings such as "wide" and "great," says he, but then more concretely, too. Again, Śaṅkara's *cogito*:

> And the existence of Brahman is a settled fact by being the self of everyone. For anyone can be aware of self as existing, and no one thinks "I am not."[9]

Everyone knows immediately, or can know, "self-existence." Immediate self-awareness is the Vedāntic gateway to Brahman-awareness—this is the subtext. That's about all that can be said without Upaniṣadic instruction, according to Śaṅkara, yet that instruction is supported by natural theology which is where the causal argument kicks in. We learn from the Upaniṣads buoyed up by rational inquiry (*BSB* 1.1.2) that the relation between Brahman and the world is a theistic emanationism. Brahman is the "Lord," *īśvara*, and not only both the self and the stuff of everything and everyone but also a first—and on-going—causal factor in everything that occurs.

It is important to keep in mind the inwardness of Vedāntic theism. A causal inwardness connects with Śaṅkara's *cogito* ("No one thinks, 'I am not'"): the Lord who out of itself fashions things is the "Inner Controller," *antar-yāmin* (*Bṛhadāraṇyaka* 3.7.1–23). Ram-Prasad (2013: 10) gleans from a range of Śaṅkara's works that for him "*ātman* is not picked out by 'I' (*ahaṃ*), as all such linguistic usage generates mistaken identification with something which is mine (*mama*) . . ." This fits Śaṅkara's insistence on a shift of *abhimāna*, "identity," to the universal, as we shall have several occasions to remark. It does not undermine Śaṅkara's *cogito*: the problem with ordinary I-consciousness is that it is not inward enough. Śaṅkara's "Lord," in any case, as the *antar-yāmin*, contrasts with the mainstream "sky-father" conception of Western theism, God as an extracosmic fashioner, standing outside his material, like a potter with clay. Vedāntic theism locates the fashioner in an inner core best manifest in self-awareness. Furthermore, there is no separate "matter" for the Lord to shape. Brahman is matter, and materially everything derives from Brahman as shown in the organic nature of the world. Both Śaṅkara and Aurobindo and many others sprinkle the Vedāntic cosmological argument with teleological spice:[10] the world is full of pleasure reflecting Brahman's characteristic "bliss" (*ānanda*), also pain, admittedly, but this is due, says Śaṅkara, to the justice of karmic debt whereby the Lord by being just is forced to acquiesce to unpleasantness. Aurobindo, in contrast, argues that our planet is gestating "divine life," a kind of "new heaven and new earth," in the biblical conception.[11] Pain and suffering have instrumental value for "soul-making," as more and more people realize the "final cause," becoming experiential knowers of the true "Self," in a material world. The end justifies the means.[12]

Aristotle's and other cosmological arguments, formulated in Greek and Arabic and Latin, rely on a premise of the impossibility of an infinite regress. If the Unmoved Mover were not unmoved, there would have to be another mover, *ad infinitum*—an impossibility. This is not part of how Brahman is known according to Śaṅkara's commentary on *Brahma-sūtra* 1.1.2, and acceptable infinite series are identified across the classical Indian schools. However, Śaṅkara makes several other elaborations that are worth a look:

> The words, "That from which," in the sūtra ("That from which the world's creation and the rest proceed") are about Brahman as cause such that the sūtra is to be filled out by understanding the cause of this world in a certain fashion: as (a

> Lord, *īśvara*) knowing everything, as entirely capable of bringing about the origin, maintenance, and destruction of this universe—a universe unfolding in multifarious individuals and types (*nāma-rūpa*) in connection with multiple agents and enjoyers, serving as the basis for particular fruits of action as conditioned by places and times. Brahman is the cause of this world whose marvelous arrangement is unimaginable even by the poetic mind.[13]

The Lord has to be all-knowing (*sarvajña*) and capable of creation (*sarva-śakteḥ kāraṇāt*) of an unimaginably complex, and beautiful, I daresay (not anachronistically, I think), universe of organically interconnected individual beings and things. Interconnectedness, I take it, is thought to reflect Brahman's unity and inclusiveness.

But what about other possibilities? Just a little later in the passage, Śaṅkara reasons:

> If the theistic thesis is put aside, that is, not positing a Lord characterized as we have ("knowing everything" and the rest) who is the cause, it would not be possible to conceive of the universe to have resulted as described in some other way, from an inconscient *pradhāna* ("primordial matter"), for example, from atoms, from nothing, or from a limited being stuck in the cosmic flux. Nor could things have so resulted on their own accord, because we observe that here in this world things occur in particular times and places with particular causes.[14]

Each of the alternative possibilities is given painstaking elaboration—and refutation—in his *Commentary* on a long stretch of sūtras in the *Brahma-sūtra*'s second chapter (2.2.1–45).

Next in his comments on *Brahma-sutra* 1.1.2, Śaṅkara turns to epistemology, imagining an interlocutor objecting that he has surrendered the thesis that Upaniṣadic instruction is required to understand—and indeed "realize"—Brahman: Śaṅkara has the *Brahma-sūtra* putting itself squarely in the camp of natural theology, with no need for Upaniṣads.

> **Objection**: You have advanced nothing other than a theistic inference establishing the existence of a Lord along with certain properties that make the Lord different from a being stuck in the cosmic flux. Natural theologians argue in this way. So here, too, as you tell it, the sūtra about the origin, etc., lays out just that view.
>
> **Answer**: Wrong, because the purpose of the sūtras is to tie together Upaniṣadic statements like flowers in a garland. For, the sūtras express reflection carried out with particular statements in mind, conveying an understanding of Brahman that arises out of reflective effort directed to the meaning of the statements, not

> from some other knowledge source such as inference. But among the propositions about a cause of the universe's origin, etc., an inference, too, that, in the face of Upaniṣadic statements, *firms up one's grasp* of the meaning is not to be denigrated as not a knowledge source so long as it is consistent with the statements.[15]

Probably Śaṅkara would not go so far as to say that Brahman can be realized in an "enlightenment" experience—"Knowledge," *vidyā*, with a capital "k"—without comprehending certain Upaniṣadic statements. It is of course the content, the meaning of those statements, that is crucial, not the actual words. In any case, his view seems to be that an intellectual understanding of Brahman *is* a prerequisite, and that understanding requires reflection on the meaning of certain "stand-out" statements, *mahā-vākya*, "Thou art That," "I am He," and "All this is the Brahman," to cite famous examples. However, Śaṅkara goes on to suggest, in the same passage, while directing an attack on Mīmāṃsaka readings, that someone could have the Brahman experience *without* studying the Upaniṣads. One could, perhaps, acquire the intellectual understanding in some other way.

> Moreover, in this matter sacred texts and company along with awareness (*anubhava*) and company are, as the case may be, the knowledge-generator, because acquiring an understanding of Brahman is completed in a special awareness (*anubhava*) and because that special knowledge has as its object an existing reality (not, like an act, something to be done).[16]

Thus, comprehension of Upaniṣadic statements appears to be on par with yogic prerequisites—"calm, self-control, compassion, and the rest," *śama-dama-dayâdi*—as discussed in the introduction here. The transcendent nature of the resultant special experience is a theme surfacing in the passage as well as in other places in Śaṅkara's *Brahma-sūtra-bhāṣya*. For example, in the "Introduction" (*avatāra*) with elegant prose he waxes dramatic to the effect that *śāstra*—including *śruti*, "scripture," Upaniṣadic statements—communicate *only* on the condition of "spiritual ignorance," *avidyā*, as pointed out. People with "spiritual knowledge," *vidyā*, cannot be said to know or act in the familiar and everyday ways. They may seem to, but the ordinary categories do not apply.

> A person ceasing to identify with the "I" and "mine" with regard to the body, the senses, and so on is not a "knower" in the ordinary sense, because the workings of a "knowledge source," *pramāṇa*, would be impossible (a "knower," a *pramātṛ*, requires a *pramāṇa*—perception, inference, testimony—likewise "knowledge," *pramā*, in the everyday sense). For without employing sense faculties and

> company, a person could not act and communicate by way of conventions with perception and the like. Nor would it be possible to have everyday exchanges involving the sense faculties without an overseeing of their operations (that is, without an overseer who uses them for an "I" and "mine"). Furthermore, without self being projected (*adhyasta*) onto the body, no one sets out to do anything. And if there is none of this, there would be "being-self" unattached such that to be a knower would be out of the question. And without a knower, there would be no operation of any knowledge source. Therefore, the sources of knowledge, perception and the rest, have objects only under the condition of "spiritual ignorance," *avidyā*. And this holds for *śāstra* (authoritative texts) as well.[17]

Those with true *vidyā* move according to different rules and forces, if "move" they do at all. Of course, we must remind ourselves, Śaṅkara embraces the notion of "living liberation," such that self-knowers would appear to know in the everyday way and are able to teach a way to enlightenment.

A final note before looking at Aurobindo's causal argument. As mentioned, Śaṅkara does not, so far as I can tell, explicitly embrace avoidance of infinite regress as part of the Vedāntic argument for Brahman. But he does cite "no stopping place," *anavasthā*, as a problem devastating Buddhist subjectivism, at *Brahma-sūtra-bhāṣya* 2.2.30: "mental dispositions," *saṃskāra*, responsible for memory and maintaining all sorts of classifications, cannot result just from earlier *saṃskāra* as opposed to real, external objects, for fear of "no stopping place," *anavasthā*. My sense is that Advaitins typically take it for granted that the same logic applies to the idea of an ungrounded series of causes, but not Śaṅkara, who says explicitly in connection with an attempt to explain away evil (see Appendix D) that infinite regress is not in every context unacceptable. Buddhists aver that the phenomenal world of cause and effect is infinite in both directions: like seed and sprout, no beginning and no end. Śaṅkara agrees largely, apparently viewing the *īśvara* as emergent as an agent from a homogeneous Brahman after a period of cosmic dissolution (*pralaya*) at the beginning of a new round. But there is no absolute origin according to him—perhaps because of knots he sees in other explanations of evil. The Lord cannot make this world a paradise because of constraints of karma made by persons in a previous round. Except for karma, the Lord out of intrinsic "bliss," *ānanda*, entailing intrinsic compassion, would have made this world nothing but a pleasure-ground.[18]

Aurobindo inherits many of the conceptual knots in Vedānta's understanding of Brahman, but launches into his own lines of solution, ignoring—though at times echoing, perhaps inevitably—disputes among the classical subschools. In an early chapter of *The Life Divine* entitled "The Methods of Vedantic Knowledge," he complains:

> We see this succession [mystic awareness called "intuition" replaced by reason as the most authoritative faculty for philosophy] in the Upanishads and the subsequent Indian philosophies. The sages of the Veda and Vedanta relied entirely on intuition and spiritual experience. . . . when the age of rationalistic speculation began, Indian philosophies, respectful of the heritage of the past, adopted a double attitude towards the Truth they sought. They recognized in the Sruti the earlier results of Intuition or, as thy preferred to call it, inspired Revelation, an authority superior to Reason. But at the same time they started from Reason and tested the results it gave them, . . . [eventually] the natural trend of Reason to assert its own supremacy triumphed in effect over the theory of its subordination.
>
> *SABCL* v. 18: 69

Like several neo-Vedāntins, Aurobindo seems wary of the argumentation of classical Vedāntins, who do indeed use tools of logic and critical reasoning (*nyāya*) to support one or another position. Neo-Vedāntins champion, in contrast, "spiritual experience." Typically they are also wary of myth and religious dogma—unless interpreted esoterically, not as about "heaven" or the like, in the fashion of Mīmāṃsakas, but as meditational props—taking Upaniṣads to record neither (a) the word of God nor (b) timeless reverberations in the cosmic "ether" (like all Veda, according to Mīmāṃsā), but rather (c) special experiences such as, in the case of Aurobindo, his own, had, he tells us, by "quieting thought." Nevertheless, it is not true that the early "sages" (*ṛṣi*-s) authoring the Upaniṣads relied *entirely* on spiritual experiences, since, as Śaṅkara says correctly, the causal argument is there at least implicitly in the *Bṛhadāraṇyaka*, *Chāndogya*, and other early Upaniṣads including the *Īśā*. Furthermore, Aurobindo himself accepts, indeed develops, the causal argument. And knots such as the problem of evil motivate his novel cosmology of "divine life." Let me explain.

Aurobindo pretty much jettisons the "inexplicability," *anirvacanīya*, notion of classical Advaita, claiming the *nêti nêti* ("Not this, not that") of the *Bṛhadāraṇyaka* is matched with an *iti iti* ("It is this, It is that"), albeit he makes much use of a concept of "spiritual ignorance," *avidyā*, which he interprets, in line with Śaṅkara, as lack of knowledge of a true "self," *ātman*.[19] For him, the Upaniṣadic negative expressions (in the *Kena Upaniṣad*, for instance) are directed to propositional thought concerning the experience, not to Brahman's "essence" (*rasa*). At places he seems to say otherwise, but the overwhelming thrust of his teachings is that Brahman *is* knowable intellectually, because Brahman is knowable experientially, through yoga practice. The intellectual knowledge is speculation, he acknowledges, but based on "spiritual experience," which is captured phenomenologically by aesthetically heightened imagery and abstractly by a plastic mentality whereby the "logic of the Infinite" can be grasped (compare again Medhananda's "Principle of Mystic Receptivity": 2020). Meditation and resultant experience have a clear message for description of what is revealed: Brahman is "Sachchidananda" (Aurobindo's spelling), *sac-chid-ānanda*, "Existence-Consciousness-Bliss."

Turning to *The Life Divine* and four early chapters devoted to elaborating each of the three terms, (a) "existence," *sat*, (b) "consciousness" or "consciousness-force," *cit* or, as he says sometimes, *cit-śakti*, and (c) "bliss," *ānanda*, we see that, despite protestations about rational theology, Aurobindo repeats the causal argument laid out by Śaṅkara: he does so quite explicitly in Book One, Chapter Ten, "Conscious Force," a chapter devoted to *cit*. Indeed, like Śaṅkara refuting Sāṃkhya (*Brahma-sūtra-bhāṣya* 2.2.1–10 and elsewhere[20]), Aurobindo expressly targets the Sāṃkhya notion of *pradhāna*, "primordial matter" (see premise 3 in the above reconstruction of Śaṅkara's argument), which he says may stand in for the "matter" of modern materialism (*SABCL* v. 18: 81–2), the stuff of the physical universe. Furthermore, Aurobindo's avowed refutation of materialism is based on there being sentient life, consciousness shown in the workings of nature (*SABCL* v. 18: 88–9). The line of thought is developed throughout the long text. He endorses a monism similar to monistic materialism: everything is made out of Brahman as some hold that there is a single material "stuff." But he adds a vitalist dimension and more: everything is at least minimally alive and potentially mental and indeed "supramental" in deriving from Brahman.

However, the thrust of Aurobindo's reasoning in that introductory chapter ("Conscious Force") and many others is far different from how Śaṅkara proceeds in his *Brahma-sūtra Commentary* and elsewhere, Śaṅkara who rests content with the attributes of "omniscience," *sarvajñatva*, and "full capability," *sarva-śaktitva*, without much elaboration anywhere. Aurobindo, in contrast, launches into hundreds of pages of detailing of Brahman's nature such that Brahman as supreme "Consciousness-Force" is willing and able to create not only, of course, the physical universe but all that is manifest phenomenologically: the emotionality, agency, and, perhaps most importantly, the meditational experiences had by us or any sentient being in any world. In other words, the project of filling out the role of "Sachchidananda" in accounting for features of our multi-dimensional reality is carried out in hundreds of pages. How, given Brahman primordially, is inconscient material possible and why does it come about? Life? Mind? "Self-experience?" And most problematically, it seems to me, evil?

The bottom line for Aurobindo with evil is that the world's originating out of Brahman as Sachchidananda (especially *ānanda*, "Bliss") means that evil has to have instrumental value for accomplishing the telos of divine life. The inconscience of matter itself has instrumental value, he reasons, "manifested" so that there can be divine life. The idea drives much of his reflection, let me stress. Evil is not, like compassion, selflessness, etc., an expression of Sachchidananda in the terms of our human universe, no direct manifestation, in any case, of Brahman through one or another of the Lord's wondrous "powers" (*śakti*). In sum, telling the story of the instrumental value of evil—evidently the worst of the knots in Vedāntic theism—is thematic throughout the thousand pages of the treatise. Our world is destined to manifest an at least much diviner life. Evil is a causal factor, necessary for a stretch but eliminable.

This chapter is not the place to rehearse the explanations of matter, life, and mind in relation to Brahman as first cause, nor how they or certain features of them are viewed as constituting evidence for Brahman. We will scrutinize the explanation of evil, both natural and moral, in the last chapter. My point now is that Aurobindo's "Brahman" is supposed to be intelligible in its workings, manifest as the physical universe along with all the phenomena of mind and life and meditational experience. And he finds at least some of the causal story in the early Upaniṣads, especially the *Īśā*.

6

Knowledge of Self (*ātman*) and Knowledge of the Occult

Īśā 9–14

The next six verses, 9 through 14, form a group topically. Note that Śaṅkara, for verses 9 and 10, takes the word *vidyā* not as he does elsewhere—as "spiritual knowledge," or "Knowledge," to use Aurobindo's spelling—but as referencing a "lower," occult knowledge, as he explains in his commentary. Aurobindo understands the word to mean self-discovery, that is, "Knowledge" in the usual Vedāntic—and Advaitic—sense of "self-discovery." To Śaṅkara's sensibilities, there is no deficiency in genuine *vidyā* and so that could not be what's meant when *vidyā* is denigrated in verse 9, whereas Aurobindo does find fault when our world of "Ignorance," ***avidyā***, is ignored, no matter that the self be found. He reasons that as Brahman cannot be ignorant of "Ignorance," neither should we. Knowledge by identity can be integrated with other modes of awareness, according to him, in an expanding "change of consciousness," as we saw in the last quotations in Chapter 4. The other verses in the sextet are read by each Vedāntin consistently with the two distinct understandings of *vidyā* and thus quite differently.

Śaṅkara:

> They enter a blinding darkness who devote themselves to (spiritual) ignorance, *avidyā*.
> Than that there is an even greater darkness. Into it go, as it were, they who are pleased with the (lower) knowledge. || 9 ||
>
> One thing, it is said, is accomplished through (lower) knowledge; something else, it is said, through (spiritual) ignorance, *avidyā*.
> So we have heard from the wise who have to us explained it all. || 10 ||
>
> Knowledge and ignorance, if together the two are engaged,

Crossing over death by the ignorance, one tastes by the knowledge the nectar of immortality. || 11 ||
They enter a blinding darkness who devote themselves to unmanifest nature.
Than that into an even greater darkness go, as it were, those who are pleased with manifest nature. || 12 ||

Just one thing is said to come from (devotion to) manifest nature; something else from the unmanifest, it is said.
So we have heard from the wise who have to us explained it all. || 13 ||

(Meditating on) the (un)manifest and dissolution, the person who knows both together
By the dissolution crosses beyond death, by the unmanifest tastes the nectar of immortality. || 14 ||

Aurobindo:

9. Into a blind darkness they enter who follow after the Ignorance, they as if into a greater darkness who devote themselves to the Knowledge alone.

10. Other, verily, it is said, is that which comes by the Knowledge, other that which comes by the Ignorance; this is the lore we have received from the wise who have revealed That to our understanding.

11. He who knows That as both in one, the Knowledge and the Ignorance, by the Ignorance crosses beyond death and by the Knowledge enjoys Immortality.

12. Into a blind darkness they enter who follow after the Non-Birth, they as if into a greater darkness who devote themselves to the Birth alone.

13. Other, verily, it is said, is that which comes by the Birth, other that which comes by the Non-Birth; this is the lore we have received from the wise who have revealed That to our understanding.

14. He who knows That as both in one, the Birth and the dissolution of Birth, by the dissolution crosses beyond death and by the Birth enjoys Immortality.

At the risk of oversimplifying the nature of Śaṅkara's audience, we may say that in addition to those who seek the supreme self, striving to be free from desire, there are two groups of Vedic adherents delineated in these verses, according to the Advaitin, two, that is, that are distinct from seekers of true "knowledge," knowledge of the universal self. The two are, first, Mīmāṃsaka ritualists, who are patently not to be followed, as we have discussed, and then, second—to say possibly anachronistically—"tantric" yogis who aim at knowledge of occult forces ("divinities") accompanied with extraordinary "powers," *siddhis*. Śaṅkara and Aurobindo do not disagree that yoga can lead to occult powers and experiences. They disagree about the value of their pursuit.

First note the profound agreement about self-discovery's prerequisite of desirelessness, much emphasized by Śaṅkara in comments on these verses. Aurobindo, let me repeat, also specifies austere demands. For example, he recommends not just celibacy but no "indulgence" of sexual feeling or any natural desire which could block meditational progress and especially occult openness to "Shakti," a divine energy (sexual feeling is apparently too engrossing for the sensitivity required). Admittedly, this judgment is based mainly on letters to people seeking yogic advice, and no strict rules are laid out in the massive *The Synthesis of Yoga*—revised in the 1940s—which paints *sādhana* in very broad strokes indeed, without much in the line of daily practice. But Aurobindo's own "integral yoga" is hardly a hippie path of free love and "vital indulgence." The ideal of "Janaka" promoted in his *Thoughts and Aphorisms* (1958/1913: *SABCL* v. 16) is not that of a family man but rather of a desire-free yogi living responsibly in the everyday world (as a just and respected king no less, in Janaka's case), not in an isolated cave or on a mountaintop.

Śaṅkara, for his part, accepting the Mīmāṃsaka understanding of action as invariably motivated by desire for a specific end or "fruit," *phala*, finds the having of desire to be the key presumption framing these six verses of the *Īśā*. The two groups he finds delineated are not on the path of the supreme knowledge although it is righteous ("dharmic") to have a desire for heaven or for a fortunate reincarnation, on the one hand (group one), or for occult knowledge and power, on the other (group two). Both would be meritorious by Vedic standards, the best of people who have a "faith-stand," *niṣṭhā*, conditioned by desire, who are nonetheless notches above ordinary folk unaware of or not practicing Vedic teachings.

Aurobindo, in contrast, finds only two groups, one, as he sees things, the likes of "nihilist," *śūnya-vāda* Buddhists, let us say, advocating absorption in the transcendence of Brahman, whom we might call from his perspective—I have to admit—"Śaṅkarites," and, two, ordinary people who are not following a yogic path. While Śaṅkara has three groupings, Aurobindo has two, both of whom he sees as going wrong when excluding the other and its practices according to the Upaniṣad. Spiritual knowledge is to be combined with worldly life, the Upaniṣad says according to him, whereas Śaṅkara apparently views that as impossible.

However, despite the direct conflict here, it should now be evident that the "Shankara" of Aurobindo's magnum opus, *The Life Divine*, is not to be mistaken for the author himself, although it is not an entire miss. The right way to understand the long arguments where the name "Shankara" appears (*SABCL* v. 18: 454–64, in particular) is that it is a generic "Mayavadin," an "Illusionist," who is being refuted by an argument series. It is best to understand Aurobindo's interlocutors as invented.[1] At places in *The Life Divine*, targeted positions doubtless reflect a popular (mis)understanding of Śaṅkara, but it is an invented opponent, really opponents, that Aurobindo takes himself to show to be wrong. Aurobindo's "Shankara" adversary is not a "straw man," as some have alleged, but there is a succession of interlocutors, as the argumentation proceeds, who are much like the voices in *pūrva-pakṣa* ("prima facie positions") of classical Sanskrit texts. As explained earlier in criticizing Thieme for finding *pūrva-pakṣa* in the the *Īśā* (anachronistically there, but no anachronism with Aurobindo), the term is tied to philosophy as a genre of literature, and as a strategy it is of course well-known in Western texts that, like the numerous classical Indian, are dialogic in form, whether overtly as with Plato or covertly as with practically the whole discipline. The point is that though historical figures may well be important and echoed, an author need not be thought of as having particular persons in mind when presenting views to be opposed. The historical Śaṅkara does not say that the world is actually an illusion; he says self-discovery is something *like* the correction of an illusion perceptually. How the world looks from Brahman's perspective cannot be explained, but for practical purposes we use the best explanation—which is that Brahman is the primeval origin and conscious cause and indeed our very own underlying subjectivity—that is, in short, an emanationist theism, a panentheism and cosmopsychism. Aurobindo does not get this quite right if the historical Śaṅkara is his intended target. But he is not.

Tradition presents Śaṅkara as a tantric yogi and the author of tantric texts, importantly the famous *Saundarya-laharī* ("Torrent of Beauty"), an occult practice manual written in florid verse, with 103 "stanzas," and the *Prapañca-sāra* ("The Quintessence of the World's Unrolling"), a much longer manual of almost 2,500 verses divided into thirty-six chapters. The problem with using these works to reconstruct Śaṅkara's philosophy and his reading of the *Īśā* is the worry that text promotion along with prestige is the real reason that a work is said—usually in a colophon—to be composed by him. Thus because of the large number of texts attributed to Śaṅkara (almost 400 according to Pande 1994: 104) coupled with rejection by Brown (1958: 25–30) of *Saundarya-laharī* authorship for Śaṅkara and of other works putatively by him by other scholars, it is now practically illegitimate to cite texts other than the commentaries on ten Upaniṣads, on the *Gītā*, and on the *Brahma-sūtra* along with the *Upadeśa-sahasrī* in reconstructing Śaṅkara's positions.[2] Many works must have been accredited falsely. Nevertheless, Pande (1994: 351–5) mounts a strong case for the kinship of Śaṅkara's teaching overall with Śāktism, which is also an Advaita emanationist theism but stressing the role of the "Goddess," *devī*, the "Energy" of Śiva. Forms of the Goddess are identified with Vedāntic "divinities" and thought to be manifest in occult forces and occult centers of consciousness (*cakras*) in on-going arrangings of the world. Brahman's manifestation is launched and kept in harmony by the supreme "Power" of the Lord, *īśvara* (sometimes "*īśvarêśvarī*," a bigendered Absolute), who remains transcendent but who is also all-encompassing, freely loosing herself forth, emanating and enlivening a very real world or worlds. Śakti branches out as a host of divinities, subordinate "energies," to accomplish her on-going tasks.

Pande is right, it seems to me, to a certain extent, that is, as he says (1994: 353), "the status of the world in Śaṅkara's *Advaita* is [not] inconsistent with that in Śākta [tantric] *Advaita*. In both, consciousness is the sole reality which manifests the world through self-limitation." This seems a fair judgment without necessarily accepting the main evidence Pande cites which consists of traditional ascriptions to Śaṅkara of both the *Saundarya-laharī* and the *Prapañca-sāra* along with traditional stories of his founding two monastic *sampradāya* (at Śṛṅgeri and Kāñci: Pande 1994: 354–5) which are tantric.[3] For, in the authenticated corpus—and right here in his commentary on the *Īśā*—Śaṅkara endorses not just yoga but, arguably, tantric yoga, as laudably Vedic and thus presumably preparatory for self-discovery and in any case a life plan that, though not the superior "path of knowledge," is still a notch above the lives of ordinary folk. Occult powers, he asserts, accrue from tantric disciplines, from "knowledge of divinities." In his commentary on *Īśā* 9–14, Śaṅkara distinguishes such seekers from Mīmāṃsaka ritualists, both groups living under the condition of *non*-renunciation of desire, as opposed to the highest type of aspirant who gives up all desire to know the self. He writes introducing verse 9 (see Appendix B):

> there is a distinct result for the "knowledge" that is directed to divinities—"divine wealth"—which is not the spiritual knowledge of the supreme self but rather knowledge that is to be put aside as combined with certain works: "By (such a lower) knowledge, one enters the world of the gods." *Bṛhadāraṇyaka Upaniṣad* 1.5.16

So, there are, according to him, two groups delineated in the six verses, neither of which is on the path of supreme knowledge, broadly (a) ritualists who aim at heaven and fortunate circumstances in reincarnation and (b) tantrics who combine meditation with other practices. Despite the denigration of both groups in verse 9, verses 10 and 11 assert a certain virtue in the combination of the occult knowledge of tantrics and proper ritual action, but still falling short of the desirelessness required by the highest path. Śaṅkara at the very beginning of his introduction to verse 9 makes the point, hearkening back to his reading of verse 1:

> The Upaniṣad's opening mantra set forth a path of knowledge that proceeds by *renunciation of all desire*: "All this is to be blocked out by the Lord, . . . you should not yearn for anyone's wealth," a first and premiere teaching of the Upaniṣad. [Emphasis mine.]

Later in that introduction to verse 9, he makes the same point referring to verses 6 and 7, and then continues:

> And then there are passages such as (*Bṛhadāraṇyaka Upaniṣad* 4.4.22) "What would we want with children, we for whom this world is the self?" where, by the method of renunciation of the triad of desires for wife and company (wealth and *loka*, "worlds," i.e., power), the path of (knowing) the self as it is in its essential nature alone is presented, a path for those who would know the self, a path that is in tension with any of works.

For him, the overall message of the six verses is that within the realm of desire one can achieve occult knowledge and *siddhi*s (the *Yoga-sūtra* enumerates many, such as creatures' fearlessness in the yogi's presence, which is tied to the practice of *ahiṃsā*, "non-injury," and being able to go unnoticed in a crowd, great physical strength, and so on). Thus, a yogi can attain the lofty goal of right combination of occult knowledge and action, as Śaṅkara says in commenting on verse 11, namely, that such a one:

> "tastes . . . the nectar of immortality," that is, attains the state of transformed consciousness characterized by knowledge of divinities. For that is called the "nectar of immortality" which amounts to attaining that divine state.

However, the overriding theme remains with him the desirelessness required by the path of knowledge. Śaṅkara, like the *Yoga-sūtra* (*YS* 3.37), denigrates the seeking of *siddhi*s presumably from the perspective of a master of the higher path. See here his commentary on *Īśā* 13 and 14 in particular where he appears to be attacking what he sees as the false goal of yogis who are nevertheless very advanced, aiming to know the primeval cause, a state entailing *siddhi*s. He uses a technical term from the *Yoga-sūtra*, *prakṛti-laya*, for that high accomplishment that yet falls short of the truly supreme end, the "supreme personal good," *parama-puruṣârtha*. From his commentary on 13:

> [F]rom devoting oneself to an "Absolute" *as an effect* the result is characterized by such yogic powers (*siddhis*) as unnoticeability and control. This is the meaning. . . . Purāṇic sources inform us that the statement, "They enter a blinding darkness," is about (what the *Yoga-sūtra* and the *Sāṃkhya-kārikā* call) "absorption in nature," *prakṛti-laya* (for the mind).

Then again from his commentary on *Īśā* 14:

> For, meditating on Hiraṇyagarbha [the Absolute as an effect], the result is to gain the *siddhis* of unnoticeability and so on. Having transcended "death" in the form of lack of control and the like, one "tastes"—by means of meditating on the unmanifest, by means of "unmanifest nature"—the nectar of immortality; that is, one attains to "absorption in nature," *prakṛti-laya* (for the mind).

"Absorption in nature," *prakṛti-laya*, is a yogic term apparently used to explain the mind's *near* complete silence and spontaneous *samādhi*—"yogic trance," "deep meditation"—in that its attainment is supposed to be, as Vācaspati explains in commenting on *Yoga-sūtra* 1.19, very close to the highest end but still requiring a future lifetime and a still greater *samādhi*. Śaṅkara's use shows familiarity with yoga psychology, and before moving to Aurobindo's reading of our *Īśā* sextet, let us explore a little further the Advaitin's relation to yoga with respect to the *Yoga-sūtra*'s central concept of *samādhi*.

Many later Advaitins identify the *summum bonum* of "immediate experience of Brahman," *brahma-sākṣātkāra*—in Śaṅkara's most perspicacious expression (from the *Bṛhadāraṇyaka*)—with the *Yoga-sūtra*'s "extreme absorption in yogic trance," *nirvikalpa-samādhi*, that is, "*samādhi* without content," without content except, to be sure, the self's self-luminosity. The idea is thematic, for example, in the *Viveka-cūḍā-maṇi*, "Crest Jewel of Discrimination," whose authorship, as mentioned, has been much discussed. The *Yoga-sūtra*'s *asamprajñāta-samādhi* and *nirbīja-samādhi*, "seedless *samādhi*," that is to say, without the "seeds" of mental dispositions that would throw one out of the transcendent state, are cognate. Despite the theory of potentially disturbing dispositions, the *samādhi* concept in the *Yoga-sūtra* seems rather metaphysics-free, its neutrality evident in the fact that Buddhists, Naiyāyikas, and so on—schools with very different views of reality—use the term. So *samādhi* is at the least "deep meditation," and is sometimes rightly rendered, "yogic trance." The word is also used in different genre of literature, for example, drama and court poetry, with this range of meaning. There is, of course, as we saw in Chapter 4 on the epistemology of mysticism, disagreement about its character and especially what the state, or states, reveal. The *Yoga-sūtra* differentiates types of *samādhi*, with "contentless" *samādhi* held up as the ultimate goal and accomplishment, not *prakṛti-laya* which is nevertheless close. Śaṅkara uses the term *samādhi* (e.g., *BSB* 2.3.39), but he does not use *nirvikalpaka-samādhi* or its cognates (this is one reason Ingalls et al. reject authorship by him for the *Viveka-cūḍā-maṇi*). The *Yoga-sūtra* interprets the highest *samādhi* as a break in the usual connection of self (*puruṣa*) and nature (*prakṛti*) such that there is no future reincarnation. Śaṅkara similarly views *prakṛti-laya* as a step below true self-knowledge and within the sphere of rebirth (*saṃsāra*), as he says in commenting on verses 13 and 14.

Aurobindo, for his part, finds the *Īśā* proposing a complex goal, "Knowledge" somehow united to "Ignorance." He in effect endorses Śaṅkara's positive position on self-discovery but not the exclusionary, negative spin given to Ignorance. On his reading of the Upaniṣad—coupled with an avowal of an existential sense of the omnipresence of the One—there has to be a story about cosmic becoming showing its worth as a fitting manifestation of the "Divine." Multiplicity is not illusion, nor the inconscience of matter nor the predatory nature of life, because these are slowly to unfold in harmony with their secret nature as manifestations of "Sachchidananda." Thus, Ignorance is not to be denigrated except when, as verse 9 says, it is not drawn towards Knowledge. Similarly, Knowledge—that is, awareness of the cosmic self, *ātman*—is incomplete without pulling towards itself in its essential characteristics beings forged in Ignorance. Ignorance is a matter of multiple false identities, but invariably false identity with a purpose, making of fragile individuality pulled to express, better and better, the self's native characteristics of consciousness and bliss, in other words, persons progressively transformed in the direction of awesome virtues, creaturely solidarity, happiness, beauty in action. Even egoism is said to have a positive purpose as scaffolding for building psychic personalities. There is to be multiple individuations but all remain the One. Although a soul is said to be becoming increasingly unique, "psychic beings" uniformly come to reflect essential characteristics of the single cosmic witness, especially "delight," *ānanda*, according to Aurobindo.

The key idea is that there has to be value in Brahman's "manifestation," and the ideal is a person's expressing the qualities of a figure like the Kṛṣṇa of the *Bhāgavata Purāṇa*, who to each encounter brings joy, or someone with the *pāramitā*s, "perfections," of a Bodhisattva (the traditional six: *dāna*, "generosity," *śīla*, "uprightness of character, sociability," *kṣānti*, "patience, endurance, acceptance," *vīrya*, "strength, energy," *dhyāna*, "concentration, meditation," *prajñā*, "wisdom") such that the cosmic loss of consciousness in material nature itself has meaning. Matter, life, and mind are challenging to Brahman because of Brahman's essential unity, Aurobindo reasons, but Brahman dares to become divided, he says, *for a purpose*, for "divine life," which justifies the long travail. The opposition of Knowledge and Ignorance—as imaged in a secluded yogi enjoying in trance the transcendent self versus a normal, egoistic person acting out of desire—has to be harmonized: this is the pragmatic message of the Upaniṣad and, Aurobindo tells us, the direction of his own yoga and spiritual experience. He calls his *sādhana* "integral yoga," aiming at what he calls "integral knowledge." And he reads the Upaniṣad accordingly.

If it is possible to break out of the "hermeneutic circle" of interpreting a text as foundational according to a touchstone preconceived, then I'd like to say that these six verses of the *Īśā* do read as a condemnation of an extreme asceticism like the *via negativa* that Aurobindo associates with "Shankara." The Upaniṣad makes an internal criticism, not a rejection premised on materialism or the delusion of self-discovery but, more in line with Aurobindo's reading, yogic advocacy coupled with denunciation of mere world-rejection as even worse than failing altogether to take up a yogic path. Aurobindo may read in some of his meliorist metaphysics, but the *Īśā* does indeed appear to endorse a kind of harmony between ascesis and ordinary life. Nevertheless, it seems unfair for Aurobindo to build into foundational yogic experience rejection of the "Nirvana" on which he sees traditional Advaita as based. But a careful reading (see again the quote at the end of Chapter 4) shows that he does not "reject" the transcendence in the experience but finds it coming to include and modify the transcended.[4] My sense of the philosophic point is that just what "spiritual experience" corrects misleading claims based on whatever other spiritual experience is a ballgame of infinite extra innings, the other side ever getting a new turn at bat.[5]

Whatever the merits of Aurobindo's reading, however, he presents a philosophy of Brahman that shares with Śaṅkara's—and all Vedāntic metaphysics—certain conceptual difficulties, I contend. Before taking them up again, let's look at a summary statement he makes about the *Īśā* which occurs in the middle of *The Life Divine*:

> The Isha Upanishad insists on the unity and reality of all the manifestations of the Absolute; it refuses to confine truth to any one aspect. Brahman is the stable and the mobile, the internal and the external, all that is near and all that is far

> whether spiritually or in the extension of Time and Space; it is the Being and all becomings, the Pure and Silent who is without feature or action and the Seer and Thinker who organizes the world and its objects; it is the One who becomes all that we are sensible of in the universe, the Immanent and that in which he takes up his dwelling. The Upanishad affirms the perfect and liberating knowledge to be that which excludes neither the Self nor its creations: the liberated spirit sees all these as becomings of the Self-existent in an internal vision and by a consciousness which perceives the universe within itself instead of looking out on it, like the limited and egoistic mind, as a thing other than itself. To live in cosmic Ignorance is a blindness, but to confine oneself to an exclusive Absolutism of Knowledge is also a blindness: to know Brahman as at once and together the Knowledge and the Ignorance, to attain to the supreme status at once by the Becoming and the Non-Becoming, to relate together realisation of the transcendent and the cosmic self, to achieve foundation in the supramundane and a self-aware manifestation in the mundane, is the integral knowledge; . . .
>
> *SABCL* v. 19: 636

The "true individual" Aurobindo finds presaged in the Upaniṣad involves what he calls a "triple transformation": (1) a psychic transformation (a soul personality made in secret over many lifetimes takes over the "surface consciousness"—cf., "by the Ignorance crosses beyond death," verse 11—(2) a spiritual transformation (difficult to imagine despite Aurobindo's undeniable eloquence), and (3) a supramental transformation (even more difficult). The latter chapters of *The Life Divine* spell these out as increasingly awesome. Let me just remark that such people would apparently be loveable saints and artists, and move on to the philosophic questions of the knots in Vedānta metaphysics and whether Aurobindo has untied them.

Picking up from the discussion in the last chapter, we have identified two conceptual difficulties vexing a Brahman-centered philosophy, whether Śaṅkara's or Aurobindo's or any other. First, there is problem of how Brahman includes the things of the world and our individual awarenesses, both of which are changing all the time. Second, there is the problem of evil. Let me make some remarks on the first, which, it is easy to show, connects with the second. The last chapter expands upon this discussion.

Is Brahman aware of being the dog lying at my feet, the particular animal, as the dog is aware? The dog is very intelligent, but I doubt he knows himself as Brahman, whereas Brahman knows itself as itself, according to all Vedānta. Or, to change examples, is Brahman aware of being Hitler the way Hitler was aware of himself, including his body, thought, and emotion but without awareness of

Brahman? If so, then Brahman loses awareness of itself as bliss (*ānanda*), etc., since neither the dog as the dog nor Hitler as Hitler was aware of supernal bliss. If not, then arguably Brahman is not all-encompassing, not "the One," in not including Hitler's own phenomenology albeit including the immediacy of his consciousness and self. Thus, Brahman is not in the widest sense "pervasive," *vibhu*. Okay, but (existence) monism is preserved in that everything *derives* from Brahman. But then there is a second aspect of the problem. Let's say Hitler's phenomenology derives from Brahman. So, first, does Brahman have parts? I think Śaṅkara's answer is clearly "Yes!" viewing material things as a separate emanation, or emanations, from that of consciousness. Brahman is the original cause and governs world-processes as *īśvara* without losing itself in them or anything finite. But then, second, how can evil derive from Brahman, from a being whose essential nature is consciousness and bliss?

Aurobindo tries to ease the tension between the homogeneous and composite ways of thinking about Brahman with his notion of the "logic of the Infinite." The true Infinite has to include the finite, he reasons. However, he also holds that Brahman cannot lose its character in becoming finite, even in becoming matter. That's why the evolution of consciousness has to occur. Aurobindo makes use of a presumed incompatibility of a totally inconscient material universe and Brahman as "Sachchidananda."[6] Interestingly, Śaṅkara says that "incompatibility" with self-knowledge, *vidyā*, is not easily determined—see the end of the commentary translated in Appendix B.

My take on this issue with respect to the views of Aurobindo is that Brahman is not aware of Hitler as Hitler was aware of Hitler, it should be said, and that Brahman does change in becoming Hitler or anyone or anything else for that matter. The Lord (*brahman* as *īśvara*) may know Hitler's deepest desires and thoughts better than Hitler himself but, on this option, not in the severely limited way characteristic of Hitler the person. That was just one horrible individual. Then to consider the *vivaraṇa* ("tranmogrification") option where Hitler's awareness would be "illusion" and even "non-existent," *asat*, note that Aurobindo, too—not only Śaṅkara, Padmapāda, and company—has to admit a degree of *māyā* in a negative sense since, as I understand him, Brahman excludes Hitler's phenomenology as lived by Hitler himself, although as both the ultimate material and an on-going agential cause and not just the cosmic witness Brahman should be said to be responsible for Hitler.

The Upaniṣadic view is that everything comes out of Brahman, but nothing is the Absolute by itself to the exclusion of others. Aurobindo insists on an essential nature for Brahman which Brahman cannot lose and which guarantees that manifestation cannot be a matter of anything goes but must be compatible with that nature. A world of unending pain, for example, is not inconceivable by a mind not presupposing Brahman but is ruled out by taking into account Brahman's essential nature.[7] Thus for Aurobindo, as I read him, the evils of not being aware of Brahman as Brahman is aware—to include inconscience, egoism, and pain and suffering—have to have justification. The justification is supposed to be "divine life."

So, our first set of knots connects with the second with respect to Aurobindo's positions. Why should Brahman lose itself in matter, life, mind, and persons living in "Ignorance?" Why are there these fundamental evils? Theodicy is the driving force in Aurobindo's *The Life Divine*, articulating a *telos* in Brahman's becoming that would justify this material "manifestation." That goal, which is supposed to be meaningful both from Brahman's and a human perspective, is "soul-making," to use the expression of John Keats popularized by John Hick (1978). The logic is, as pointed out, that the end justifies the means. But what about how excessive evil seems, *all* the pain and suffering, some of which seems patently *dis*teleological on Aurobindo's conception of a *telos* as on any other?

I have written on this in other places, in particular, "God's Last World: Sri Aurobindo's Argument for Divine Life" (2008/2016), where to his theory I add the following thought experiment. God creates many worlds much better than this, the heavens, for instance, of the gods, but in those worlds I do not exist. Our world is definitely not the best of all possible worlds, but it is the one where I exist. So, I am grateful that God in Her graciousness suffers it. Indeed, this could be God's "last world," a world that is only barely possible as bordering on incompatibility with Brahman's nature as "Sachchidananda" (in Aurobindo's conception). This may be called the Parallel-Worlds Defense of God's Goodness in the Face of Evil.

Leibniz reasoned that God should create the best of all possible worlds. The problem is that this world does not seem to be that world, because of evil. But suppose that God does create the best of all possible worlds. What about the second-best world, the runner-up in world competition? Should not God give the creatures in the second-best world their day in the sun? Why should some flaw, in comparison with the champion world, prevent God from letting the runner-up world come to be? God, it seems, would create the second best as a parallel universe, with its own space and time, etc., alongside the first prize. Similarly, the third place, the fourth, the fifth, and so on down to a world where the balance of good and evil is so tenuous that God decides, "Okay, this one and finished." That last world would be ours. Thus, so long as we judge that there is not so much evil in this world that God would refuse to give us our day in the sun, then the evil here is compatible with the idea of God as good. The defense has the further virtue that it matches our gratitude for being at all. That is, so long as we are, all told, glad we exist, we would feel thankful toward a Creator, despite evil.

This idea I got from Aurobindo's "planes of being," which line up with conceptions in certain Upaniṣads especially as interpreted by tantrics. That is, our neo-Vedāntin maintains that there are indeed other worlds, not my separate, parallel universes, but "levels of being" both accessible occultly and expressed in everyday life. The epic poem *Savitri* has a long "book" on these ("The Book of the Traveller of the Worlds") which range from ours and the "kingdom of subtle matter" through life worlds—of the "Little Life" and the "Greater Life"—and worlds of mentality—"Kingdoms and Godheads of the Little Mind" and "Kingdoms and Godheads of the Greater Mind"—to "Heavens of the Ideal" and "Kingdoms of the Greater Knowledge" (*Savitri*, *SABCL* v. 28: 93–302). These are not supposed to be just matters of poetic fancy—though surely imagination is addressed—and the figure of "King Ashwapati," who is the "traveller," is, though of course fictional, commonly supposed to stand for Aurobindo himself in his yogic explorations. Like Śaṅkara, Aurobindo assumes there is a subtle body of non-material psychological continua that Vedāntins, following the *Taittirīya Upaniṣad*, call "sheaths," *kośa*.

Aurobindo also uses—whereas Śaṅkara does not (apart from the works of dubious authorship such as the *Saundarya-laharī*)—a tantric, "chakric" psychological model. According to the *kośa* schema, consciousness has five spheres of embodiment: (1) physical, *annamaya*, (2) vital—or "breath-made," pranic, *prāṇamaya*—(3) lower-mind, *manomaya*—the sensuous intelligence humans share with animals—(4) higher-mind, *vijñānamaya*—more profoundly connective intelligence—and (5) blissful, *ānandamaya*, the sheath nearest in character to the self, *ātman*. The *Taittirīya Upaniṣad* seems to have these bodies concentrically ordered, each interior (*antara*) to its predecessor beginning with the most exterior, the physical body, the "food" (*annamaya*) sheath. However, the meaning of the word "interior" does not, in this context, concern relative location but rather relative "essentiality" or "nearness" to the self, ideas cashed out with respect to relative endurance among other factors. The physical sheath perishes at the most rapid rate. Each sheath connects with a world or environment consonant with its constituents. The food sheath has as its universal counterpart the physical world, the pranic the life world (or worlds), the lower-mind and higher-mind sheaths connect with mental worlds, and then bliss and spirit contain or suffuse all planes of being. The "inner" sheaths enliven the outer, and the outer can die and fall away while the inner continue on. For Śaṅkara, the main point is that while they are all Brahman one needs to learn to differentiate self from transitory formations occurring in any of these bodies. For Aurobindo, the point is to let them be transformed from, so to say, the inside out.

The tantric view of chakras has a string of them connected by "channels," *nāḍi*, which are sometimes viewed as lines of spiritual light connecting also the sheaths. Chakras are conceived as broadcasting and receiving channels for occult energies. Aurobindo views awareness of chakric exchanges as part of a developing soul personality that justifies our universe, whereas Śaṅkara—again outside of tantric texts perhaps wrongly ascribed—sees occult matters as a distraction in regard to the path of knowledge. And that is how he reads these verses of the *Īśā*. For Aurobindo, or at least for his yogic recommendations, awakening and transformation of the chakras works best from the top down, by descent of "Shakti" through the top of the head in through the most major *nāḍi* or "channel," the "Royal Road," the *suṣumṇa*, the central channel in the conception of tantrics—who, we may add, seem by and large to differ from Aurobindo in at least one crucial respect. The mainstream tantric view has a sleeping "serpent energy," *kuṇḍalinī*, in the lowest chakra located near the base of the spine that when awakened by meditation rises up, opening all the "centers" in an experience of self-discovery. Aurobindo uses the tantric imagery but urges seekers to call upon a "descent" of Shakti into the higher chakras, especially the heart chakra (*anāhata*), or to try to recenter identity in the chakra just above the head (*sahasra-dala*).

Psychologically Aurobindo points to what he calls the "war of the members," echoing Plato's argument for a tripartite "soul": conflict is possible only if there are distinct factors. Our hearts need not line up with our desires, and our mental will—our ethical sense—has to check baser impulses. From a Vedāntic perspective, Plato leaves out, surprisingly, the body (the *annamaya-kośa*), and, maybe not so surprisingly, a spiritual self or witness (*ātman*) to include the psychic as championed by Aurobindo. But Plato does have the appetitive and emotional—both "pranic" in the *kośa* classification—and the rational which is capable of contemplating "Forms." According to the Vedāntic theory, the rational would be the "mental," mentality dividing into a higher type in contrast with a lower shared with animals (*manomaya* and *vijñānamaya*). In Plato's view, the rational is to control the appetitive and emotional parts, and, consonantly in the social and political spheres, he dreams of a "philosopher-king" and an authoritarian state, where unruliness is prevented by police. In Aurobindo's richer utopian idea of "divine life," no police would be necessary, every person self-regulating in harmony with everyone else. A psychic element would be psychologically dominant; so, he envisages a possible future. Actually, the psychology put forth by Aurobindo is yet more complex, in that he purports to identify several levels of a "higher mind." Intuitively, the best I can do with that is to point to inspiration, which, just to consider the poetic kind, does seem to come from some better part of ourselves than whatever voices hunger. For Aurobindo, the best mantras come from some such exalted level of mind, and he sees the last verses of the *Īśā* as in this way particularly luminous.[8]

However elaborate Aurobindo's cosmology, it is difficult to understand how there could be so much evil if Brahman as understood by him ("Sachchidananda") were really real. We may be grateful for our less than perfect world, and yet it still seems like there should be a lot less pain and suffering on any theistic theory including Aurobindo's. We take up theodicy again in the last chapter.

7

A Theistic Way to Self-Discovery

Īśā 15 and 16

Śaṅkara:

> The face of truth is covered by a golden lid.
> Pūṣan! Nourisher! Make it open, for one whose *dharma* is true, for experience.
> || 15 ||
>
> Pūṣan! Nourisher! Solo Traveler! Death, Yama the Controller! Sun! Child of Prajāpati, Father of Creatures! Disperse your (blinding) rays. Concentrate your energy (*tejas*).
> The form of yours that is the most auspicious, that I would see. That yonder Person, I am He (*so 'ham*). || 16 ||

Aurobindo:

> 15. The face of Truth is covered with a brilliant golden lid; that do thou remove, O Fosterer, for the law of the Truth, for sight.
>
> 16. O Fosterer, O sole Seer, O Ordainer, O illumining Sun, O power of the Father of creatures, marshal thy rays, draw together thy light; the Lustre which is thy most blessed form of all, that in Thee I behold. The Purusha there and there, He am I.

Śaṅkara reads the *Īśā*'s last four verses, 15–18, as a unit framed by the speaker's dying and knowing death is near.[1] We'll take them up two at a time because of their richness, poetic and propositional, and the richness of the commentaries to boot. The four verses have an aesthetic unity that may be the reason they were borrowed from the *Bṛhadāraṇyaka* (*Bṛ* 5.15.1–4). (Possibly it was the other way around, but scholarly opinion has the *Bṛhadāraṇyaka* as the oldest Upaniṣad.) The immediately preceding passage in the *Bṛhadāraṇyaka* praises a certain "Gāyatrī" mantra, so named for the meter, *gāyatrī*, whose twenty-four syllables fall into three sets of eight, precisely ordered in terms of longs and shorts. That mantra is echoed by the sixteen syllables in the lines here as well as by it being the "Sun" who is the addressee in both cases. And most loudly we are reminded of the Gāyatrī with the end of verse 16, "The form of yours that is the most auspicious, that I would see." Compare the Gāyatrī: "That most excellent form of the god that is the Sun, Savitri, on that we would meditate, that which would best elevate our consciousness" (*tat savitur vareṇyam bhārgo devasya dhīmahi dhiyo yo naḥ pracodayāt*, *Ṛg Veda* 3.62.10). If we may extend Śaṅkara's reading, it seems as though the speaker in the *Īśā* is showing that through meditational practice the Gāyatrī has been internalized and there is nothing more to do now but await the Lord's action, which would be the final step, the removal of an occult lid at the top of the inner vision.

Having said that the speaker is near the end in the introduction to 15, Śaṅkara tells us more about the person in commenting on 16.[2] And what he says is in tension with his theme of the incompatibility of knowledge and action. I think he knows this. There has been tension all along, a kind of pragmatic contradiction, a form of exaggeration, in my opinion, for emphasis, or possibly a false generalization made for emphatic effect, concerning action and "knowledge." Śaṅkara says the speaker is praying, which is a "speech act," as we moderns have learned from Wittgenstein and J.L. Austin. Indeed, is not meditation an act? Yes, and a difficult one at that, requiring disciplined attention. Śaṅkara understands the reference to *dharma* in verse 15 as the *action* taken by a person committed to the path of "knowledge," *vidyā*, but who has not yet reached the goal. A good translation for *dharma*—which is a very weighty term in Sanskrit—is in English "right action," used with both ethical and prudential significance.

Mayeda (1992: 88–94), addressing the question of Śaṅkara's view of ethics, homes in on the apparent contradiction and says flat out, "our examination has revealed that Śaṅkara's treatment of action is self-contradictory" (1992: 88–9). If this is correct, the contradiction appears right here in Śaṅkara's framing of the *Īśā*'s last four verses, specifically, in his introducing verse 15 against having lauded the speaker as having *acted* entirely in accord with the requirements of the path of knowledge. From Appendix B:

> The results of the disciplines that provide human and divine wealth, which are set forth in the śāstras, have their culmination in "absorption in nature," *prakṛti-laya* (which guarantees *samādhi* in another incarnation). All of it occurs within the realm of rebirth (*saṃsāra*). Beyond that, there is a distinct result, as proclaimed in the verse, "(When) 'Nothing but myself has come to be,' when in

> this way someone knows (all beings)." This is nothing other than the state of having become the self of everyone and everything, which is the result of the path of knowledge requiring renunciation of desire in its entirety.
>
> In this way, the teachings of the Veda (including the Upaniṣads) run in two modes, one characterized by action, the other by inaction. This is made plain here.

Mayeda considers and rejects, with respect to the teachings of the *Upadeśa-sāhasrī*, three explanations of the (apparent) contradiction between Śaṅkara's specifying "right action" in pursuit of self-knowledge and claiming a person in touch with the true self, *ātman*, doesn't act: (a) that Śaṅkara's target is Mīmāṃsaka ritual and only that kind of action,[3] (b) that Śaṅkara sees Brahman as "beyond good and evil" and so too the self of each of us, thus transcending action whether good or bad (motivated by desire, I may add),[4] and (c) that Śaṅkara's target includes those who would combine ritual with Vedāntic meditation (*jñāna-karma-samuccaya-vādins*)[5] who—Mayeda theorizes about Śaṅkara's perspective—appear to need a drastic message to help shake off attachment to that path (this explanation seems not much different from the first). He favors (d) that Śaṅkara's overriding concern is to lay out the most direct path to the true *summum bonum*—called literally "the best," *śreyas*, the "supreme personal good," *parama-puruṣârtha*, which is immediate Brahman awareness—and everything has to be viewed in that light. As Mayeda says at the end and climax of his introduction: "Śaṅkara's view of ethics may be vague or self-contradictory, but this is because its real aim is the highest possible effectiveness in leading his pupils to the final goal" (1992: 94).

Although the scholar's reasons for rejecting (a) through (c) are weak in my opinion, he seems on track in his overall assessment that Śaṅkara's principal voice is that of a spiritual preceptor, as I have argued all along, emphasizing meditation.[6] Still, as partial explanations there is nothing wrong with (a)—(c), that is, as illumining particular instances of assertion or appearance of incompatibility. Furthermore, Mayeda fails to bring out that the trope, well-known to literary critics (*alaṁkārikas*), "contradiction," *virodha*, is used for emphasis in poetry.[7] Śaṅkara may have learned from those folks to claim an incompatibility everyone knows has to be false since teaching itself is an act. Śaṅkara's purpose is to encourage a certain kind of meditation—and supporting conduct—at the expense of whatever other course of action one might contemplate. And he reveals here in his commentary on these last verses of the *Īśā* that he sees certain kinds of action not only as compatible with the path of knowledge but constitutive of it at least in part. We'll take this up again in the next chapter, the last, along with views of the *Gītā* on knowledge and action. For the Advaitin closes his *Īśā* commentary with a summary paragraph about *vidyā*, "knowledge," two meanings of the word in the Upaniṣad as he sees things, and the issue of incompatibility.

Śrī Śaṅkara sees the poet, the speaker of these last four verses, as having followed the right path—the speaker is "one whose *dharma* is true," that is, someone who has been wholeheartedly devoted to the path of knowledge, trying to fulfill all the prerequisites. From Appendix B:

> The phrase, "for one whose *dharma* is true," is to be construed as follows: for one who has true *dharma* through meditating on the truth as I have, for such a person, for me—alternatively, for the practitioner of *dharma* as it should be—"for experience," that is, so that the person should experience the reality of the self.

The verse expresses a prayer—or a prayer within an occult meditative experience ("a golden lid")—a prayer directed to the highest self as *īśvara*. Now this "Lord" is not the Western acosmic "God" but a pantheist Unity—or pan*en*theist—something like a pagan divinity but all-encompassing, immanent in everything as well as transcendent. Thus, God can be symbolized in many ways, as the "Sun," as the "Father of creatures," and so on. Śaṅkara takes the epithets in 16 to be for the Sun and the references to include the physical "ball of gas," the most awesome entity, we may remark, within the world of material stuff, from our everyday perspective. It is a material symbol as opposed to any drawn from the spheres of life or mind or spirit, which are different emanations according to him.[8] But of course the principal reference is to the Lord as the highest self. The "Sun" is also, so Aurobindo emphasizes, a symbol for self-discovery.

The aesthetic excellence of verse 15 makes it less a prayer than an offering, the words directed to the Wordless for a culmination of yoga. "Golden" in Sanskrit is not the ordinary word for the metal; instead, the mellifluous *hiraṇyamaya* is used, a word whose consonants are all soft and whose five vowels are all short resulting in a smooth flow right into the next word "lid" which in Sanskrit is an internal rhyme (in virtue of the instrumental case, setting up a sentence whose verb is in the passive voice), all poetically fine moves. Śaṅkara's path of knowledge turns in this way theistic, with an offering of a beautiful mantra directed to the final goal. It is by the Lord's "grace," *prasāda*, that the last block is removed.[9] The speaker presumes it is the self's energy that both binds through blinding brightness and brings mystical sight. This may not be the emotional, *avatāra-*

oriented theism of *bhakti*, "loving devotion," directed to a divine "incarnation" (such as Rāma, Kṛṣṇa, or Jesus), but it is a theistic path, nonetheless.

The speaker is no ordinary worshipper. Śaṅkara sees the prayer as offered by a *kavi*, a "seer-poet," a kind of cosmic person, as he elaborates at the end of the commentary on 16. From Appendix B:

> to you I do not pray as a servant but rather as the Person consisting of speech who lives in the solar globe, "That yonder Person, I am He"—which is true because of the personal form, alternatively, because of the entire world being filled by this self of life and intelligence. . . . the meaning of "I am He" is that I am that one.

The speaker is "the Person consisting of speech," that is to say, the perfect poet, who has given up everyday *abhimāna*, "identity," to become the "self of life" filling the entire world. But the change of consciousness is not complete. God, Pūṣan, O Sun the Nourisher, please remove the golden lid. Cosmicization makes one ready for a final transcendence, but that is not brought on through practice but by *ātman* itself, as *īśvara*. Given that the mantra is being intoned by someone dying, it echoes the Buddhist idea of *parinirvāṇa*, the further experience of the "enlightened" at death, and in yoga circles *mahā-samādhi*, the "great *samādhi*."

Aurobindo's reading of *Īśā* 16 is less theistic than Śaṅkara's, at least in the abstract, since he does not understand the proper names to refer to *īśvara* as one or another of God's "faces" but gives a psychological gloss. This he does with a long footnote to verse 15 and then further explanation in an essay published as an "Analysis" of the Upaniṣad in his *Arya* period (*The Upanishads*, 67 and 125–6). First from the footnote:

> In the inner sense of the Veda, Surya, the Sun-God, represents the divine illumination of the Kavi . . . His realm is described as the Truth, the Law, the Vast. He is the Fosterer or Increaser, for he enlarges and opens man's dark and limited being into a luminous and infinite consciousness. He is the sole Seer, Seer of Oneness and Knower of the Self, and leads him to the highest Sight. His rays . . . become deflected and distorted, broken up and disordered in the reflecting and dividing principle, Mind. They form there the golden lid which covers the face of the Truth. The seer prays to Surya to cast them into right order . . . The result of this inner process is the perception of the oneness of all beings in the divine Soul of the Universe.

Here Vedic symbolism as understood by Aurobindo guides his reading as much as his metaphysics, I dare say. About his deciphering, let me add only that his is not much out of line with the portrayal of Vedic symbolism by the academic

Vedist Jan Gonda (*The Vision of the Vedic Poets*, 1963) or even L. Renou (the greatest of all Western sanskritists, in my opinion).[10] Interpreting the Vedic symbols in the *Īśā*, Aurobindo seems able to bring out the phenomenology of steps along the path of "knowledge" as delineated by Śaṅkara with more specificity than provided by the Advaitin himself.[11] His vision of "divine life" does, however, color his reading, as we can see in his *Arya* essay:

> Surya is Pushan, fosterer or increaser. His work must be to increase this enlargement of the divided self-perception and action of will into the integral will and knowledge. He is sole seer and replacing other forms of knowledge by his unifying vision enables us to arrive finally at oneness. That intuitive vision of the totality, of one in All and All in one, becomes the ordainer of the right law of action in us, the law of the Truth. For Surya is Yama, the Ordainer or Controller who assures the law, the Dharma. Thus we arrive at the fullness of action of the Illuminer in us, accomplish the entirety of the Truth-Consciousness.

Aurobindo envisages divine action—"right law of action in us"—through beings like us—well, not exactly like us—as conduits of divine determinations. "Psychic transformation" is required, he says, which appears to involve, for just about everyone, serious *sādhana*, serious yoga, including, to be sure, meditation à la Śaṅkara.

According to Śaṅkara, a sense of oneself as a cosmic person, having solidarity with everything embodied—like Marx's "conscious species being" except expanded to include non-human species—is depicted in the Upaniṣad. This state precedes self-discovery which is brought about in the end by divine grace, according to him. Renunciation of desire, which is, he insists, the premier precondition for the *summum bonum*, demands a certain impersonality, a certain universality, like Kant's "pure will" not ramified in terms of rules, "imperatives," but rather "identity," *abhimāna*. Cosmicize and then find transcendence seems to be the message. The idea is echoed in plenty of passages in Aurobindo, but there is also with him the equally important theme of the "Divine" expressing itself in life.

Now as early as the *Bṛhadāraṇyaka* and the *Chāndogya*, an ideal of universalization is presented, captured by an abstract word, *vaiśvānara*, "the self of everyone," specifically of "humans," *nara* (compare the humanist motto, *humani ne alienum puto*, from Terence). The word is sometimes used (e.g., *Chāndogya* 5.11.2) as a synonym for *ātman* and at *Māṇḍūkya* 3 as the "waking state," the first of four "feet" attributed to the universal self.[12] Apparently in Vedic usages, as in the *Maitrī* (e.g., *Maitrī* 6.9), it is associated with "Fire," *agni*, "the fire in everyone." Aurobindo interprets *agni* as the "psychic" reality that dwells occultly in a "cave" behind the *anāhata cakra*, the "heart center," which, he says, expresses itself in the "surface being" as "aspiration for the Divine," that is to say, for realization of *ātman and* bringing native characteristics of the cosmic self into life, conjointly.

This would make artists of the yogi and yogini, or would-be artists. At the least, everyone is in this view "the artist of her own life," as proclaimed by the existentialist Nietzsche, but I think Aurobindo means something more. Probably there is Nietzschean influence on his thought, but it is not obvious and there is more definitely in the Indian context influence in the "aesthetic turn" of Abhinava Gupta (and learned followers) in elaborating *rasa*, "taste, juice, essence, aesthetic experience," as comparable to "the rapturous bliss of Brahman."[13] The analogy is turned around by Aurobindo, providing in effect a *rasa* theodicy: the psychic, "true individual" aestheticizes daily life, finding wondrous color and taste, *rasa*, in every experience, no matter how apparently negative.[14] Mallarmé quipped, "Everything exists to fill out a novel" ("*Tout existe pour aboutir à un livre*"). With Aurobindo, everything exists for *rasa*; everything *feeds*—or is to feed for those advanced along the "integral" path—an aesthetic delight, a somehow spiritualized aesthetic delight, *rasa*+. And this is what justifies Brahman's world-becoming.

Traditionally, there are two sides to the analogy in tantric texts, also in the *bhakti* Vedānta of at least a few Vaiṣṇava theologians such as Caitanya and Vallabha (fifteenth century). Kashmiri tantrics reincarnate the Sāṃkhya teaching of the disinterested "witness," *sākṣi*, with a Vedāntic twist. The truest part of ourselves simply witnesses, without reaction, our lives' unfolding. The twist is that the witnessings are tinged with delight, *ānanda*. According to Aurobindo, the psychic part in us pushes our natures "upwards," to the saintly as well as the charming and beautiful, like Whitehead's "God" who lures but does not coerce all actual entities towards the sublime and interconnected. The second side of the analogy between *rasa* and self-realization is creativity. In a "tantric turn," metaphysics—as articulated principally by Kashmiri Shaivites—recognizes creative energies expressing themselves through us in life.

Abhinava (eleventh century) was a renowned literary critic as well as a tantric guru and metaphysician, and he seems to be Aurobindo's most important precursor.[15] It would be, then, by cultural osmosis that Aurobindo continues the paradigm shift, since, so far as we know, he was not initiated into a tantric lineage (albeit some initiations are secret) nor did he read Abhinava's or any tantric texts, that is, at least he makes no references.[16] Śāktism was prominent in Bengal in the nineteenth and early twentieth centuries, and as early as his Baroda period

Aurobindo began reading Swami Vivekananda (1863–1902) and admiring the tantric saint Sri Ramakrishna (1836–86), Vivekananda's guru.[17] Anecdotally, I would say that the small tract entitled "The Mother" is, among Aurobindo's disciples, his most popular work. There he personifies creative psychological forces as the goddesses Sarasvatī ("Mahasaraswati"), Kālī ("Mahakali"), Lakṣmī ("Mahalakshmi"), and Maheśvarī ("Maheshwari," traditionally, Pārvatī), all forms of "Mahashakti, the universal Mother." Now Pārvatī ("Daughter of the Mountain") is traditionally "Earth," the "Earth Mother," and I suspect from his poetry—see "Ahana" in particular—that this was his own "preferred divinity," *iṣṭa-devatā*, in a *bhakti* practice. As a poet he was a lover of nature, or at least of nature poetry, both of Kālidāsa (especailly *Megha-dūta*) and cohorts in Sanskrit and Shelley (especially "The Cloud" and *The Revolt of Islam*) and so on in English.[18] He viewed poetry, as did Romantics, as a means to see the beauty and enchantment of nature, but also, like pagan polytheists, indwelling divinities.

Aurobindo understands the "golden lid" of verse 15 differently from Śaṅkara who takes it to represent a high state of consciousness but not the highest. Aurobindo takes it to represent everyday mentality which he views much more positively than Śaṅkara. Mind is a mode of manifestation of Brahman and though everyday thinking obscures the true self it is nevertheless a light that guides our activities. The suggestion seems to be that with the right intellectual picture we can mentally see through to the other side or at least become ready to do so existentially. In any case, the prayer, according to him, is in part to have the right connections among mental formations: "The seer prays to Surya to cast them into right order."

Śaṅkara says in contrast (from Appendix B):

> salutations to the sun who makes itself up out of its "rays"—life energies (*prāṇa*) and sensory experiences—the Sun, "Sun!" ... "Disperse" in the sense of "make depart" your own (blinding, blocking) rays. "Concentrate" means "unify, bring together." "Energy," yogic energy, is what becomes concentrated, heat made by yoga practice, (spiritual) light.

Then again as part of his commentary on the lines in the *Bṛhadāraṇyaka*, at the very end, under verse 18, he explains the imagery. From Appendix B, Addendum:

> "Disperse," that is to say, "Make go away," "(blinding, blocking) rays." "Concentrate," "bring together," spiritual energy (*tejas*), that is, the energy of the self (*ātman*) whereby I can have mystic vision. For, it is energy that has cut off vision such that right now thy true nature I am unable to "see." It is like lightning with things' colors and shapes (so blinding they cannot be seen). So unify thy energy (*tejas*).

In other words, the "life energies" of emotions, desires, and breath (*prāṇa*) together with sensory presentations blind us by their brightness. Nevertheless, they are energies belonging to the *ātman* who is capable of controlling them, funneling them into a kind of "exclusive concentration" (to use Aurobindo's term) to break through to self-discovery. The self's energy needs curbing but also concentrated. A penultimate stage of meditation would be unification of all the brightness internally. Parallel to this is the *Yoga-sūtra*'s presumption of the *power* of consciousness (*citi-śakti*) to bring mental fluctuation to a halt (*YS* 4.34), in flat contradiction, by the way, with its dualist metaphysics that has all power on the side of *prakṛti*, "nature." Śaṅkara understands the word *tejas*, which appears at the end of the first line of verse 16 (thus receiving emphasis), as "yogic heat," the heat built up by yoga practice. It is the purest energy of the self. "Please, Lord, turn it all up so that there may be the concentration necessary to break through to the other side." This is the yogic message, he implies, rendering the symbols of the Upaniṣad.

Finally, a word about the *so 'ham* mantra in verse 16, "I am He." It is surprising that it is not taken by Śaṅkara to mean self/Brahman identity but rather the speaker's identity with a cosmic person who needs the grace of the Lord to achieve the final transcendence. Aurobindo takes it to express self-discovery. Intoning it is a common tantric practice. From Satyananda Saraswati, the founder of the Bihar School of Yoga, *A Systematic Course in the Ancient Tantric Techniques of Yoga and Kriya* (1989: 548):

> try to be aware of the breath and the sound *Soham* that it makes. It does not matter whether the breath is fast or slow; only be aware of it and the associated mantra. It can be done while walking, talking, eating, working, sleeping or whatever you do in your daily life. Everyday activities are continued but with a background of the *Soham* mantra. . . . It is a method that is widely mentioned in many well-known scriptures such as the *Yogasiksha Upanishad* and the *Kularnava Tantra*. . . . [From] the *Kularnava Tantra*: "The more you repeat this mantra, the greater the fruits both temporal and spiritual. Therefore with intense effort, in all conditions, at all times, you should repeat the mantra." Continuous repetition makes the mantra penetrate the deeper levels of the mind, and the mind becomes harmonized and one-pointed, leading to meditation.

Indeed, practically the whole of third chapter of the *Kulārṇava Tantra* is devoted to *so 'ham*, "He am I." Mueller-Ortega (White 2000: 585) and others say it is the favorite mantra of Abhinava, and it seems Swami Satyananda follows tradition in claiming that the natural sound of the breath is *sa* (*so* or *sā*), in-breath, and *ha* (*ham*), out-breath. There is elision of the letter *a* with *'ham*—in Sanskrit *aham* means "I"—and *saḥ,* nominative singular masculine pronominal "he," becomes *so* by *sandhi* ("euphonics"). There is a variation, *sâham,* (the equally grand) "I am She"—*sā* being nominative singular feminine, absorbing the first *a* of *aham.* A second or double meaning depends on reversing the syllables: *haṃsa,* which means "royal bird"—a mythic or trans-himalayan crane or swan or eagle, in any case the most awesome of fowls—is commonly taken to symbolize the transmigrating individual, *jīvâtman.* Repeating the two syllables hundreds or even thousands of times, the syllables are easily reversed and the meanings of "I am the cosmic *ātman*" and "I am the transmigrating soul" fused. Historically, across sect, the mantra has extraordinary resonance, second perhaps only to *om*—whose meditational and symbolic value is elaborately analyzed in the *Māṇḍūkya Upaniṣad* and Gauḍapāda's *kārikās* and which is intoned as part of our next verse, *Īśā* 17.

8

Aspiration and Surrender

Īśā 17 and 18

Śaṅkara:

> Air to Wind, to the Immortal, to the Nectar of Immortality; then there is this body that will turn now to ash (let it be an offering).
> Om! Doer! Remember the deeds, remember. Doer! Remember the deeds, remember. || 17 ||
>
> Fire! Show us the true path to happiness. Divine Being! You know us, you know every state of mind.
> Fight, please, to separate us from deviating evil and sin. Salutations, extreme salutations to you we urge. || 18 ||

Aurobindo:

> 17. The Breath of things is an immortal Life, but of this body ashes are the end. OM! O Will, remember that which was done, remember! O Will remember, that which was done, remember!
>
> 18. O god Agni, knowing all things that are manifested, lead us by the good path to the felicity; remove from us the devious attraction of sin. To thee completest speech of submission we would dispose.

Śaṅkara has the speaker praying for the dissolution of the subtle body, breath back into air, etc., the body to universal earth. From the "Addendum" to Appendix B, here is the Advaitin's commentary on identical verses in the *Bṛhadāraṇyaka*:

> When the body falls away, the truth, the immortal, which I am, well, let my life energy (*prāṇa*) return to "Wind" (universal *prāṇa*). Let my breath go back to the external air. Likewise, all my other faculties—the divinities of sensation and action—let them go to their respective natures, *prakṛti*. Then also this body, "which will turn to ash," may it go to earth.

Robert Hume (1931/1971: 365n1) makes an illuminating remark apropos of verse 17:

> The idea that at death the several parts of the microcosmic man revert to the corresponding elements of the macrocosm is expressed several times in Sanskrit literature. With the specifics mentioned here, compare "his spirit (*ātman*) to the wind (*vāta*)" in the Cremation Hymn, RV [*Ṛg Veda*] 10.16.3a; . . . [and other references].

According to Śaṅkara, it is important to note, the dissolution is not automatic. A "subtle body," *sūkṣma-śarīra*, normally survives death, and karmic dispositions together with subtle "sheaths," *kośa*, hang together to determine a new personality in the next incarnation which is continuous with the old. Śaṅkara reads the verse as expressing an *ideal* of disentanglement—the universal becoming manifest in the individual—in contrast with inevitable physical reëmbodiment of a subtle body. He says pointedly, "What is implied is, 'And may this subtle body purified of cognition and karma ascend,'" where "ascend" appears to mean for him "disjoin, separate into individual strands merging with their respective 'divinities,'" that is to say, with their universal forms, which are distinct emanations of Brahman. Thus, no longer would there be a composite individual with a subtle body who could reincarnate.

However unattractive this picture may seem, let us hasten to remind ourselves that according to the Advaitin such disentanglement and universalization are possible for a living person. Indeed, that is one way of looking at self-discovery. And that's also why *action*—in the everyday since of "action" as undertaken by an egoistic person—a false composite—who moves to get something wanted, or to avoid something undesirable—is not possible for a realized yogi. The self-knower seems to act like everyone else, but the bodily movements are entirely natural, in tune with the Lord in the Lord's on-going creative energy, which moves in universal rhythms as distinct emanated "divinities."

Verse 18 is yet blatantly about personal action, highlighting the action of speech, which in the Vedic tradition of the *kavi*, "seer-poet," is the most important action of all. After a cursory explanation of certain words, Śaṅkara launches into a dialectic on knowledge and action in general, to close his commentary on the Upaniṣad. The excursion, which does not appear in his *Bṛhadāraṇyaka* commentary on the four verses, takes us back to the double meaning he finds for the word *vidyā* in earlier verses of the *Īśā*. But in order fully to appreciate Śaṅkara's stance and how precisely it makes his reading different from Aurobindo's, we need a somewhat wider view of the relevant literature, especially certain pronouncements in the *Bhagavad Gītā*.

Indeed, I think that Śaṅkara may well have been motivated by the *Gītā* on knowledge and action to make exaggerated statements, echoing a flirtation with paradox that occurs in the *Gītā* (for instance, 4.18: "If one were to see inaction in action and action in inaction, that person among mortals would be wise; . . ."). Furthermore, to say, as Śaṅkara does in interpreting the *Gītā*'s *karma-yoga*, the "yoga of action," that certain kinds of action, certain practices, are *preparatory* for the path of knowledge is not to denigrate them but, at least often, I would say, to point to their helpfulness for meditation. I think this is key to his reading of verse 18 of the *Īśā*. Like the speaker's behavior her whole life, we need to increase our sensitivity by adopting basic attitudes of "non-injury," *ahiṃsā*, "telling the truth," *satya*, etc., trying to act out of a sense of the welfare of others as opposed to personal desire and attachment. Śaṅkara is well aware that everyone in some sense has to "act." Kṛṣṇa in the *Gītā* presents a holistic view of nature and of realized yogis as "acting" for, and delighted in, the "good of all," *sarva-bhūta-hite ratāḥ* (*Gītā* 5.25). Śaṅkara could be taking certain passages from the *Gītā* as framing his statements, echoing tropes used for emphasis.

It may seem digressive to look now at some of these verses, but I should like to presuppose that everyone is familiar with the *Gītā* selections in Appendix C, Part Two.[1] The verses address action and inaction in general, and are, if not invariably lucid, rework the old idea of sacrifice, "internalizing" it, such that practically anything done can become a sacrifice, a ritual offering. Thus, profane action carried out in a spirit of giving can count as "sacrifice" in the sense of a sacred act.[2] Furthermore, these verses, one would imagine, were well-known to at least many in Śaṅkara's audience as regarded by him. The dialogue between Kṛṣṇa, the yoga teacher (a description sufficient for present purposes), and Arjuna, a warrior worried about an immediate course of action, occurs as the two are about to join a great action, a battle depicted in the epic, the *Mahābhārata*.

My view is that Śaṅkara accepts what is said in these *Gītā* verses, including, of course, the theism expressed in 5.29. His point about the oppositions he finds in the *Īśā* is to stress the importance of the kind of meditation indicated by *Gītā* 5.27–8 (note also in particular 4.29 in a complete convergence of *karma-yoga* with the meditative path). Do not be misled by the labels of the chapters (chapter 3, "The Yoga of Action," *karma-yoga*, chapter 4, "The Yoga of Knowledge and Renunciation of Action," *jñāna-karma-saṃnyāsa-yoga*, and chapter 5, "The Yoga of Renunciation," *saṃnyāsa-yoga*), which are not part of the discourse despite their prevalence in manuscripts; they are commonly viewed as provided by copyists. For throughout these chapters not three separate paths are laid out but rather meditation instruction is interwoven with advice about what attitude to take whatever one does, basically *karma-yoga* supplementing *jñāna-yoga* (often called by Kṛṣṇa, *sāṃkhya*). All action becomes a profound meditation with the right attitude (5.8: "The knower of the truth of things, disciplined in yoga practice, would think, 'I do nothing whatsoever,' while seeing, hearing, touching, smelling, eating, moving about, sleeping, breathing"). Then there is mystical inclusion of action in the "sacrifice" that Brahman constantly supports—like a standing wave, a halo in a river—expressed in 4.24, touching the core of Vedāntic monism: "Brahman is the giving, Brahman the oblation; by Brahman into the Brahman-fire it is poured. It is just to Brahman where one goes achieving the ecstatic trance of Brahman-action." This is the quintessence of *karma-yoga* according to the *Gītā*, which, like Śaṅkara says, is supposed to culminate in, first, the disinterested witnessing of the path of knowledge and then the experience of self-discovery.[3]

Aurobindo takes a similar view about the "yoga of action," about which he says, "works fulfill themselves in knowledge" (*The Synthesis of Yoga*, *SABCL* v. 21: 521). And he quotes *Gītā* 4.33 in Sanskrit (*sarvam karmâkhilam jñāne parisamāpyate*): "All (yogic) action in its entirety is fulfilled in knowledge." The idea seems to be that the change of consciousness to know immediately the cosmic self, *ātman*, is nothing but awareness, not a motor ability. Yet later in the same passage Aurobindo goes on to say (*SY* 522): "But knowledge is not complete without works; for the Will in being also is God … and if works find their culmination in knowledge, knowledge also finds its fulfillment in works." Then he adds a dimension of "love," *bhakti*, to the conceptualization of the transformative experience, as intrinsic to it, not like Śaṅkara as preparation for *vidyā* but as integral to the yogic end.

Granting that Śaṅkara composed at least a few of the devotional poems ascribed to him as well as that he is shy of characterizing "self-discovery" beyond what he finds in "scripture," *śruti*, and that right here in the *Īśā* he waxes theistic, finding the last step on the path to be a matter of divine grace, granting all this, we must still concede that Aurobindo describes something a little different, something like an expanding self-realization that comes to include emotion, as he says, "godward emotion." This seems to be the reason why some scholars align Aurobindo's teaching more with the radically theistic *bhakti* movement of the later centuries of the classical period more than with Śaṅkara or (even) his (tantric) legacy—a mistake in my opinion since Śaṅkara is not shy about echoing Upaniṣadic declarations of self-discovery as "bliss," *ānanda*. It is absolutely wrong to think that Aurobindo is a dualist about the relation of Brahman to the individual, in the manner of Dvaita Vedānta. His denial of dualism is like

Śaṅkara's, albeit he finds value, where Śaṅkara does not, in "soul personality" for its own sake and not just to make one ready for self-discovery. Nevertheless, in many passages Aurobindo stresses a *bhakti* dimension, for example, from *The Synthesis of Yoga* (*SABCL* v. 21: 579):

> We throw up all the passions of the heart against him, till they are purified into a sole ecstasy of bliss and oneness. But that too is monotony; it is not possible for the tongue of human speech to tell all the utter unity and all the eternal variety of the Ananda of divine love. Our higher and our lower members are both flooded by it, the mind and life no less than the soul: even the physical body takes its share of the joy, feels the touch, is filled in all its limbs, veins, nerves with the flowing of the wine of the ecstasy, *amṛta*. Love and Ananda are the last word of being, the secret of secrets, the mystery of mysteries.

Meditation even at its core can have more content, it seems with Aurobindo, than the "block of consciousness" that Śaṅkara touts.

Śaṅkara reads the second half of verse 17 along with 18 differently from how he reads the first half of 17. He says that the word "Doer!" in 17's second line is addressing an individual formation of self, "you whose nature is intention (*saṅkalpa*)." "Intention" belongs to the "mental sheath," the *manomaya-kośa*, which is responsible for memory. Furthermore, the subtle body is often said to consist of karma and intention, immaterial dispositions hanging together somehow non-physically. The prayer is addressed to the speaker's own individual self at a mental or "mental-dispositional" level. The shift, which Śaṅkara fails to signal, from (a) an offering and prayer to the Lord to (b) a plea to a subtle individual form of oneself for continuity, seems to be a back-up strategy: my intentions and actions having been of the very best, let them continue as the "I" without a physical body: "Om![4] Doer! Remember the deeds! Remember!" repeated for emphasis, *krato smara kṛtaṃ smara krato smara kṛtaṃ smara*. The idea anticipates Aurobindo's theme of psychic continuity and development, but for him individuality—in a translife sense (metaphysically, there is only one "individual")—takes shape at a more essentially "Divine" level, the psychic, not the mental.

Psychic expansion is, as we have discussed, the keynote in material "manifestation," according to Aurobindo. In Vedic symbolism, he takes the first word of verse 18, *agne*, "Fire!" (vocative singular)—"O god Agni," in his rendering—to mean the indwelling, individual or potentially individual, divine being that develops "psychic personality" over a series of lives. The very first word of the very first hymn of the *Ṛg Veda* (*RV* 1.1.1), is *agnim*—"*Fire* (we call)"—said in that verse to deliver the sacrifice to the gods and to return with their beneficence ("Fire, priest of the sacrifice, bringing to us divine riches"). Aurobindo takes the Vedic symbol to represent the "psychic" in human beings and all life, remaining hidden for most, "behind a veil," but when surfacing bringing the "divine riches" of self-discovery and expanding spiritual experience. Whether we feel or identify with it, it is this soul principle that profits from our lives: "psychecization" in his view makes this creation/manifestation compatible with—indeed worthy of—Brahman as "Existence-Consciousness-Bliss," "Sachchidananda."

The "doer" of Śaṅkara—the Sanskrit word is *kratu*, a derivative of the widely employed root √*kṛ*, "to make," "to do"—Aurobindo interprets as the "mental will" that guides activity, so far like the Advaitin, but that can also *merge with* a "divine Will" immanent in our world, called "Agni," and be divinized, "psychecized."

> The Upanishad solemnly invokes the Will to remember the thing that has been done, so as to contain and be conscious of the becoming, so as to become a power of knowledge and self-possession and not only a power of impulsion and self-formation. It will thus more and more approximate itself to the true Will and preside over the co-ordination of the successive lives with a conscious control. Instead of being carried from life to life in a crooked path, as by winds, it will be able to proceed more and more straight in an ordered series, linking life to life with an increasing force of knowledge and direction until it becomes the fully conscious Will moving with illumination on the straight path towards the immortal felicity. The mental will, *kratu*, becomes what it at present only represents, the divine Will, Agni.
>
> *SABCL* v. 12: 131–2

"Will" inherent in the consciousness of Brahman-knowers is such that, as Kṛṣṇa says in the *Gītā*, they act in harmony with the general weal. The ensoulment of psychic "Fire," "Agni," is God's presence in the material universe and in us as individuals, in Aurobindo's worldview.[5]

To pick up the discussion of evil and theodicy with regard to the ideas of verse 17, I should like to reiterate that despite a parallel-worlds defense of God as Brahman and Aurobindo's "Sachchidananda" supplementing Aurobindo's "soul-making" theodicy, the overall issue with his view suffers from the cold reality of excessive evil: there seems to be way too much evil in our world for any theism to be, if not eliminated, at all plausible. "Natural evil," let me add, is not the only reason Christianity's "free-will defense" fails. God may get off the hook for moral evil—the evil that humans perpetrate—but not the natural kind, so goes the standard line in philosophy. However, because our choices are not entirely free but are determined, at least in part, by desires natural to all members of our species (and other species), God is not absolved even for the evil that seems to be due to creaturely choice. In the philosophic literature, examples commonly cited against the mainstream theology of a God having unlimited goodness and power are natural disasters, disease, and other misfortunes which, it is supposed, could have been prevented by an omnipotent being and would have been prevented by an all-loving God. A version of this argument was formulated as early as the third-century BCE by Epicurus, as Hume points out in his famous *Dialogues* (1776). Acts by humans are excluded as due to a good thing in God's creation, namely, free will, choice. However, if God is taken to have created our natures as beings of desire and self-interest, the Lord *is* responsible for the evil committed by the likes of Hitler and indeed everyone else. The famous dictum (from Milton) "Sufficient to have stood, though free to fall" leaves out the strength of impulses and temptations, so to say.

Frankfurt (1971) analyzes "freedom of the will" as a matter of "second-order desires," distinguishing freedom from wantonness in the capacity of a person to choose which desires to act out of and which to suppress, a "wanton" being someone like a heroin addict who cannot resist heroin (imagine the drug etc. right in front). Personal "will" gives weight to, or subtracts from, "first-order desires." The idea reverberates with traditional free-will theodicy in the West *and* Śaṅkara's karma theodicy also (see Appendix D). But Aurobindo's view is different. Like Augustine and Whitehead, Aurobindo advances an "aesthetic" explanation of evil, defending not so much Brahman's goodness as "delight," *ānanda*. As Augustine conceived of the world as chock full of being, as much as possible in the "Great Chain of Being," Aurobindo conceives of the world as chock full of "joy," this to range from animal pleasures to the supernal bliss of self-discovery. Living exclusively in a "surface consciousness" we are not privy to all that is going on in terms of delightful experience, he insists. Indeed, our everyday ups and downs are said to be like aesthetic experience, *rasa*, to the truest part of ourselves, our psychic being. Something at our core relishes whatever happens.

The view is subject to the objection that appeals to delight as a "hidden justifier" is illicit, because, to name just one reason, an ordinary person has pleasures and pains differently from the experience of a psychic being as imagined by Aurobindo and so a combined hedonic score seems impossible (apples and oranges). And if, as with utilitarians, each is to count as one, there seems to be way too much pain and suffering and not enough delight in any form for the theory to fly.

Tallying up hidden experience is not the whole story with Aurobindo, however. To the aesthetic justification, he adds the telos of "divine life," where for many the psychic being would have come to the "surface" and where others would be more clearly on that path. All kinds of evil are rooted in the nescience of matter, he reasons, but we have material bodies (for which we should be grateful, an attitude I think is presupposed) and so too would the spiritual persons living the divine life. Matter is thus instrumental to the divine telos, he argues. The end is to justify the means. The linchpin of Aurobindo's theodicy is that misery can be experienced in different ways and even when experienced just as misery can be viewed as instrumental to a worthy goal, like toiling for practically anything, athletic training, for instance. Still, I dare say it would remain hard to see benefit in many cases, no matter how "enlightened" you were. (What if someone you loved died suddenly, say, a child?)

So why does Brahman manifest? Aurobindo answers that it is because Brahman's dynamic side contributes a certain value, "delight," namely, expressed in finite forms. Choice does not have much to do with the value added to Brahman through cosmic manifestation, although it may have a lot to do with our own yogic development. In Aurobindo's view, natural desires make choice limited and, by the way, at their core, he reasons, are not all bad. As he says commenting on the Upaniṣad (*SABCL* v. 12: 136):

> the renunciation [intended by the Upaniṣad] is an absolute renunciation of the principle of desire founded on the principle of egoism and not a renunciation of world-existence. This solution depends on the idea that desire is only an egoistic and vital deformation of the divine Ananda or delight of being from which the world is born; by extirpation of ego and desire Ananda again becomes the conscious principle of existence.

Without desire "founded on . . . egoism" our lives would enrich the Absolute like the action in a beautiful drama or dance, but even now they enrich it. The main point of yoga, I take it, is that we would be let in on the play (*līlā*) and also act delighted. This reminds me of Yeats' "Dialogue of Self and Soul," as the Self declares at the end: "We must laugh and we must sing,/ We are blest by everything,/ Everything we look upon is blest." Aurobindo imagines, similarly, a transformed state of enjoyment of Ananda. From the end of his essay on the *Īśā*, including in effect a summary gloss of verse 18 (*SABCL* v. 12: 141):

> when we have the sight and live in the Truth-Consciousness, our will becomes the spontaneous law of the truth in us and . . . leads straight to the human goal, which was always the enjoyment of the Ananda, the Lord's delight

> in self-being, … In our acts also we become one with all beings and our life grows into a representation of oneness, truth and divine joy and no longer proceeds on the crooked path of egoism full of division, error and stumbling. In a word, we attain to the object of our existence which is to manifest in itself whether on earth in a terrestrial body and against the resistance of Matter or in the worlds beyond or enter beyond all world the glory of the divine Life and divine Being.

An insurmountable problem with this as a theodicy for Aurobindo's "Brahman" is, as I argued in an earlier book (Phillips 1986: 143–4), that the egoistic human being gets used. It is only the psychecized person who makes Brahman's cosmic becoming (*prapañca*) worthwhile on Aurobindo's premises. And how used we are! being subject not only to, as Buddhists are fond of saying, the three evils of disease, old age, and death, but also to the inhumanity of war and tyranny and torture. There is just way too much evil of all kinds in our world for any theism to pass muster, including Aurobindo's, although I want to slightly soften this judgment below. From the human perspective, God, in Aurobindo's conception, looks like a bully, not a being "worthy of worship," to use philosophers' touchstone phrase. Aurobindo finds divine purpose in psychecization, but that leaves out ordinary human and animal pain and suffering except as instrumental to that end. It does not seem fair that the suffering person reaps no benefit but only somehow an indwelling "soul."

It is important, nevertheless, to understand the character of Aurobindo's theism against this shortcoming and its connection to yoga and meditation as opposed to metaphysics. For that is where the human meets the inner divinity most lucidly and dramatically according to his teaching. Perhaps his view will prove resilient—I cannot help but wish that something like his view were true. But religious views of survival seem pretty obviously to reflect, as Freud argued,[6] *wishful thinking*, desire for personal continuity. And that may well be the best explanation of eschatology in general. Longing for retribution may also play in some traditions an eschatological role—Kant saw this in formulating his "moral argument"[7]—retribution that is unavailable except by divine means, especially the desire for punishment of horrendous moral failure. Buddhists imagine hells for murderers and not only Dante and John Edwards. It seems that Aurobindo would have us believe that Brahman delights even in the sadist and torturer, somehow from the inside, like a novelist expert in portraying phenomenology. However, this objection may well be unfair in that its language ("delights") crosses a theological border without the right documentation: the Lord in Aurobindo's conception would not "delight" in the torturer in the way a sick tyrant might. But then just how are we to understand "Ananda" and *rasa* in his view? We seem in danger of losing our grip! The thrust of his yoga teaching, in any case, is that the psychic being pushes the ordinary person towards the supererogatory, towards beneficence, munificence, self-sacrifice, and creativity as well as happiness and the ideal action of a divinely directed life in the sense not of following rules but of better ethical sensibilities and a heightened sense of beauty.

Aurobindo is often critical of ethical views and mores, especially moral rules, which he condemns as normally only intellectual and not sufficiently wide and flexible to govern the behavior of an emerging psychic being. If anything, he is a "virtue ethicist," like Confucius and Aristotle. In a chapter of *The Synthesis of Yoga* entitled "Standards of Conduct and Spiritual Freedom," he writes (*SABCL* v. 20: 192–3):

> A moral law can be imposed as a rule or an ideal on numbers of men who have not attained that level of consciousness or that fineness of mind and will and psychic sense in which it can become a reality to them and a living force. As an ideal it can be revered without any need to practice. As a rule it can be observed in its outsides even if the inner sense is missed altogether. The supramental and spiritual life cannot be mechanised in this way; it cannot be turned into a mental ideal or an external rule. It has its own great lines, but these must be made real, must be the workings of an active Power felt in the individual's consciousness and the transcriptions of an eternal Truth to transform mind, life and body. . . . In that alone can all these lower discords resolve themselves into a victorious harmony of the true relations between manifested beings who are portions of the one Godhead and children of one universal Mother.

In answer to the question of the ethical criterion, or criteria, upon which ethical judgments are to be made, it is open for the virtue ethicist to respond that ethical judgment requires training. This is one of Confucius's great themes. To know the good, one has to be good, a position that dovetails with ethical intuitionism: we intuit what's right in particular circumstances, that is, so do those of us who have developed a kind of ethical sense organ, a "conscience," along with, let us say, "rules of thumb." Aurobindo is an ethical intuitionist of an extreme sort, almost an outright ethical skeptic.[8] However, yoga in his view provides ethical training. Through yoga a person assists, he says, psychic growth which is supposed to transform natural desires towards the beautiful and the saintly.

Now to bring these views to bear on the theodicy question, let me say that, personally, I want the likes of Stalin to suffer, and Nazis reborn as feral pigs, despised, hunted down, even by vegetarians. Śaṅkara finds justice in human and animal pain and suffering; bad karma gets repaid. This is a central premise in his theodicy. Aurobindo does not go along, partly because he sees human choice as not nearly as consequential for events as natural forces. His ideal of divine life involves spontaneous acts motivated by desires transformed into expressions of "Delight." It seems natural to ask whether the idea of this telos elevates the credibility of his theism, as with the goal of traditional theodicy. But Aurobindo's meliorist theory is not so much an epistemic plus for his theism as it is the keystone of a metaphysics of meditation, mutually supported by and supporting other propositions in the system.

In interpreting verse 18, Aurobindo provides a theistic gloss, but not quite like Śaṅkara who has the speaker awaiting the action of the Lord. Aurobindo envisages what in other places he calls "surrender" (*SABCL* v. 12: 132–3):

> It is the divine will [Agni], one with divine knowledge, which leads us towards felicity, ... All that belongs to the deviations of the ego, all that obscures and drives or draws us into this or that false path with its false lures and stumblings are put away from us by it. These things fall away ... and cease to find lodging in our consciousness.
>
> Therefore the sign of right action is the increasing and finally the complete submission of the individual to the divine Will which the illumination of Surya reveals in him. Although manifested in his consciousness, this Will is not individual. It is the will of the Purusha who is in all things and transcends them. It is the will of the Lord.

Since the religious idea of "surrender" is familiar in religious studies—*islam* means "surrender" in Islam, that is, follow the Law, follow revealed rules as interpreted by scholar/priests—it is worth emphasizing that Aurobindo does not mean "rule-abiding." Surrender is not for him a mental act, as though the mind were strong-armed, held at gun-point, coërced into conformity. Neither is it a matter of prayer or acceptance of mental guidance, but, I take it, more like giving into a feeling of love.[9] Baptism may be a good model, physically falling back into trusted arms. According to Aurobindo's yogic teaching, this can occur, or typically occurs, only at an advanced stage of "discipline," *sādhana*, like, on Śaṅkara's interpretation of verse 18, the speaker's prayer for a final enlightenment.

What Aurobindo calls "aspiration" is different, the starting point of *sādhana*, not the culmination. By nature, he says, the psychic being longs for the "Beloved," for commerce with the "Divine"; by nature it has *bhakti*. Classically, this is epitomized by love for Kṛṣṇa by gopis ("cowgirls") as recounted in the *Bhāgavata*

Purāṇa and elsewhere, an almost erotic *bhakti* that comes spontaneously, prompted by Kṛṣṇa's beauty. According to Aurobindo, the psychic element inspires all sorts of goals, skill development, and so on, and excellence in practically any dimension of life (*Gītā* 2.50, "Yoga is skill in works," *yogaḥ karmāsu kauśalam*).[10] Psychic love motivates yoga and meditation to include *karma-yoga*, the yoga of making an offering of whatever you do. This is "Agni . . . lead[ing] by the good path to the felicity" in his understanding of verse 18.

Emotionally—as can be gathered from Aurobindo's letters to followers—aspiration is often identified as an intense feeling deep in the middle of the breast. It is, by his account, not so much mental but does motivate prayer as well as meditation. The idea of it is not uncommon in Eastern soteriology (in Buddhism, for example, it is sometimes said that desire for Nirvāṇa is not an ordinary desire). Aurobindo sees aspiration as the clearest expression of the psychic being. He speaks of its emergence as joyful, accompanied sometimes by tear-inducing gratitude, and philosophically he sees it taking many forms. For example, he finds it referred to as the "daemon" of Socrates in Plato's early dialogues.[11]

Avoidance of the "devious attraction of sin" in verse 18 he sees as mentioned because a sort of psychological purification is considered necessary to have "Knowledge," *vidyā*. Sinning by others is not so much our business, but we want to be free of sin's power to obscure awareness of our true self. This last view compares favorably with the dovetailing of the prudential and the ethical in the *Yoga-sūtra*. One practices *ahiṃsā*, "non-injury," for example, for oneself as well as for others, specifically to make it easier to meditate, as well as to respect fellow creatures. And it is a commonplace in classical Vedānta that one does things to make the psychological quality of *sattva*—"luminous intelligence, calm contentment"—predominant over two other *guṇas*, *rajas*—"passion, energy, intensity"—and *tamas*—"torpitude, stupidity"—all three made famous by Sāṃkhya passages in the early Upaniṣads and the *Gītā*. A flaw in the classical conception is, it seems to me (and I think Aurobindo would agree, though I know of no passage where he says as much precisely), *sattva* is supposed to be inactive, a person requiring an admixture of *rajas* to get anything done. For Aurobindo, the indwelling psychic being pushes the "surface being" not only towards luminosity, etc., but towards creativity, to actively bring "Delight" (*ānanda*) into life. Psychic expression of *rajas* would seem to occur—to elaborate in this vein—in characteristics such as courage and love, adventurism even, and of *tamas* in steadfastness, fortitude, and loyalty.

However, to judge from letters to disciples and in *The Mother*, a small manual of *sādhana* popular among them, the schema of the three *guṇas* is not Aurobindo's preference for picturing the commingling of the Divine and the human but rather normally unperceived forces made familiar in tantra. It is true that in *Essays on the Gita* and *The Synthesis of Yoga* he uses practically all of Vedānta's conceptual tools including the "*guṇa*s of *prakṛti*," "the main constituent qualities of personality," but for his followers, to whom he wrote hundreds of letters, he cashes out psychecization as involving openings of chakras and attunement to occult energies, which seem to be Śaṅkara's "divinities" of the early Upaniṣads. The most important of these are lines, or formations, of "Shakti"—of the "Divine Mother"—Maheshwari (goddess of wisdom), Mahasaraswati (goddess of diligence as well as of music and art), Mahalakshmi (goddess of beauty and wealth), Mahakali (goddess of righteousness).

In winding up, we should note a Sāṃkhya echo in Aurobindo's conception of matter. In classical Sāṃkhya, *prakṛti*, "nature," has no consciousness, not in any form, including, especially, gross physical stuff. *Yoga-sūtra* 2.18 says *prakṛti* includes the *guṇa*s along with the material elements and even the organs of sight and the rest. But the same sūtra also says that nature has embedded purpose, enjoyment (for conscious beings, *puruṣa*) and self-discovery (*bhogâpavargârtha*). In other words, as the commentators bring out, nature *serves* the conscious being, and herself eventually provides a person with the right desires and attitudes such that she or he will practice yoga and achieve the *summum bonum*. Aurobindo envisages, similarly, a rather natural psychic emergence, for many at least, although whether in the current lifetime seems for some, I must say, dubious(!). But despite what he calls the negative resistance of matter and the physical "sheath," he thinks that eventually a significant number of people will rather naturally come to have the right attitudes, that is to say, come to practice yoga and meditation. As he says in *Savitri*, "God shall grow up while wise men talk and sleep" (*SABCL* v. 28: 55).

Appendix A

Śaṅkara's Reading of the *Īśā* (Translated according to Śaṅkara's Commentary) and Aurobindo's Translation (without his notes or analysis)[1] and the Sanskrit text (with and without *sandhi*, "euphonic combination")[2]

om

īśāvāsyôpaniṣat

oṃ pūrṇamadaḥ pūrṇamidaṃ pūrṇāt pūrṇamudacyate |
pūrṇasya pūrṇamādāya pūrṇamevâvaśiṣyate ||

oṃ śāntiḥ śāntiḥ śāntiḥ |

om

īśāvāsyôpaniṣat

Om. That is the Full. This is the Full. From the Full, the Full proceeds.
Taking the Full from the Full, it is just the Full that remains.

Om. Peace. Peace. Peace.

om
īsā vāsyamidaṃ sarvaṃ yatkiṃca jagatyāṃ jagat |
tena tyaktena bhuñjīthā mā gṛdhaḥ kasyasvid dhanam || 1 ||

om
īsā vāsyam idaṃ sarvaṃ yat kiṃ ca jagatyām jagat |
tena tyaktena bhuñjīthā mā gṛdhaḥ kasyasvid dhanam || 1 ||

Śaṅkara:

All this is to be blocked out by the "Lord," *īś*, whatever is moving in the moving world.
By that renounced, you should enjoy (the Lord, *īś*). You should not yearn for anyone's wealth.

Aurobindo:

All this is for habitation by the Lord, whatever is individual universe of movement in the universal motion. By that renounced thou shouldst enjoy; lust not after any man's possession.

• • •

kurvannevêha karmāṇi jijīviṣecchatāṃ samāḥ |
evaṃ tvayi nânyathêto'sti na karma lipyate nare || 2 ||

kurvann eva iha karmāṇi jijīviṣec chatāṃ samāḥ |
evaṃ tvayi na anyathā ito 'sti na karma lipyate nare || 2 ||

Śaṅkara:

Just in doing works here in this world, one may desire to live a hundred years.
Thus it is so—not otherwise than this—that karma sticks not to you as an individual.

Aurobindo:

Doing verily works in this world on should wish to live a hundred years. Thus it is in thee and not otherwise than this; action cleaves not to a man.

• • •

asuryā nāma te lokā andhena tamasā"vṛtāḥ |
tāṃste pretyâbhigacchanti ye ke ca ātmahano janāḥ || 3 ||

asuryā nāma te lokā andhena tamasā āvṛtāḥ |
tāṃs te pretya abhigacchanti ye ke ca ātma-hano janāḥ || 3 ||

Śaṅkara:

"Ungodly" are those other worlds, with blinding darkness covered.
And it is to them, on deceasing, that self-slayers go.

Aurobindo:

Sunless are those worlds and enveloped in blind gloom whereto all they in their passing hence resort who are slayers of their souls.

• • •

anejadekaṃ manaso javīyo nainad devā āpnuvan pūrvamarṣat |
tad dhāvato'nyānatyeti tiṣṭhat tasmin napo mātariśvā dadhāti || 4 ||

anejad ekaṃ manaso javīyo na enad devā āpnuvan pūrvam arṣat |
tad dhāvato 'nyān atyeti tiṣṭhat tasminn apo mātariśvā dadhāti || 4 ||

Śaṅkara:

Not moving the One is swifter than the mind. The gods do not catch it, which goes ever in front.
Standing still, it surpasses everything else though speeding along. It is that in which Mātariśvā puts the waters.

Aurobindo:

One unmoving that is swifter than Mind, That the Gods reach not, for It progresses ever in front. That, standing, passes beyond others as they run. In That the Master of Life establishes the Waters.

• • •

tadejati tannaijati taddūre tadvantike |
tadantarasya sarvasya tadu sarvasyâsya bāhyataḥ || 5 ||

tad ejati tan na ejati tad dūre tad v antike |
tad antarasya sarvasya tad u sarvasya asya bāhyataḥ || 5 ||

Śaṅkara:

That moves, that moves not. That's far, that's near.
That is on the inside of all this, of all this that is on the outside.

Aurobindo:

That moves and That moves not; That is far and the same is near; That is within all this and That also is outside all this.

• • •

yastu sarvāṇi bhūtāni ātmanyevânupaśyati |
sarva-bhūteṣu câtmanaṃ tato na vijugupsate || 6 ||

yas tu sarvāṇi bhūtāni ātmany eva anupaśyati |
sarva-bhūteṣu ca ātmanaṃ tato na vijugupsate || 6 ||

Śaṅkara:

Whoso sees all beings in nothing but the self,
And the self in all beings, shrinks therefore from nothing.

Aurobindo:

But he who sees everywhere the Self in all existences and all existences in the Self, shrinks not thereafter from aught.

• • •

yasmin sarvāṇi bhūtāni ātmaivâbhūd vijānataḥ |
tatra ko mohaḥ kaḥ śoka ekatvamanupaśyataḥ || 7 ||

yasmin sarvāṇi bhūtāni ātmā eva abhūd vijānataḥ |
tatra ko mohaḥ kaḥ śoka ekatvam anupaśyataḥ || 7 ||

Śaṅkara:

When "Nothing but myself has come to be," when in this way one knows all beings,
How then can there be delusion? What grief can there be? For a person realizing oneness?

Aurobindo:

He in whom it is the Self-Being that has become all existences that are Becomings, for he has the perfect knowledge, how shall he be deluded, whence shall he have grief who sees everywhere oneness?

• • •

sa paryagācchukramakāyamavraṇamasnāviraṃ śuddhamapāpaviddham |
kavir manīṣī paribhūḥ svayambhūr yāthātathyato'rthānvyadadhācchāśvatībhyaḥ samābhyaḥ || 8 ||

sa paryagāc chukram akāyam avraṇam asnāviraṃ śuddham apāpa-viddham |
kavir manīṣī paribhūḥ svayam-bhūr yāthātathyato 'rthān vyadadhāc chāśvatībhyaḥ samābhyaḥ || 8 ||

Śaṅkara:

That one has become all-encompassing, the bright, the bodiless, the flawless, not sectioned, pure, not pierced by evil or sin;
The poet, the seer, the thinker, who is everywhere, the self-created (*svayam-bhū*) has set things in order, as they should be, for years immemorial.

Aurobindo:

It is He that has gone abroad—That which is the bright, bodiless, without scar of imperfection, without sinews, pure, unpierced by evil. The Seer, the Thinker, the One who becomes everywhere, the Self-existent has ordered objects perfectly according to their natures from years sempiternal.

• • •

andhaṃ tamaḥ praviśanti ye 'vidyāmupāsate |
tato bhūya iva te tamo ya u vidyāyāṃ ratāḥ || 9 ||

andhaṃ tamaḥ praviśanti ye 'vidyām upāsate |
tato bhūya iva te tamo ya u vidyāyāṃ ratāḥ || 9 ||

Śaṅkara:

They enter a blinding darkness who devote themselves to (spiritual) ignorance, *avidyā*.
Than that there is an even greater darkness. Into it go, as it were, those who are pleased with (lower) knowledge.

Aurobindo:

Into a blind darkness they enter who follow after the Ignorance, they as if into a greater darkness who devote themselves to the Knowledge alone.

• • •

anyadevâhur vidyayā anyadāhuravidyayā |
iti śuśruma dhīrāṇāṃ ye nastad vicacakṣire || 10 ||

anyad eva āhur vidyayā anyad āhur avidyayā |
iti śuśruma dhīrāṇāṃ ye nas tad vicacakṣire || 10 ||

Śaṅkara:

One thing, it is said, is accomplished through (lower) knowledge; something else, it is said, through (spiritual) ignorance, *avidyā*.
So we have heard from the wise who to us have explained it all.

Aurobindo:

Other, verily, it is said, is that which comes by the Knowledge, other that which comes by the Ignorance; this is the lore we have received from the wise who revealed That to our understanding.

• • •

vidyāṃ câvidyāṃ ca yas tad vedôbhayaṃ saha |
avidyayā mṛtyuṃ tīrtvā vidyayā'mṛtamaśnute || 11 ||

vidyāṃ ca avidyāṃ ca yas tad veda ubhayaṃ saha |
avidyayā mṛtyuṃ tīrtvā vidyayā 'mṛtam aśnute || 11 ||

Śaṅkara:

Knowledge and ignorance, if together the two are engaged,
Crossing over death by the ignorance, one tastes by the knowledge the nectar of immortality.

Aurobindo:

He who knows That as both in one, the Knowledge and the Ignorance, by the Ignorance crosses beyond death and by the Knowledge enjoys Immortality.

• • •

andhaṃ tamaḥ praviśanti ye'sambhūtimupāsate |
tato bhūya iva te tamo ya u sambhūtyāṃ ratāḥ || 12 ||

andhaṃ tamaḥ praviśanti ye 'sambhūtim upāsate |
tato bhūya iva te tamo ya u sambhūtyāṃ ratāḥ || 12 ||

Śaṅkara:

They enter a blinding darkness who devote themselves to unmanifest nature.
Than that into an even greater darkness go, as it were, those who are pleased with manifest nature.

Aurobindo:

Into a blind darkness they enter who follow after the Non-birth, they as if into a greater darkness who devote themselves to the Birth alone.

• • •

anyadevâhuḥ sambhavādanyadāhurasambhavāt |
iti śuśruma dhīrāṇāṃ ye nastad vicacakṣire || 13 ||

anyad eva āhuḥ sambhavād anyad āhur asambhavāt |
iti śuśruma dhīrāṇāṃ ye nas tad vicacakṣire || 13 ||

Śaṅkara:

Just one thing is said to come from (devotion to) manifest nature; something else from the unmanifest, it is said.
So we have heard from the wise who have to us explained it all.

Aurobindo:

Other, verily, it is said, is that which comes by the Birth, other that which comes by the Non-Birth; this is the lore we have received from the wise who revealed That to our understanding.

• • •

sambhūtiṃ ca vināśaṃ ca yastad vedôbhayaṃ saha |
vināśena mṛtyuṃ tīrtvā'sambhūtyā'mṛtam aśnute || 14 ||

sambhūtiṃ ca vināśaṃ ca yas tad veda ubhayaṃ saha |
vināśena mṛtyuṃ tīrtvā 'sambhūtyā 'mṛtam aśnute || 14 ||

Śaṅkara:

(Meditating on) the (un)manifest and dissolution, the person who knows both together
By the dissolution crosses beyond death, by the unmanifest tastes the nectar of immortality.

Aurobindo:

He who knows That as both in one, the Birth and the dissolution of Birth, by the dissolution crosses beyond death and by the Birth enjoys Immortality.

• • •

hiraṇmayena pātreṇa satyasyâpihitaṃ mukham |
tat tvaṃ pūṣannapāvṛṇu satya-dharmāya dṛṣṭaye || 15 ||

hiraṇmayena pātreṇa satyasya apihitaṃ mukham |
tat tvaṃ pūṣann apāvṛṇu satya-dharmāya dṛṣṭaye || 15 ||

Śaṅkara:

The face of truth is covered by a golden lid.
Pūṣan! Nourisher! Make it open, for one whose *dharma* is true, for experience.

Aurobindo:

The face of Truth is covered with a brilliant golden lid; that do thou remove, O Fosterer, for the law of the Truth, for sight.

• • •

pūṣannekarṣe yama sūrya prājāpatya vyūha raśmīn samūha tejas |[3]
yat te rūpaṃ kalyāṇatamaṃ tat te paśyāmi yo 'sāvasau puruṣaḥ so 'hamasmi || 16 ||

pūṣann ekarṣe yama sūrya prājāpatya vyūha raśmīn samūha tejas |[4]
yat te rūpaṃ kalyāṇatamaṃ tat te paśyāmi yo 'sāv asau puruṣaḥ so 'ham asmi || 16 ||

Śaṅkara:

Pūṣan! Nourisher! Solo Traveler! Death, Yama the Controller! Sun! Child of Prajāpati, Father of Creatures! Disperse your (blinding) rays. Concentrate your energy (*tejas*).
The form of yours that is the most auspicious, that I would see. That yonder Person, I am He (*so 'ham*).

Aurobindo: O Fosterer, O sole Seer, O Ordainer, O illumining Sun, O power of the Father of creatures, marshal thy rays, draw together thy light; the Lustre which is thy most blessed form of all, that in Thee I behold. The Purusha there and there, He am I.

• • •

vāyuranilamamṛtamathêdaṃ bhasmāntaṃ śarīram |
oṃ krato smara kṛtaṃ smara krato smara kṛtaṃ smara || 17 ||

vāyur anilam amṛtam atha idaṃ bhasmāntaṃ śarīram |
oṃ krato smara kṛtaṃ smara krato smara kṛtaṃ smara || 17 ||

Śaṅkara:

Air to Wind, to the Immortal, to the Nectar of Immortality; then there is this body that will turn now to ash (let it be an offering).
Om! Doer! Remember the deeds, remember. Doer! Remember the deeds, remember.

Aurobindo:

The Breath of things is an immortal Life, but of this body ashes are the end. OM! O Will, remember, that which was done remember! O Will, remember, that which was done, remember.

• • •

agne naya supathā rāye asmān viśvāni deva vayunāni vidvān |
yuyodhyasmajjuhurāṇameno bhūyiṣṭhāṃ te nama-uktiṃ vidhema || 18 ||

agne naya supathā rāye asmān viśvāni deva vayunāni vidvān |
yuyodhy asmaj juhurāṇam eno bhūyiṣṭhāṃ te nama-uktiṃ vidhema || 18 ||

Śaṅkara:

Fire! Show us the true path to happiness. Divine Being! You know us, you know every state of mind.
Fight, please, to separate us from deviating evil and sin. Salutations, extreme salutations to you we urge.

Aurobindo:

O god Agni, knowing all things that are manifested, lead us by the good path to felicity; remove from us the devious attraction of sin. To thee completest speech of submission we would dispose.

• • •

ity upaniṣat || oṃ pūrṇam adaḥ iti śāntiḥ ||

Here ends the Upaniṣad. Om! "That is the Full." Peace.

Appendix B

Śaṅkara's Commentary on the *Īśā Upaniṣad*

om

īśā-vāsyôpaniṣat

om pūrṇam adaḥ pūrṇam idaṃ pūrṇāt pūrṇam udacyate |
pūrṇasya pūrṇam ādāya pūrṇam evâvaśiṣyate ||

om śāntiḥ śāntiḥ śāntiḥ |

om

The *Īśā Upaniṣad*

Om. That is the Full. This is the Full. From the Full, the Full proceeds.
Taking the Full of the Full, it is just the Full that remains.

Om. Peace. Peace. Peace.

"īśā vāsyam" ity ādayo mantrāḥ karmasv aviniyuktāḥ, teṣām akarma-śeṣasya ātmano yāthātmya-prakāśakatvāt | yāthātmyaṃ ca ātmanaḥ śuddhatvâpāpa-viddhatva-ekatva-nityatvâśarīratva-sarva-gatatvâdi vakṣyamāṇam | tac ca karmaṇā virudhyeta iti yukta eva eṣāṃ karmasv aviniyogaḥ | na hy evaṃ lakṣaṇam ātmano yāthātmyam utpādyaṃ vikāryam āpyaṃ saṃskāryaṃ kartṛ-bhoktṛ-rūpaṃ vā, yena karma-śeṣatā syāt, sarvāsām upaniṣadām ātma-yāthātmya-nirūpaṇena eva upakṣayāt, gītānāṃ mokṣa-dharmāṇāṃ ca evaṃ paratvāt | tasmād ātmanaḥ 'nekatva-kartṛtva-bhoktṛtvâdi ca aśuddhatvâpāpaviddhatvâdi ca upādāya loka-buddhi-siddha[1]-karmāṇi vihitāni ||

yo hi karma-phalena arthī dṛṣṭena brahma-varcasâdinā adṛṣṭena svargâdinā ca dvi-jātir ahaṃ na kāṇatva-kubjatvâdy-anadhikāra-prayojaka-dharmavān ity ātmānaṃ manyate so 'dhikriyate karmasv iti hy adhikāra-vido vadanti | tasmād ete mantrā ātmano yāthātmya-prakāśanena ātma-viṣayaṃ svābhāvika-karmavijñānaṃ[2] nivartayantaḥ śoka-mohâdi-saṃsāra-dharma-vicchitti-sādhanam ātmaikatvâdi-vijñānam utpādayanti | ity evam uktâdhikāry-abhidheya-sambandha-prayojanān mantrān saṃkṣepato vyākhyāsyāmaḥ ||

Śaṅkara: The Vedic verses, the "mantras," that begin *īśā vāsyam* are not directed to sacrifices, "works." For they illumine the nature of the "self," *ātman*, which has nothing to do with ritual. And this teaching about the self's nature, this truth of what the self is, is its being undefiled, not touched by evil or sin, constant, bodiless, cosmic, and other qualities as will be laid out. And that the teaching about the self stands opposed to a doctrine of works is the only view that fits (the Upaniṣad). The verses are not directed to works, not to a ritual or any action. For, so understood, the nature of the self is that it is not produced, modified, achieved, or purified, not a matter of the person who acts and enjoys things in everyday life. If it were, then the verses could be taken as subordinate to a doctrine of "works" (as taught by Mīmāṃsakas, "Vedic Exegetes"), but they are not. Upaniṣadic teachings in their entirety exhaust themselves in making plain the nature of the self, *ātman*. The *Gītā* and the *Mokṣa-dharma* (portions of the *Mahābhārata*) are also about that. Therefore, works, which are accomplished with a mind-set directed to the everyday world, are to be taken as prescribed when the topic is the sort of "self" taken to be multiple, to be individually a doer, an enjoyer, and so on (but not here).

For, a person who undertakes a course of action to achieve a certain result is the one who is "entitled," the "fit," fit for undertaking a ritual or any path of "works," so say the experts about qualifications for ritual acts. One entitled to perform a ritual thinks about himself (for example), "By virtue of the splendor of the priesthood, which is plain to all, or by virtue of non-evident Fate ("Unseen Force," *adṛṣṭa*, translife karma), *I* am a twice-born (high-caste person) who has none of the disqualifications for the ritual, being blind or dwarfed or the like."

Therefore, by lighting up the right view of the nature of the self and making concern with our native action cease, these mantras that are the *Īśā* aim to produce a spiritual experience of the unitive *ātman*. Such an experience would serve to pull one away from grief, delusion, and other qualities rooted in *saṃsāra*, the realm of rebirth.

(As is the rule for a śāstric text) the audience, the topic, the audience's relation to the topic, and the purpose of the mantras have now been given. We proceed now to explain them briefly.

om īsā vāsyam idaṃ sarvaṃ yat kiṃ ca jagatyām jagat |
tena tyaktena bhuñjīthā mā gṛdhaḥ kasyasvid dhanam || 1 ||

Om. All this is to be blocked out by the "Lord," *īś*, whatever is moving in the moving world.

By that renounced, you should enjoy (the Lord, *īś*). You should not yearn for anyone's wealth. || 1 ||

īśā vāsyam iti | īśā īṣṭe iti īṭ tena īśā | īśitā paramêśvaraḥ paramâtmā sarvasya | sa hi sarvam īṣṭe, sarva-jantūnām ātmā san pratyag-ātmatayā | tena svena rūpeṇa ātmanā īśā vāsyam ācchādanīyam | kim idaṃ sarvaṃ yat kiñ ca yat kiñcij jagatyāṃ pṛthivyāṃ jagat tat sarvaṃ svena ātmanā | īśena pratyag-ātmatayā aham eva idaṃ sarvam iti paramârtha-satya-rūpeṇa anṛtam idaṃ sarvaṃ carâcaram ācchādanīyaṃ, paramâtmanā[3] | yathā candana-agarv-āder udakâdi-sambandha-ja-kledâdi-jam aupādhikaṃ daurgandhyaṃ tat-sva-rūpa-nigharṣaṇena ācchādyate svena pāramârthikena gandhena, tad-vad eva hi svâtmani adhyastaṃ svābhāvikaṃ kartṛtva-bhoktṛtvâdi-lakṣaṇaṃ jagad advaita-rūpaṃ jagatyāṃ pṛthivyām, jagatyām iti upalakṣaṇârthatvāt sarvam eva nāma-rūpa-karmâkhyaṃ vikāra-jātaṃ paramârtha-satyâtma-bhāvanayā tyaktaṃ syāt | evam īśvarâtma-bhāvanayā yuktasya putrâdy-eṣaṇā-traya-saṃnyāsa eva adhikāro na karmasu | tena tyaktena tyāgena ity arthaḥ | na hi tyakto mṛtaḥ putro vā bhṛtyo vā ātma-sambandhitāyā abhāvāt ātmānaṃ pālayati atas tyāgena ity ayam eva vedârthaḥ | bhuñjīthāḥ pālayethāḥ | evaṃ tyakta-eṣaṇas tvaṃ mā gṛdhaḥ, gṛdhim ākāṅkṣāṃ mā kārṣīr dhana-viṣayām | kasyasvid dhanaṃ kasyacit parasya svasya vā dhanaṃ mā kāṅkṣīr ity arthaḥ | svid ity anarthako nipātaḥ | athavā, mā gṛdhaḥ | kasmāt? kasyasvid dhanam ity ākṣepârtho na kasyacid dhanam asti yad gṛdhyeta | ātmā eva idaṃ sarvam iti īśvara-bhāvanayā sarvaṃ tyaktam ata ātmana eva idaṃ sarvam ātmā eva ca sarvam | ato mithyā-viṣayāṃ gṛdhim mā kārsīr ity arthaḥ || 1 ||

Śaṅkara: The verse reads "to be blocked out by the Lord." Here the word "by-the-Lord," *īśā*, is gotten from the verb for "ruling." The word for ruler, "Lord," *īś*, is an etymological derivative. "*By* that one" gives us "*by* the Lord."

The lord mentioned, the ruler, is the Supreme Lord, the supreme self of everyone. For, the Lord rules everything, being the self of every creature in that the individual self is *īś*. "By the Lord," by the Lord in its native state, that is, as self, "By the Lord . . . to be blocked out," that is, covered up, shaded. What is to be so? "All this," "whatever is moving in the moving world." "Moving world" means the earth (etc.). "World," well, that is everything here. Everything is to be blocked out by the self in its native form. "Just I am all this," is that which the individual self realizes in realizing the meaning of "by the Lord." With respect to a genuine experience of the supreme self, all this here in everyday life—the unmoving as well as the moving—seems false, that is, is to be put in the shade by realization of the supreme self.

There is an analogy in sandalwood, aloe, and the like coming into contact with water or the like taking on an uncharacteristically foul smell. But the foulness is blocked out by rubbing, bringing out the thing's true nature and its true, genuine fragrance. For, just like this, the world, which is taken to involve agency, enjoyment, etc., is by nature experience superimposed on the true self. Its true nature, which is non-duality, lies "in the moving world," in the earth (etc.). With the phrase, "in the moving world," absolutely everything is meant through indirect indication (as with "where the crows are hovering" indicating an otherwise unmentioned house), everything, that is to say, designated by (the Upaniṣadic expression) "name, form, and karma," all of which is a departure from the native state. It should all be put aside through concentrating on the true nature of the self in the highest sense, enlivening it, the supreme reality.

In this way, the qualifications, which are implicit, for Upaniṣadic entitlement simply amount to giving up the triad of desires—for children, etc. (children, wealth, and *loka*, power or "worlds": "*putra-eṣaṇāyāś ca vitta-eṣaṇāyāś ca loka-eṣaṇāyāś ca*," *Bṛhadāraṇyaka Upaniṣad* 4.4.22)—entitlement that is not specified for rituals, not for "works." A person becomes disciplined (*yoga-yukta*) in this way through concentrating on the Lord, on the self, enlivening that reality. "By that renounced" means "by giving up" (the desires). For, it is not the case that a child or another dependent who is dead is "given up" in this sense because those are not the ways they are related to the true self. One does not secure or maintain experience of the self through their relinquishment in the sense of their dying (for example). Hence, relinquishing the three desires is the Upaniṣadic meaning.

The phrase, "you should enjoy (the self, the Lord)," means "you should diligently maintain" (the experience). In this way, you who have given up the desires "should not yearn for"—which means "do not have expectations," "yearning" amounting to that—expectations, that is to say, centered on wealth, belonging to anyone whatsoever, "anyone's" meaning another's or indeed your own. Don't have expectations like that. This is the meaning. In the verse (as expressed in Sanskrit), there is a blank particle *svid* (inserted for the sake of the meter) in the expression "anyone's."

Alternatively, the reading goes: "You should not yearn for . . ." Yearn for what? The implication is that you should not yearn for that for which you would yearn if you had not given up the three desires.

"Just the self is all this" (an Upaniṣadic theme) which means that through concentrating on the Lord, enlivening that state, everything is given up. Hence, everything is related to the self alone. Furthermore, just the self is everything. Hence, do not yearn for—do not make expectations directed to—the non-genuine (anything except the self as it is in itself). This is the meaning. || 1 ||

evam ātma-vidaḥ putrâdy-eṣaṇā-traya-saṃnyāsena ātma-jñāna-niṣṭhatayā ātmā rakṣitavya ity eṣa vedârthaḥ | atha itarasya anātma-jñatayā ātma-grahaṇāya aśaktasya idam upadiśati mantraḥ —

Śaṅkara: Thus the self is secured for the would-be knower of the true self by a stand being taken in self-knowledge through rejection of the three desires, for children and the rest—such is the meaning of the Upaniṣadic verse (verse 1). Now for someone else who is not capable of grasping the self because of a mentality not directed to it, the next mantra teaches something different:

kurvann eva iha karmāṇi jijīviṣec chatāṃ samāḥ |
evaṃ tvayi na anyathā ito 'sti na karma lipyate nare || 2 ||

Just in doing works here in this world, one may desire to live a hundred years. Thus it is so—not otherwise than this—that karma sticks not to you as an individual. || 2 ||

kurvann eva iha nirvartayann eva hi karmāṇy agni-hotrâdīni jijīviṣej jīvitum icchec chataṃ śata-saṅkhyākāḥ samāḥ saṃvatsarān | tāvad dhi puruṣasya paramâyur nirūpitam | tathā ca prāptânuvādena yaj jijīviṣec chataṃ varṣāṇi tat kurvann eva karmāṇi ity etad vidhīyate | evam evam-prakāreṇa tvayi jijīviṣati nare nara-mātrâbhimānini ita etasmād agni-hotrâdīni karmāṇi kurvato vartamānāt prakārād anyathā prakārântaraṃ na asti yena prakāreṇa aśubhaṃ karma na lipyate, karmaṇā na lipyata ity arthaḥ | ataḥ śāstra-vihitāni karmāṇy agni-hotrâdīni kurvann eva jijīviṣet || kathaṃ punar idam avagamyate, pūrveṇa mantreṇa saṃnyāsino jñāna-niṣṭhā uktā, dvitīyena tad-aśaktasya karma-niṣṭhā iti, ucyate — jñāna-karmaṇor virodhaṃ parvata-vad akampyaṃ yathā uktaṃ na smarasi kim | iha apy uktaṃ, yo hi jijīviṣet sa karmāṇi kurvann eva iti | "īśā vāsyam idaṃ sarvam" "tena tyaktena bhuñjīthāḥ mā gṛdhaḥ kasya svid dhanam" iti ca | "na jīvite maraṇe vā gṛdhiṃ kurvīta araṇyam iyād iti padam tato na punar eyāt" iti sannyāsa-śāsanāt | ubhayoḥ phala-bhedaṃ ca vakṣyati | "imau dvāv eva panthānāu anuniṣkrāntatarau bhavataḥ kriyā-pathaś ca eva purastāt sannyāsaś ca uttareṇa,"[4] tayoḥ sannyāsa-patha eva atirecayati "nyāsa eva atyarecayat" iti ca taittirīyake | "dvāv imāv atha panthānau yatra vedāḥ pratiṣṭhitāḥ | pravṛtti-lakṣaṇo dharmo nivṛttaś ca vibhāvitaḥ" ity-ādi putrāya vicārya niścitam uktaṃ vyāsena vedâcāryeṇa bhagavatā | vibhāgaṃ ca anayoḥ darśayiṣyāmaḥ || 2 ||

Śaṅkara: "Just in doing works here in this world" means simply carrying out rituals (and other enjoined actions) such as the Agnihotra ("Fire-oblation") sacrifice. Doing so, "one may desire to live a hundred years," that is, to have a desire to live that long would be right and appropriate, twelve month-long periods to number a hundred. For, the maximum life-span of a man or a woman is determined to be about that long. And, likewise, that it is in performing just the works whereby one's desire to live a hundred years is good (that is, in performing enjoined actions) because they are enjoined, is the meaning that makes the verse accord with what already has been explained.

"Thus" in the sense of "in such a manner," thus for you who so wish to live, that is, a human being—someone who thinks of himself or herself only as human (nothing more)—"than this," that is, "otherwise" than what has just been said there is no other means than performing—doing right now—(prescribed) works such as the Agnihotra whereby bad karma would not stick: "karma does not stick to you as an individual." This is the meaning.

Interlocutor: Hence, work, action enjoined in the śāstras such as the Agnihotra, is what is meant by "just in performing works . . . one may desire to live . . ." How, then, is this verse to be understood in accordance with what was said earlier, namely, that a renouncer takes a stand in knowledge (self-knowledge)? According to this second verse the stand recommended is works for those of us who are incapable of that knowledge.

Śaṅkara: We can answer. (The paths of) knowledge and works are opposed, unshakably, like a mountain, as has been pointed out. Don't you recall?[5] Here it is said again. For, (the verse says) the one just performing works may wish to live (a hundred years). This contrasts with (verse 1) "All this is to be blocked out by the Lord" as well as with "By that renounced, you should enjoy (the self, the Lord). You should not yearn for anyone's wealth." The teaching of renunciation (*sannyāsa*) runs, "One should not yearn for anything, one should take to the forest. Then you should not come back from there to this state." And the difference in the results of the two will be explained. Two quotes from the *Taittirīyaka Āraṇyaka* are on point: First, "Just the two paths have definitively emerged at present: at the first solely the path of works and later renunciation"; (in other words) of the two, only the path of renunciation excels; second, "Putting aside (*nyāsa*) has excelled." The blessed Vyāsa, the Vedic teacher, having reflected, said with certainty to his son: "There are two paths whereon the Vedas are founded: *dharma*, "(worldly) righteousness," which is characterized by voluntary action (*pravṛtti*), and *dharma*, "(transcendent) righteousness," which is a matter of inaction, clearly distinct from the other." And the difference between the two will be explained. || 2 ||

atha idānīm avidvan-nindârtho 'yaṃ mantra ārabhyate —

Śaṅkara: Now commences a mantra whose purpose is to denigrate failure to spiritually know:

asuryā nāma te lokā andhena tamasā āvṛtāḥ |
tāṃs te pretya abhigacchanti ye ke ca ātma-hano janāḥ || 3 ||

"Ungodly" are those other worlds, with blinding darkness covered.
And it is to them, on deceasing, that self-slayers go. || 3 ||

asuryāḥ paramâtma-bhāvam advayam apekṣya devâdayo 'py asurās teṣāṃ ca sva-bhūtā lokā asuryā nāma | nāma-śabdo 'narthako nipātaḥ | te lokāḥ karma-phalāni lokyante dṛśyante bhujyanta iti janmāni | andhena adarśanâtmakena ajñānena tamasā āvṛtā ācchāditāḥ tān sthāvarântān pretya tyaktvā imaṃ deham abhigacchanti yathā-karma yathā-śrutam | ye ke ca ātma-hanaḥ ātmānaṃ ghnanti ity ātma-hanaḥ | ke te janāḥ ye'vidvāṃsaḥ | kathaṃ te ātmānaṃ nityaṃ hiṃsanti ? avidyā-doṣeṇa vidyamānasya ātmanaḥ tiraskaraṇāt | vidyamānasya ātmano yat kāryaṃ phalam ajarâmaratvâdi-saṃvedana-lakṣaṇaṃ tad-dhatasya iva tiro-bhūtaṃ bhavati iti prākṛtā avidvāṃso janāḥ ātma-hana ucyante | tena hy ātma-hanana-doṣeṇa saṃsaranti te || 3 ||

Śaṅkara: Here "ungodly" is used with respect to non-dual experience of the supreme self such that even the gods and their likes (in pleasure-grounds but without the experience) count as "ungodly." And the "worlds" they inhabit are "ungodly," too. In the verse (in Sanskrit), there is a blank particle *nāma* (inserted for emphasis). All these worlds (including heavens) are shaped by the results of karma, "action." They are called "worlds," *loka*, because they are constituted by what one *sees*—*lokyante* means "they see," in other words, "what they experience"—constituted by what sort of creature there is. "Blinding" means "of a non-seeing character." By the "darkness" of a lack of self-experience, the worlds are "covered," that is to say, "shaded," the experience blocked out. With death, these worlds down to the life-world are left behind. Creatures take new bodies according to their karma, as declared in sacred texts. "And ... the self-slayers" refers to *slaying* of self-experience; creatures born in those worlds are "slayers" of self-experience. Those folk do not have self-knowledge.

Interlocutor: How could they forever and ever slay the *self*?

Śaṅkara: By fault of "spiritual ignorance," *avidyā*, the self, though spiritually aware, is hidden. The result of being spiritually aware is characterized by awareness of the self as not subject to the likes of old age and death. So for whom that awareness is, as it were, "slain," it is hidden. Thus those who are like that, who are "spiritually ignorant" as discussed, are called "self-slayers," "slaying" self-experience. For by fault of the self-slaying they are reborn in those worlds again and again. || 3 ||

yasya ātmano hananād avidvāṃsaḥ saṃsaranti, tad-viparyayeṇa vidvāṃso janā mucyante te 'nātma-hanaḥ, tat kīdṛśam ātma-tattvam ity ucyate —

Śaṅkara: As those lacking spiritual knowledge are reborn because of such slaying of the self, those who are the opposite have spiritual knowledge. They are "liberated from rebirth," these who are not "self-slayers."

Interlocutor: Then what kind of reality is this "self?"

Śaṅkara: The next verse answers.

anejad ekaṃ manaso javīyo na enad devā āpnuvan pūrvam arṣat |
tad dhāvato 'nyān atyeti tiṣṭhat tasminn apo mātariśvā dadhāti || 4 ||

Not moving the One is swifter than the mind. The gods do not catch it, which goes ever in front.
Standing still, it surpasses everything else though speeding along. It is that in which Mātariśvā puts the waters. || 4 ||

anejat na ejat | ejṛ kampane | kampanaṃ calanaṃ svâvasthā-pracyutiḥ tad-varjitaṃ sarvadā eka-rūpam ity arthaḥ | tac ca ekaṃ sarva-bhūteṣu | manasaḥ saṅkalpâdi-lakṣaṇāj javīyo javavattaram | kathaṃ viruddham ucyate — dhruvaṃ niścalam idaṃ, manaso javīya, iti ca | na eṣa doṣaḥ | nirupādhy-upādhimattvena upapatteḥ | tatra nirupādhikena svena rūpeṇa ucyate 'nejad ekam iti | manaso 'ntaḥkaraṇasya saṅkalpa-vikalpa-lakṣaṇasya upādher anuvartanāt iha deha-sthasya manaso brahma-lokâdi-dūra-gamanaṃ saṅkalpena kṣaṇa-mātrād bhavati ity ato manaso javiṣṭhatvaṃ loke prasiddham | tasmin manasi brahma-lokâdīn drutaṃ gacchati sati prathama-prāpta iva ātma-caitanyâvabhāso gṛhyate 'to manaso javīya ity āha | na enad devā dyotanād devāś cakṣurâdīni indriyāṇy etat prakṛtam ātma-tattvaṃ na āpnuvan na prāptavantaḥ | tebhyo mano javīyo, mano-vyāpāra-vyavahitatvād ābhāsa-mātram api ātmano na eva devānāṃ viṣayībhavati | yasmāj javanān manaso 'pi pūrvam arṣat pūrvam eva gataṃ, vyoma-vad vyāpitvāt | sarva-vyāpi tad ātma-tattvaṃ sarva-saṃsāra-dharma-varjitaṃ svena nirupādhikena sva-rūpeṇa avikriyam eva sad upādhi-kṛtāḥ sarvāḥ saṃsāra-vikriyā anubhavati iva avivekināṃ mūḍhānām anekam iva ca pratidehaṃ pratyavabhāsata ity etad āha — tad dhāvato drutaṃ gacchato 'nyān ātma-vilakṣaṇān mano-vāg-indriya-prabhṛtīn atyeti atītya gacchati iva | ivârthaṃ svayam eva darśayati | tiṣṭhad iti | svayam avikriyam eva sad ity arthaḥ | tasminn ātma-tattve sati nitya-caitanya-sva-bhāve, mātariśvā mātary antarikṣe śvayati gacchati iti mātariśvā vāyuḥ sarva-prāṇa-bhṛt kriyâtmako yad-āśrayāṇi kārya-karaṇa-jātāni yasminn otāni protāni ca yat-sūtra-saṃjñakaṃ sarvasya jagato vidhārayitṛ sa mātariśvā | apaḥ karmāṇi prāṇināṃ ceṣṭā-lakṣaṇāni, agny-āditya-parjanyâdīnāṃ jvalana-dahana-prakāśâbhivarṣaṇâdi-lakṣaṇāni dadhāti vibhajati ity arthaḥ, dhārayati iti vā "bhīṣā asmād vātaḥ pavate"[6] ity-ādi śrutibhyaḥ | sarvā hi kārya-karaṇâdi-vikriyā nitya-caitanyâtma-sva-rūpe sarvâspada-bhūte saty eva bhavanti ity arthaḥ || 4 ||

Śaṅkara: "Not moving" means that "moving" does not apply. The phrase is derived from the verb "to move," here in the sense of "stirring," the stirring of motion, which would be a departure from the natural state. The "One" always has that form, the form of unity, without departure from its natural state. This is the meaning. And this, the "One," applies to all beings. "Swifter than the mind" mentions the mind, the *manas*, which is characterized by imagination, thought, and the like, while "swifter" means "more swift."

Interlocutor: Why the inconsistency?

Śaṅkara: That can be explained. It is certain that the One is motionless, and it is also certain that it is "swifter than the mind"—seemingly a contradiction—but no fault occurs in that what is without accidental attributes can appear to have them. In its native form, that which is beyond attributes is said to be "not moving," the "One."

The "mind" is the "internal organ." It is characterized by imaginings and thoughts which are accidental attributes. In conformity with that character, the mind as embodied right here in this world can go very far, all the way to the world of Brahmā (the Creator) through imagination in no more than an instant. Hence, it is commonly recognized that utter quickness belongs to the mind. Consciousness as belonging to the self appears to have already arrived, as it were, where the mind goes, however quickly, to the world of Brahmā, for example. Hence, it is said to be "swifter than the mind." "The gods do not . . ." do not, that is, with respect to illumination—the "gods" being here the sense organs, sight and so on—"catch it," do no reach the self in its true nature as discussed, they do not get at it. The mind is more swift than the sense organs. Since the mind mediates information from the sense organs, those "gods" never have the self as object even in mere appearance. The mind may be swift but, no matter, the One "goes ever in front," that is, has already arrived, so to speak, because it is pervasive, like the sky.

The nature of this all-pervasive self is that it is without accidental attributes. It excludes, in its proper form, all characteristics native to transmigratory existence.

Although its nature is absolutely unchanging, the One experiences, as it were, all sorts of changes in the transmigratory realm, changes formed as accidental attributes. To those without spiritual discrimination, that is to say, to the deluded, it appears as things multiple and, as it were, looks like something different with each body.

In this light, the verse's next line reads, "speeding along," that is, moving rapidly, "everything else," that is, whatever is not to be characterized as the genuine self—the mind, speech, the sense organs, and so on—"that surpasses," goes beyond, as it were. The meaning of "as it were" is suggested by the verse itself as it says, "Standing still." Intrinsically the One is absolutely changeless—this is the sense.

"It is that in which," meaning the self in its true nature as constant, conscious, self-existent, in that reality, Mātariśvā—things breathe, move, in the "mother," *mātṛ*, thus "Mātariśvā," in the intermediate space, in the air that supports all life, itself active—"puts" things supported by it, things, that is, whose origins are causal, things that are woven warp and weft in it, which may be called the thread of everything, well, that is "Mātariśvā," the supporter of everything in the world. Mātariśvā puts "the waters," deeds, namely, works of living beings, works characterized by movement, works characterized by such movements as flaming, burning, illumining, sprinkling, etc., on the part of fire, the sun-god, rain, and so on, Mātariśvā "puts," that is to say, maintains, distributes—this is the meaning—alternatively, instigates, as is said (*Taittirīya Upaniṣad* 2.8.1), "Through fear of him, the wind blows . . ." and in other sacred texts. For all changes—effects, causes, whatever—come to be only in view of the existence of that which is the basis of everything, that which in its intrinsic nature is the ever-conscious self. || 4 ||

na mantrāṇāṃ jāmitā asti iti pūrva-mantrôktam apy artha punar āha —

Śaṅkara: Since the mantras are unflagging in their emphasis, the meaning given by a previous verse is put forth again:

tad ejati tan na ejati tad dūre tad v antike |
tad antarasya sarvasya tad u sarvasya asya bāhyataḥ || 5 ||

That moves, that moves not. That's far, that's near.
That is on the inside of all this, of all this that is on the outside. || 5 ||

tad ātma-tattvaṃ yat prakṛtaṃ tad ejati calati tad eva ca na ejati svato na eva calati svato 'calam eva sat calati iva ity arthaḥ | kiñ ca tad dūre varṣa-koṭi-śatair apy aviduṣām aprāpyatvād dūra iva | tad u antike samīpe 'tyantam eva viduṣām, ātmatvān na kevalaṃ dūre 'ntike ca | tad antar abhyantare 'sya sarvasya, "ya ātmā sarvântaraḥ"[7] [iti śruteḥ] asya sarvasya jagato nāma-rūpa-kriyâtmakasya | tad u api sarvasya asya bāhyato vyāpakatvād ākāśa-van niratiśaya-sūkṣmatvād antaḥ | "prajñāna-ghana eva"[8] [iti ca] śāsanān nirantaraṃ ca || 5 ||

Śaṅkara: "That" refers to the self in its true nature which has been the primary focus so far. "That moves, that moves not," where "moves" means "is in motion," conveys the sense of "moves *as it were*," since in itself it is absolutely beyond motion. Further, there is the sense of "as it were" in the phrase "That's far," intimating that even with hundreds of millions of years it will be "far," so to say, because unattained by those lacking spiritual knowledge. "That's near" is to be taken in the sense of being in the utterly immediate vicinity for those who have spiritual knowledge. Because it is the genuine self that's being talked about, it is of course not solely far and not solely near.

With the phrase, "That is on the inside of all this," "inside" means psychologically internal, as is said in the sacred text (*Bṛhadāraṇyaka Upaniṣad* 3.4.1), "This self lies within all." The words, "all this," mean the world in its character as "name and form" (*nāma-rūpa*, "individuality") and action. And "of all this that is on the outside" is said because of its pervasiveness, like the (all-pervasive) ether (*ākāśa*). Because of unsurpassed subtlety, it's the boundary. And we have been taught (*Bṛhadāraṇyaka Upaniṣad* 4.5.13) that it is undivided: "just a mass of 'intuitive consciousness' (*prajñāna*)." || 5 ||

yas tu sarvāṇi bhūtāni ātmany eva anupaśyati |
sarva-bhūteṣu ca ātmanaṃ tato na vijugupsate || 6 ||

Whoso sees all beings in nothing but the self,
And the self in all beings, shrinks therefore from nothing. || 6 ||

yas tu parivrāṭ mumukṣuḥ sarvāṇi bhūtāny avyaktâdīni sthāvarântāni ātmany eva anupaśyaty ātma-vyatiriktāni na paśyati ity arthaḥ | sarva-bhūteṣu ca teṣv eva ca ātmānaṃ teṣām api bhūtānāṃ svam ātmānam ātmatvena, yathā asya dehasya kārya-kāraṇa-saṅghātasya ātmā ahaṃ sarva-pratyaya-sākṣi-bhūtaś cetayitā kevalo nirguṇo 'nena eva sva-rūpeṇa avyaktâdīnāṃ sthāvarântānām aham eva ātmā iti sarva-bhūteṣu ca ātmānaṃ nirviśeṣaṃ yas tv anupaśyati, sa tatas tasmād eva darśanān na vijugupsate vijugupsāṃ ghṛṇāṃ na karoti | prāptasya eva anuvādo 'yam | sarvā hi ghṛṇā ātmano 'nyad duṣṭaṃ paśyato bhavati, ātmānam eva atyanta-viśuddhaṃ nirantaraṃ paśyato na ghṛṇā-nimittam arthântaram asti iti prāptam eva | tato na vijugupsate iti || 6 ||

Śaṅkara: "Whoso," namely, an ascetic seeking liberation, "sees all beings," beings ranging from the unmanifest down to plants (and minerals), whoso perceives them "in nothing but the self," that is to say, whoso does not see things as distinct from the self—this is the meaning of the first line. And the person who perceives "the self in all beings," that is, perceives her very own self even in these things as self, like "I am, for this body, for this combination of causes and effects, the self, witnessing thoughts and all the psychological occurrences." In other words, the seeker sees the self as the sole conscious being, without qualities, as it is in itself, sees it as the self of everything from plants up to the unmanifest—this is what "(sees) the self in all beings" means—"there is nothing but me, the self"—whoso perceives such an essential self, without attributes, "shrinks therefore from nothing," the word "therefore" meaning "just for that reason," in other words, because of that experience, "shrinks from nothing," that is, has no bad feeling. This is how it is to be interpreted for anyone who has gotten there, since all negative feeling arises on the condition that a person perceives something disagreeable as other than self. For the person who experiences nothing but the self, which is supremely pure, there follows immediately a state devoid of the causes of negativity which would be something seeming to be different. Hence, the person "shrinks therefore from nothing."

imam eva artham anyo 'pi mantra āha—

Śaṅkara: This very same meaning is conveyed by yet another mantra:

yasmin sarvāṇi bhūtāni ātmā eva abhūd vijānataḥ |
tatra ko mohaḥ kaḥ śoka ekatvam anupaśyataḥ || 7 ||

When "Nothing but myself has come to be," when in this way someone knows all beings,
How then can there be delusion? What grief can there be? For a person realizing oneness? || 7 ||

yasmin sarvāni bhūtāni | yasmin kāle yathôktâtmani vā tāny eva bhūtāni sarvāṇi paramârthâtma-darśanād ātmā eva abhūd ātmā eva saṃvṛttaḥ paramârtha-vastu vijānataḥ, tatra tasmin kāle tatra ātmani vā ko mohaḥ kaḥ śokaḥ | śokaś ca mohaś ca kāma-karma-bījam ajānato bhavati, na tv ātmaikatvaṃ viśuddhaṃ gaganôpamaṃ paśyataḥ | ko mohaḥ kaḥ śoka iti śoka-mohayor-avidyā-kāryayor ākṣepeṇa asambhava-pradarśanāt sakāraṇasya saṃsārasya atyantam eva ucchedaḥ pradarśito bhavati || 7 ||

Śaṅkara: For the line that begins "When . . ." which means "at which time," alternatively, "for such a self-realized person as described," absolutely all these creatures being known in an experience of the supreme self and reality, "Nothing but myself has come to be," "then," which means "at that time," alternatively, "for that person," "how can there be delusion, what grief can there be?" Delusion and grief arise out of desire and action. Their arising happens to the person who is not having the self-experience, not for one who sees the self's oneness, which is surpassingly pure. An analogy is the sky.

"How . . . can there be delusion? What grief can there be?" The suggestion here is to teach their impossibility, that is, that delusion and grief, being effects of lack of spiritual knowledge, would end, an occurrence that would be, it is taught, a matter of an utter breaking away from the realm of rebirth along with what brings it about. || 7 ||

yo 'yam atītair mantrair ukta ātmā sa svena rūpeṇa kiṃ lakṣaṇa ity āha ayaṃ mantraḥ —

Śaṅkara: To the question of what the self is like in its own nature, that is, the self talked about in the previous mantras, the next mantra answers.

sa paryagāc chukram akāyam avraṇam asnāviraṃ śuddham apāpa-viddham |
kavir manīṣī paribhūḥ svayam-bhūr yāthātathyato 'rthān vyadadhāc chāśvatībhyaḥ samābhyaḥ || 8 ||

That one all-encompassing has become, the bright, the bodiless, the flawless, not sectioned, pure, not pierced by evil or sin;
The poet, the seer, the thinker, who is everywhere, the self-created has set things in order, as they should be, for years immemorial. || 8 ||

sa paryagāt sa yathôkta ātmā paryagāt pari samantād agād gatavān ākāśa-vad vyāpī ity arthaḥ | śukraṃ śubhraṃ jyotiṣmad dīptimān ity arthaḥ | akāyam aśarīraṃ liṅga-śarīra-varjita ity arthaḥ | avraṇam akṣatam | asnāviraṃ snāvāḥ śirā yasmin na vidyanta ity asnāviram | avraṇam asnāviram ity ābhyāṃ sthūla-śarīra-pratiṣedhaḥ | śuddhaṃ nirmalam avidyā-mala-rahitam iti kāraṇa-śarīra-pratiṣedhaḥ | apāpa-viddhaṃ dharmâdharmâdi-pāpa-varjitam | śukram ity-ādīni vacāṃsi pul-liṅgatvena pariṇeyāni, sa paryagād ity upakramya kavir manīṣī ity-ādinā pul-liṅgatvena upasaṃhārāt | kaviḥ krānta-darśī sarva-dṛk | "na anyo 'to 'sti draṣṭā"[9] ity-ādi-śruteḥ | manīṣī manasa īṣitā sarva-jña īśvara ity arthaḥ | paribhūḥ sarveṣāṃ pary upari bhavati iti paribhūḥ | svayam-bhūḥ svayam eva bhavati iti yeṣām upari bhavati yaś ca upari bhavati sa sarvaḥ svayam eva bhavati iti svayam-bhūḥ | sa nitya-mukta īśvaro yāthātathyataḥ sarvajñatvād yathā-tathā-bhāvo yāthātathyaṃ tasmāt yathā-bhūta-karma-phala-sādhanato 'rthān kartavya-padârthān vyadadhād vihitavān yathā anurūpaṃ vyabhajad ity arthaḥ | śāśvatībhyo nityābhyaḥ samābhyaḥ saṃvatsarâkhyebhyaḥ prajāpatibhya ity arthaḥ || 8 ||

Śaṅkara: The words, "That one all-encompassing has become," refer to the self, the one already discussed. The self "encompassing has become" in that the self in becoming is all around, is all-surrounding, that is, in that way comes to be, like the ether (*ākāśa*), pervasive—this is the meaning. "The bright" is the beautiful, the radiant, like a lamp. This is the meaning. The sense of "bodiless" includes being free (even) of a subtle body. The word "flawless" has the sense of "unharmed." "Not sectioned" (*asnāviram*) is to be linguistically analyzed as "That in which sections—heads (and so on)—do not exist." The use of the words, "flawless" and "not sectioned," in both cases targets the gross physical body to exclude it. The word "pure," which means "untainted" or "devoid of the taint of spiritual ignorance, *avidyā*," is used to exclude the causal body. The phrase, "not pierced by evil or sin," is used to exclude *dharma and adharma*, "righteousness" *and* "unrighteousness," and everything associated with evil and sin. The words, "the bright one" and others (with seemingly neuter case endings) are to be taken as masculine (in grammatical agreement with *ātman*). With "That one all-encompassing has become" as the beginning, the verse proceeds with "The poet, the seer, the thinker," which are masculine in gender as words, to make a grammatically unified statement.

"The poet, the seer" is the one who "sees beyond," who sees everything. "There is none other than this" (*Bṛhadāraṇyaka Upaniṣad* 3.8.11) is said in a sacred text. The words "the thinker" are used in the sense of "overseer of the mind," which is the all-knowing Lord (*īśvara*). This is the meaning. The phrase, "who is everywhere" (*paribhūḥ*), is to be analyzed as "around" (*pari*) everything, that is to say, to be (*upari*) "beyond" it.

"The self-created" (*svayam-bhūḥ*) is said because just by itself (*svayam*) it comes to be (*bhavati*). Coming to be beyond those (created things) and coming to be as beyond, that is the "all" who comes to be just by itself, thus "the self-created."

This is the Lord (*īśvara*) who is eternally liberated. The words "in order" are used because the Lord is all-knowing. The *state* of being "in order" is the precise meaning. Thus the Lord "has set things," that is, determined their relationships, determined that things, the possible referents of words—including things brought about because of the fruition of karma as it is in fact—determined that things be in order, that is, as they should be. That's how the Lord "has set" them. This is the meaning. "Immemorial" gives the sense of "eternal, constant," a sense that, conjoined with "for years," renders the meaning of "throughout what we call years," that is to say, for the (all) the Prajāpatis, (all) the "Fathers of creatures" (each commencing a new round of creation). This is the meaning. || 8 ||

atra ādyena mantreṇa sarva-eṣaṇā-parityāgena jñāna-niṣṭhā uktā prathamo vedârthaḥ "īśā vāsyam idaṃ sarvaṃ" "mā gṛdhaḥ kasyasvid dhanam" iti | ajñānāṃ jijīviṣūṇāṃ jñāna-niṣṭhâsambhave "kurvann eva iha karmāṇi jijīviṣet" iti karma-niṣṭhā uktā dvitīyo vedârthaḥ | anayoś ca niṣṭhayor vibhāgo mantra-pradarśitayor bṛhadāraṇyake 'pi pradarśitaḥ "so 'kāmayata jāyā me syāt"[10] ity-ādinā ajñasya kāminaḥ karmāṇi iti | "mana eva asya ātmā vāg jāyā"[11] ity-ādi-vacanāt ajñatvaṃ kāmitvaṃ ca karma-niṣṭhasya niścitam avagamyate | tathā ca tat-phalaṃ saptânna-sargas teṣv ātma-bhāvena ātma-sva-rūpâvasthānam | jāyâdy-eṣaṇā-traya-saṃnyāsena ca ātma-vidāṃ karma-niṣṭhā-prātikūlyena ātma-sva-rūpa-niṣṭhā eva darśitā "kiṃ prajayā kariṣyāmo yeṣāṃ no 'yam ātmā ayaṃ lokaḥ"[12] ity-ādinā | ye tu jñāna-niṣṭhāḥ saṃnyāsinas tebhyo "asuryā nāma te" ity-ādinā avidvan-nindā-dvāreṇa ātmano yāthātmyaṃ "sa paryagāt" ity etad antair mantrair upadiṣṭam | te hy atra adhikṛtā na kāmina iti | tathā ca śvetāśvat arāṇāṃ mantrôpaniṣadi "atyāśramibhyaḥ paramaṃ pavitraṃ provāca samyag ṛṣi-saṅghajuṣṭam"[13] ity-ādi vibhajya uktam | ye tu karmiṇaḥ karma-niṣṭhāḥ karma kurvanta eva jijīviṣavas tebhya idam ucyate—"andham tamaḥ" ity-ādi | kathaṃ punar evam avagamyate na tu sarveṣām ity ucyate—akāminaḥ sādhya-sādhana-bhedôpamardena "yasmin sarvāṇi bhūtāny ātmā eva abhūd vijānataḥ | tatra ko mohaḥ kaḥ śoka ekatvam anupaśyataḥ" iti yad ātma-ekatva-vijñānam, tan na kenacit karmaṇā jñānântareṇa vā hy amūḍhaḥ samuccicīṣati | iha tu samuccicīṣayā avidvad-ādi-nindā kriyate | tatra ca yasya yena samuccayaḥ sambhavati nyāyataḥ śāstrato vā tad iha ucyate | tad daivaṃ vittaṃ devatā-viṣayaṃ jñānaṃ karma-sambandhitvena upanyastaṃ na paramâtma-jñānam "vidyayā deva-lokaḥ"[14] iti pṛthak-phala-śravaṇāt | tayor jñāna-karmaṇor iha eka-ekânuṣṭhāna-nindā samuccicīṣayā, na nindā-parā eva eka-ekasya, pṛthak-phala-śravaṇāt "vidyayā tad ārohanti" "vidyayā deva-lokaḥ"[15] "na tatra dakṣiṇā yanti" "karmaṇā pitṛ-lokaḥ"[16] iti na hi śāstra-vihitaṃ kiñcid akartavyatām iyāt | tatra

Śaṅkara: The Upaniṣad's opening mantra set forth a path of knowledge that proceeds by renunciation of all desire: "All this is to be blocked out by the Lord, . . . you should not yearn for anyone's wealth," a first and premiere teaching of the Upaniṣad. A second teaching is for persons not following the path of knowledge, for those for whom spiritual knowledge is not possible. These, desiring long life, are given a path of works and action, "Just in performing works here in this world, one may desire to live . . ." And the difference between the two paths (*niṣṭhā*, "where one takes one stand") as laid out in the two verses is also taught in the *Bṛhadāraṇyaka Upaniṣad* in the statement (1.4.17) for the non-knower, for the person filled with desire, that begins, "He made for himself a desire, 'Let me have a wife,'" and others including (in the same passage, *Bṛhadāraṇyaka*

Upaniṣad 1.4.17), "Mind alone was his self, speech his wife," where the statement makes it easy to infer that it is not about spiritual knowledge but about the state of having desires. They are part of a teaching of a path of works. And in this way there is spelled out the result of the path, which involves seven kinds of fruition.[17] On this path, the person thinks of the self as these.

And then there are passages such as (*Bṛhadāraṇyaka Upaniṣad* 4.4.22) "What would we want with children, we for whom our world is the self?" where, by the method of renunciation of the triad of desires for wife and company (wealth and *loka*, power or "worlds"), the path of (knowing) the self as it is in its essential nature alone is presented, a path for those who would know the self, a path that is in tension with that of works.

But then those who are on the path of knowledge, renunciants, are given a warning with (the third mantra) "Ungodly are those worlds . . ." which, through denigration of the state of lack of spiritual knowledge, directs one to the self as it is in itself. This teaching continues with the last mantra we have studied (number eight), "That one all-encompassing . . ." For, the eligible who are addressed are not those stricken with desire. Moreover, there what's said is said in a verse from the *Śvetāśvatara Upaniṣad* (6.21), "After distinguishing the two paths, (Śvetāśvatara) taught the supreme way of purification to those of the most advanced stage, which was rightly welcome to the rishi assembly." But to active people, the followers of the path of works, who were addressed with (the second mantra) "Just in performing works here in this world, one may desire to live a hundred years," now in the next mantra there is for them concordantly, ". . . into a blinding darkness . . ."

Interlocutor: But why should it be supposed that two groups are addressed in this way and not everyone at once?

Śaṅkara: The answer is that to those who are free from desire it is taught that there is tension between the paths which are distinct both in what is to be accomplished and in the means of accomplishing. This goes along with the teaching of spiritual knowledge of the oneness of the self, to wit, "When 'Nothing but myself has come to be,' when in this way someone knows all beings,/ How then can there be delusion? What grief can there be? For a person realizing oneness?" In other words, no non-deluded person would desire to combine the knowledge of the self's oneness with any action whatsoever or any other kind of knowledge.

But here, coupled with a desire to combine, there is denigration of the state of the non-knower along with what goes with it. And just what can be combined with what, whether according to reason or sacred texts, is stated here in the

Upaniṣad. For, there is an Upaniṣadic declaration to the effect that a distinct result comes from the "knowledge" that is directed to divinities—"divine wealth"—which is not the spiritual knowledge of the supreme self but rather knowledge that is to be put aside as combined with certain works: (*Bṛhadāraṇyaka Upaniṣad* 1.5.16) "By (such a lower) knowledge, one enters the world of the gods."

In the verse coming up, denigration of separate practice of such (lower) knowledge or of works is not simply a matter of denigration—presuming a desire to combine—since there are Upaniṣadic declarations to the effect that a distinct result for each obtains, (*Bṛhadāraṇyaka Upaniṣad* 1.5.16) "By that knowledge, they rise to it . . ." "By (such a lower) knowledge, one enters the world of the gods," "Following the southern path, they do not go there," "By works, one gains the ancestral world (*pitṛ-loka*)." For, with what's ordained by *śāstra*, there is not even a smidgen that is not to be done.

Accordingly, there comes next:

andhaṃ tamaḥ praviśanti ye 'vidyām upāsate |
tato bhūya iva te tamo ya u vidyāyāṃ ratāḥ || 9 ||

They enter a blinding darkness who devote themselves to (spiritual) ignorance, *avidyā*.
Than that there is an even greater darkness. Into it go, as it were, those who are pleased with (lower) knowledge. || 9 ||

andhaṃ tamaḥ adarśanâtmakaṃ tamaḥ praviśanti | ke ye 'vidyāṃ vidyāyā anyā avidyā tāṃ karma ity arthaḥ karmaṇo vidyā-virodhitvāt | tām avidyām agni-hotrâdi-lakṣaṇām eva kevalām upāsate tat-parāḥ santo 'nutiṣṭhanti ity abhiprāyaḥ | tatas tasmād andhâtmakāt tamaso bhūya iva bahutaram eva te tamaḥ praviśanti | ke, karma hitvā ye u ye tu vidyāyām eva devatā-jñāne eva ratāḥ abhiratāḥ || 9 ||

Śaṅkara: "They enter a blinding darkness," that is, a darkness characterized by absence of spiritual experience.

Interlocutor: Who do?

Śaṅkara: Those who devote themselves to "(spiritual) ignorance," *avidyā*, an ignorance that is something other than spiritual knowledge, (devoting themselves) to that, namely, a path of works. This is the meaning, since works are opposed to knowledge. This "ignorance" is characterized by the performance of rituals such as the Agnihotra ("Fire-oblation"). Some "devote themselves" to such acts alone. In other words, intent on such practices they take their stand. This is the gist.

"Than that" means "than that darkness characterized by spiritual blindness," that is to say, "even greater" than that darkness, that is, into even more intense darkness they "go, as it were."

Interlocutor: Who?

Śaṅkara: Those who, abandoning the path of works, "are pleased," that is to say, are delighted with, (lower) knowledge alone, delighted solely with knowledge of divinities. || 9 ||

tatra avāntara-phala-bhedaṃ vidyā-karmaṇoḥ samuccaya-kāraṇam āha | anyathā phalavad-aphalavatoḥ sannihitayor aṅgāṅgitā eva syāt iti —

Śaṅkara: The next mantra talks about intermediate, separate results of the paths of (lower) knowledge and works brought about by their being practiced together. Otherwise, it might be thought that when something efficacious and something non-efficacious were combined, the relation would be subordination of one to the other.

anyad eva āhur vidyayā anyad āhur avidyayā |
iti śuśruma dhīrāṇāṃ ye nas tad vicacakṣire || 10 ||

One thing, it is said, is accomplished through (lower) knowledge, *vidyā*;
something else, it is said, through (spiritual) ignorance, *avidyā*.
So we have heard from the wise who to us have explained it all. || 10 ||

anyat pṛthag eva vidyayā kriyate phalam ity āhur vadanti "vidyayā deva-lokaḥ" "vidyayā tad ārohanti"[18] iti śruteḥ | anyad āhur avidyayā karmaṇā kriyate "karmaṇā pitṛ-lokaḥ"[19] iti śruteḥ | ity evaṃ śuśruma śrutavanto vayaṃ dhīrāṇāṃ dhīmatāṃ vacanam | ye ācāryā no 'smabhyaṃ tat karma ca jñānaṃ ca vicacakṣire vyākhyātavantas teṣām ayam āgamaḥ pāramparyâgata ity arthaḥ || 10 ||

Śaṅkara: "One thing," that is to say, just one separate thing, "through (lower) knowledge" is made to come about, that is, just one result, "it is said," or "they say." Sacred texts teach as much, to wit, (*Bṛhadāraṇyaka Upaniṣad* 1.5.16) "By (such a lower) knowledge, one enters the world of the gods" and "By that knowledge, they rise to it . . ." "Something else, it is said, through spiritual ignorance, *avidyā*," that is, by way of the path of works something else results, as proclaimed in the sacred text, (*Bṛhadāraṇyaka Upaniṣad* 1.5.16) "By works, one gains the ancestral world." The word "so" means "in this way": "So we have heard"—we have listened and learned—these proclamations "from the wise," from people with wisdom, "who," namely, these teachers (*ācāryāḥ*), who "to us have explained it all," that is, have explained the paths of works and of (lower) knowledge. They have explained it all in that they have illumined sacred lore that has come down to us through a lineage of one teacher after another. This is the meaning. || 10 ||

yata evam ataḥ

Śaṅkara: So, in this way, there is the following:

vidyāṃ ca avidyāṃ ca yas tad veda ubhayaṃ saha |
avidyayā mṛtyuṃ tīrtvā vidyayā 'mṛtam aśnute || 11 ||

Knowledge and ignorance, if together the two are engaged,
Crossing over death by the ignorance, one tastes by the knowledge the nectar of immortality. || 11 ||

vidyāṃ ca avidyāṃ ca devatā-jñānaṃ karma ca ity arthaḥ | yas tad etad ubhayaṃ saha ekena puruṣeṇa anuṣṭheyaṃ veda tasya evaṃ samuccaya-kāriṇa eva eka-puruṣârthaṃ sambandhaḥ krameṇa syād ity ucyate — avidyayā karmaṇā agni-hotrâdinā mṛtyuṃ, svābhāvikaṃ karma jñānaṃ ca mṛtyu-śabda-vācyam, ubhayaṃ tīrtvā atikramya vidyayā devatā-jñānena amṛtaṃ devatâtma-bhāvam aśnute prāpnoti | tad dhy amṛtam ucyate yad devatâtma-gamanam || 11 ||

Śaṅkara: By "knowledge" and "ignorance" is meant "awareness of divinities" and "works." If a person practices both together, knows them in the sense of being engaged with them, then a connection would be made serially for that person who, trying to do them together, has a single goal (e.g., knowledge of divinities). "By the ignorance" which means "by the performance of rituals such as the Agnihotra ("Fire Oblation")," (crossing over) "death," here, namely, everyday action and everyday knowledge—such is what the word expresses—thus "crossing over" them both in the sense of "transcending" them both, a person "by the knowledge," that is, by awareness of divinities, "tastes . . . the nectar of immortality," attains the state of transformed consciousness characterized by knowledge of divinities. For that is called the "nectar of immortality" which amounts to attaining that divine state. || 11 ||

adhunā vyākṛtâvyākṛtôpāsanayoḥ samuccicīṣayā pratyekaṃ nindā ucyate |

Śaṅkara: Next, with respect to a desire to combine the two practices of worship, the one involving manifest objects (divinities), the other unmanifest, hidden (works, rituals), there is denigration of each separately.

andhaṃ tamaḥ praviśanti ye 'sambhūtim upāsate |
tato bhūya iva te tamo ya u sambhūtyāṃ ratāḥ || 12 ||

They enter a blinding darkness who devote themselves to unmanifest nature.

Than that into an even greater darkness go, as it were, those who are pleased with manifest nature. || 12 ||

andhaṃ tamaḥ praviśanti ye 'sambhūtiṃ sambhavanaṃ sambhūtiḥ sā yasya kāryasya sā sambhūtiḥ tasyā anyā asambhūtiḥ prakṛtiḥ kāraṇam avidyā avyākṛtâkhyā tām asambhūtim avyākṛtâkhyāṃ prakṛtiṃ kāraṇam avidyāṃ kāma-karma-bīja-bhūtām adarśanâtmikām upāsate ye te tad-anurūpam eva andhaṃ tamo 'darśanâtmakaṃ praviśanti | tatas tasmād api bhūyo bahutaram iva tamaḥ te praviśanti ya u sambhūtyāṃ kārya-brahmaṇi hiraṇyagarbhâkhye ratāḥ || 12 ||

Śaṅkara: With "They enter a blinding darkness who devote themselves to *unmanifest nature*," these last words are to be analyzed as proposing that an unmanifest nature—the term is to be analyzed as other than what would be a bringing-to-be whose effect would be *nature*, to wit, *unmanifest nature*, nature to be—nature, *prakṛti*, that is to say, itself viewed as a cause, in other words, a state of spiritual ignorance, *avidyā*, which is called "the unmanifest." Those who "devote themselves to" this so-called unmanifest nature viewed as a cause, as a state of spiritual ignorance which comes to be the seed of desire and action in an unconscious way, well, ironically, in accordance with that idea these people "enter a blinding darkness": such a nature would be unconscious. The words "than that" insinuate "*even* than that," "greater . . . as it were," meaning "*even* more, as it were." "They enter (such) a blinding darkness ... who are pleased with *a manifest nature*," that is, an "Absolute" (*brahman*) as an effect which they call Hiraṇyagarbha (the "Golden Womb"). || 12 ||

adhunā ubhayor upāsanayoḥ samuccaya-kāraṇam avayava-phala-bhedam āha —

Śaṅkara: Next a verse stating the distinct results of the separate parts combined, that is, for each of the two paths —

anyad eva āhuḥ sambhavād anyad āhur asambhavāt |
iti śuśruma dhīrāṇāṃ ye nas tad vicacakṣire || 13 ||

Just one thing is said to come from (devotion to) manifest nature; something else from the unmanifest, it is said.
So we have heard from the wise who have to us explained it all. || 13 ||

anyad eva pṛthag eva āhuḥ phalaṃ sambhavāt sambhūteḥ kārya-brahmôpāsanād aṇimâdy-aiśvarya-lakṣaṇaṃ vyākhyātavanta ity arthaḥ | tathā ca anyad āhur asambhavād asambhūter avyākṛtād avyākṛtôpāsanād yad uktam "andhaṃ tamaḥ praviśanti" iti, prakṛti-laya iti ca paurāṇikair ucyate | ity evaṃ śuśruma dhīrāṇāṃ vacanaṃ ye nas tad vicacakṣire vyākṛtâvyākṛtôpāsana-phalaṃ vyākhyātavanta ity arthaḥ || 13 ||

Śaṅkara: "Just one thing," that is to say, just one separate thing, "from (devotion to) manifest nature"—from (devotion to) a "bringing-to-be"—just one separate thing comes about, that is, one result, so "(it) is said." That is, from devoting oneself to an Absolute *as an effect* the result is characterized by such yogic powers as unnoticeability and control. This is the meaning. And so "something else from the unmanifest, it is said," that is, from something that is not a "bringing-to-be," from something unmanifest; that is, from devoting oneself to an unmanifest (there is a distinct result). Purāṇic sources inform us that the statement, "They enter a blinding darkness," is about (what the *Yoga-sūtra* and the *Sāṃkhya-kārikā* call) "absorption in nature," *prakṛti-laya* (for the mind). "So," which means "in this way," "we have heard from the wise" this proclamation, the wise "who have to us explained it all," that is, they have illumined the proclamation about the results of the meditative practices targeting the manifest and the unmanifest. This is the meaning. || 13 ||

yata evam ataḥ samuccayaḥ sambhūty-asambhūty-upāsanayor yukta eva eka-puruṣârthatvāc ca ity āha —

Śaṅkara: Since the results are this way, combination of the practices targeting manifest nature and the unmanifest can be appropriate. And there also could be a single goal. Thus the next mantra runs:

sambhūtiṃ ca vināśaṃ ca yas tad veda ubhayaṃ saha |
vināśena mṛtyuṃ tīrtvā 'sambhūtyā 'mṛtam aśnute || 14 ||

(Meditating on) the (un)manifest and dissolution, the person who knows both together
By the dissolution crosses beyond death, by the unmanifest tastes the nectar of immortality. || 14 ||

sambhūtiṃ ca vināśaṃ ca yas tad veda ubhayaṃ saha, vināśena vināśo dharmo yasya kāryasya sa tena dharmiṇā abhedena ucyate vināśa iti | tena tad-upāsanena anaiśvaryam adharma-kāmâdi-doṣa-jātaṃ ca mṛtyuṃ tīrtvā, hiraṇyagarbhôpāsanena hy aṇimâdi-prāptiḥ phalam tena anaiśvaryâdi-mṛtyum atītya asambhūtyā 'vyākṛtôpāsanayā 'mṛtaṃ prakṛti-laya-lakṣaṇam aśnute | sambhūtiṃ ca vināśaṃ ca ity atra a-varṇa-lopena nirdeśo draṣṭavyaḥ | prakṛti-laya-phala-śruty-anurodhāt || 14 ||

Śaṅkara: Now in the verse "(Meditating on) the (un)manifest and dissolution, the person who knows both together, by the dissolution . . ." the phrase, "by the dissolution," is to be understood in terms of a property—destruction, namely—whose effect would be non-distinct from the meaning of the noun referring to the property-bearer: the property-bearer's destruction is said to be simply "destruction." Thus by meditating, by devotion to that, one "crosses beyond death," "death" in the sense of "lack of control," which is born of faults such as wrongdoing (*adharma*) and lust. For, meditating on Hiraṇyagarbha, the result is to gain the powers of unnoticeability and so on (as was pointed out). Having transcended "death" in the form of lack of control and the like, one "tastes"—by means of meditating on the unmanifest, by means of "unmanifest nature"—the nectar of immortality; that is, one attains to "absorption in nature," *prakṛti-laya* (for the mind).

"(Meditating on) the (un)manifest and dissolution" has (in Sanskrit) elision of the letter *a* (meaning "not-" or "un-") such that the instruction has to be read as targeting the "*un*manifest" in accordance with the sacred text about the result which is "absorption in nature," *prakṛti-laya*.[20] || 14 ||

> mānuṣa-daiva-vitta-sādhyaṃ phalaṃ śāstra-lakṣaṇaṃ prakṛti-layântam | etāvatī saṃsāra-gatiḥ | ataḥ paraṃ pūrvôktam "ātmā eva abhūd vijānata" iti sarvâtma-bhāva eva sarva-eṣaṇā-saṃnyāsa-jñāna-niṣṭhā-phalam | evaṃ dvi-prakāraḥ pravṛtti-nivṛtti-lakṣaṇo vedârtho 'tra prakāśitaḥ | tatra pravṛtti-lakṣaṇasya vedârthasya vidhi-pratiṣedha-lakṣaṇasya kṛtsnasya prakāśane pravargyântaṃ brāhmaṇam upayuktam | nivṛtti-lakṣaṇasya vedârthasya prakāśane 'ta ūrdhvaṃ bṛhadāraṇyakam upayuktam | tatra niṣekâdi-śmaśānântaṃ karma kurvan jijīviṣed yo vidyayā saha apara-brahma-viṣayayā, tad uktaṃ "vidyāṃ ca avidyāṃ ca yas tad veda ubhayaṃ saha | avidyayā mṛtyuṃ tīrtvā vidyayā 'mṛtam aśnute" iti | tatra kena mārgeṇa amṛtatvam aśnuta ity ucyate — "tad yat tat satyam asau sa ādityo ya eṣa etasmin maṇḍale puruṣo yaś ca ayaṃ dakṣiṇe 'kṣan-puruṣaḥ"[21] etad ubhayaṃ satyam brahmôpāsīno yathôkta-karma-kṛc ca yaḥ so 'nta-kāle prāpte saty ātmānam ātmanaḥ prāpti-dvāraṃ yācate —

Śaṅkara: The results of the disciplines that provide human or divine wealth, which are set forth in the *śāstra*s, have their culmination in "absorption in nature," *prakṛti-laya* (which guarantees *samādhi*, "yogic trance," in another incarnation). All of it occurs within the realm of rebirth (*saṃsāra*). Beyond that, there is a distinct result, as proclaimed in the verse, "(When) 'Nothing but myself has come to be,' when in this way someone knows (all beings)." This is nothing other than the state of having become the self of everyone and everything, which is the result of the path of knowledge requiring renunciation of desire in its entirety.

In this way, the teachings of the Veda (including the Upaniṣads) run in two modes, one characterized by action, the other by inaction. This is made plain here.

Of the two, the *Śatapatha Brāhmaṇa* through the section on the Pravargya ritual (preliminary to a Soma sacrifice) is rightly consulted for illumination of Vedic teachings involving action, filled out by injunctions and prohibitions. It is rightly consulted for its illumination, that is to say, for all those Vedic teachings that consist of injunctions and prohibitions. Later in the corpus, the *Bṛhadāraṇyaka Upaniṣad* is what should be consulted for illumination of Vedic teachings involving inaction.

Of the two teachings, doing the "works" enjoined between the sprinkling (done ritually at birth) and the cremation ground, one "may wish to live (a hundred years)." Such a person practices by knowing the "lower" (*apara*) Brahman (the determinate Absolute). It was proclaimed above: "Knowledge and ignorance, if together the two are engaged,/ Crossing over death by the ignorance, one tastes by the knowledge the nectar of immortality." This is the answer to the question of which of the two routes (*mārga*) leads to "tasting the nectar of immortality."

Then there is, (*Bṛhadāraṇyaka Upaniṣad* 5.5.2) "That which is this reality (Brahman) is this sun. The very person who is in this globe and this very one who is in the right eye," both are this reality. And a person, having practiced meditation on Brahman and having performed works as specified, prays at the time of death to the self for the door to self-realization to open:

hiraṇmayena pātreṇa satyasya apihitaṃ mukham |
tat tvaṃ pūṣann apāvṛṇu satya-dharmāya dṛṣṭaye || 15 ||

The face of truth is covered by a golden lid.
Pūṣan! Nourisher! Make it open, for one whose *dharma* is true, for experience. || 15 ||

hiraṇmayena pātreṇa hiraṇmayam iva hiraṇmayaṃ jyotirmayam ity etat | tena pātreṇa iva apidhāna-bhūtena satyasya eva āditya-maṇḍala-sthasya brahmaṇo 'pihitam ācchāditaṃ mukhaṃ dvāram tat tvaṃ he pūṣann apāvṛṇv apasāraya | satya-dharmāya tava satyasya upāsanāt satyaṃ dharmo yasya mama so 'haṃ satya-dharmā tasmai mahyam athavā yathā-bhūtasya dharmasya anuṣṭhātre dṛṣṭaye tava satyâtmana upalabdhaye || 15 ||

Śaṅkara: In the verse, "by a golden lid . . ." "golden" is a metaphor for "being made of light." By that "lid," as it were, by that covering, the "face," that is to say, the truth that is the means to the reality of Brahman dwelling in the globe of the sun, "is covered," is blocked out. "Pūṣan, make it open," make it transcended. The phrase, "for one whose *dharma* is true," is to be construed as follows: for any who has true *dharma* through meditating on the truth as I have, for such a person, for me—alternatively, for the practitioner of *dharma* as it should be—"for experience," that is, so that that person should experience the reality of the self. || 15 ||

pūṣann ekarṣe yama sūrya prājāpatya vyūha raśmīn samūha tejas |[22]
yat te rūpaṃ kalyāṇatamaṃ tat te paśyāmi yo 'sāv asau puruṣaḥ so 'ham asmi || 16 ||

Pūṣan! Nourisher! Solo Traveler! Death, Yama the Controller! Sun! Child of Prajāpati, Father of Creatures! Disperse your (blinding) rays. Concentrate your energy (*tejas*).
The form of yours that is the most auspicious, that I would see. That yonder Person, I am He (*so 'ham*). || 16 ||

he pūṣan! jagataḥ poṣaṇāt pūṣā raviḥ | tathā eka eva ṛṣati gacchati ity ekarṣiḥ he ekarṣe ! tathā sarvasya saṃyamanād yamaḥ he yama ! tathā raśmīnāṃ prāṇānāṃ rasānāṃ ca svīkaraṇāt sūryaḥ he sūrya ! prajāpater apatyaṃ prājāpatyaḥ he prājāpatya ! vyūha vigamaya raśmīn svān | samūha ekīkuru upasaṃhara tejas tāpakaṃ jyotiḥ | yat te tava rūpaṃ kalyāṇatamam atyanta-śobhanaṃ tat te tava ātmanaḥ prasādāt paśyāmi | kiṃ ca ahaṃ na tu tvāṃ bhṛtya-vad yāce yo 'sāv āditya-maṇḍala-stho vyāhṛty-avayavaḥ puruṣaḥ puruṣâkāratvāt, pūrṇaṃ vā anena prāṇa-buddhy-ātmanā jagat samastam iti puruṣaḥ, puri śayanād vā puruṣaḥ so 'ham asmi bhavāmi || 16 ||

Śaṅkara: "Pūṣan!" The sun is called the "Nourisher," "Pūṣan," because it nourishes the world. Likewise, the sun travels alone across the sky; "traveling" means "going." Thus the appellation, "solo Traveler." "Solo Traveler!" Similarly, because death controls everyone ultimately, death is called "Yama the Controller" (*yama* = control), "Yama the Controller!" So, too, salutations to the sun who makes itself up out of its "rays"—life energies (*prāṇa*) and sensory experiences—the Sun, "Sun!" Projeny of Prajāpati are each called a child of Prajāpati, the Father of Creatures, "Child of Prajāpati!"

"Disperse" in the sense of "make depart" your own (blinding, blocking) rays. "Concentrate" means "unify, bring together." "Energy," yogic energy, is what becomes concentrated, heat made by yoga practice, (spiritual) light. "That form of yours that is the most auspicious"—"auspicious" in the sense of "most effectively purifying"—"that I would see," I would see by way of the self's grace (*prasāda*).

Furthermore, to you I do not pray as a servant but rather as the Person consisting of speech who lives in the solar globe, "That yonder Person, I am He"—which is true because of the personal form, alternatively, because of the entire world being filled by this self of life and intelligence. Etymologically, the word *puruṣa*, "person," comes from "sleeping" (*śaya*) in the city (the body, *pur*), to take up another possibility. Then the meaning of "I am He" is that I am that one. || 16 ||

vāyur anilam amṛtam atha idaṃ bhasmāntaṃ śarīram |
om krato smara kṛtaṃ smara krato smara kṛtaṃ smara || 17 ||

Air to Wind, to the Nectar of Immortality; then there is this body that will turn now to ash (let it be an offering).
Om! Doer! Remember the deeds, remember. Doer! Remember the deeds, remember. || 17 ||

atha idānīṃ mama mariṣyato vāyuḥ prāṇo 'dhyātma-paricchedaṃ hitvā adhidaivatâtmānaṃ sarvâtmakam anilam amṛtaṃ sūtrâtmānaṃ pratipadyatām iti vākya-śeṣaḥ | liṅgaṃ ca idaṃ jñāna-karma-saṃskṛtam utkrāmatv iti draṣṭavyam mārga-yācana-sāmarthyāt | atha idaṃ śarīram agnau hutaṃ bhasmāntaṃ bhūyāt | om iti yathā upāsanam om-pratīkâtmakatvāt satyâtmakam agny-ākhyaṃ brahmâbhedena ucyate | he krato saṅkalpâtmaka smara yan mama smartavyaṃ tasya kālo 'yaṃ pratyupasthitaḥ, ataḥ smara etāvantaṃ kālaṃ bhāvitaṃ kṛtam agne smara yan mayā bālya-prabhṛty-anuṣṭhitaṃ karma tac ca smara | krato smara kṛtaṃ smara iti punar vacanam ādarârtham || 17 ||

Śaṅkara: The word "now" is used in the sense of "at this time," which, for me (the person saying the mantra), is the time of dying. "Air," being breath and life (*prāṇa*), is leaving the limitation of the body for divinity, for the "Wind" that is everywhere, for the "Nectar of Immortality," which is the core of being: "May it attain that goal" is how the verse is to be filled out. What is implied is, "And may this subtle body purified of cognition and karma ascend," because such a prayer for direction along a journey can carry that implication. "Let 'this body that will turn now to ash,' let it be an offering into Agni, the Flame"—this is how the line continues.

Om! is in the mantra, because engaging with it, voiced as inscribed, meditating on *om*, which symbolizes the self, is called *agni*, the "Fire" that is said to be non-distinct from Brahman the Absolute. "Doer!" amounts to "Hey you whose nature is intention (*saṅkalpa*, 'intention,' which along with karma makes an individual capable of a subtle body)." "Remember . . ." that is to say, "what I have done please preserve, I who now at this last moment have come to you." For this reason, the mantra continues, "Doer! Remember the deeds, remember," the repetition expressing respect. That is, "Remember what is done at this very moment by me engaged in prayer at just such a moment, and remember, O Fire, what I have performed from childhood on, remember that, remember the deeds."

punar anyena mantreṇa mārgaṃ yācate —

Śaṅkara: Again, the prayer is for a path (*mārga*) with another mantra:

agne naya supathā rāye asmān viśvāni deva vayunāni vidvān |
yuyodhy asmaj juhurāṇam eno bhūyiṣṭhāṃ te nama-uktiṃ vidhema || 18 ||

Fire! Show us the true path to happiness. Divine Being! You know every state of mind.
Fight, please, to separate us from deviating evil and sin. Salutations, extreme salutations to you we urge. || 18 ||

ity upaniṣat || om pūrṇam adaḥ iti śāntiḥ ||

Here ends the Upaniṣad. Om! "That is the Full." Peace.

agne naya iti | he agne naya gamaya supathā śobhanena mārgeṇa | supathā iti viśeṣaṇaṃ dakṣiṇa-mārga-nivṛtty-artham | nirviṇṇo 'haṃ dakṣiṇena mārgeṇa gatâgata-lakṣaṇena, ato yāce tvāṃ punaḥ punaḥ gamanâgamana-varjitena śobhanena pathā naya | rāye dhanāya karma-phala-bhogāya ity arthaḥ | asmān yathôkta-dharma-phala-viśiṣṭān viśvāni sarvāṇi he deva vayunāni karmāṇi prajñānāni vā vidvāñ jānan | kiñ ca yuyodhi viyojaya vināśaya asmad asmatto juhurāṇaṃ kuṭilaṃ vañcanâtmakam enaḥ pāpam | tato vayaṃ viśuddhāḥ santa iṣṭaṃ prāpsyāma ity abhiprāyaḥ | kin tu vayam idānīṃ te na śaknumaḥ paricaryāṃ kartum, bhūyiṣṭhāṃ bahutarāṃ te tubhyaṃ nama-uktiṃ namas-kāra-vacanaṃ vidhema namas-kāreṇa paricarema ity arthaḥ |

Śaṅkara: "Fire!" "Show us," lead us by way of the "true path," the path that purifies. The modifier ("true") in "true path" is used to exclude the "southern" way (on the post-mortem journey). "I am disenchanted with the southern way with its coming and going, its death and rebirth. Thus I pray to you to show the path that purifies without going and coming again and again." The words "to happiness" mean "to wealth" in terms of enjoyment (*bhoga*) of the fruits of action. This is the point. The word "us" refers to us insofar as our character includes fruits, results of action, that are *dharmic* (righteous), as has been laid out. "Divine Being! You know," you are aware of, "every state," acts or states of mind, namely, all of them (physical and mental).

Furthermore, "fight" in the sense of "separate from us, destroy for us," "deviating," that is to say, meandering, deceptive, "evil and sin," wrong-doing. Thus thoroughly cleansed, we would be able to attain the wished-for end. This is the idea.

(The background is that) we, however, at this moment right now are unable to serve you (sufficiently well). This is why the verse closes with a kind of service voiced: "Salutations, extreme salutations"—"extreme" in the sense of "very intense"—"to you," to you yourself, "we urge . . ." that is, "we urge honoring of you to be voiced." This is the meaning.

"avidyayā mṛtyuṃ tīrtvā vidyayā 'mṛtam aśnute" "vināśena mṛtyuṃ tīrtvā 'sambhūtyā 'mṛtam aśnute" iti śrutvā kecit saṃśayaṃ kurvanti | atas tan-nirākaraṇârthaṃ saṅkṣepato vicāraṇāṃ kariṣyāmaḥ | tatra tāvat kin-nimittaḥ saṃśaya ity ucyate — vidyā-śabdena mukhyā paramâtma-vidyā eva kasmān na gṛhyate amṛtatvaṃ ca | nanu uktāyāḥ paramâtma-vidyāyāḥ karmaṇaś ca virodhāt samuccayânupapattiḥ | satyam | virodhas tu na avagamyate virodhâvirodhayoḥ śāstra-pramāṇakatvāt | yathā avidyânuṣṭhānaṃ vidyôpāsanaṃ ca śāstra-pramāṇakaṃ tathā tad-virodhâvirodhāv api | yathā ca "na hiṃsyāt sarva-bhūtāni" iti śāstrād avagataṃ punaḥ śāstreṇa eva bādhyate "adhvare paśuṃ hiṃsyād" iti | evaṃ vidyâvidyayor api syāt | vidyā-karmaṇoś ca samuccayaḥ | na "dūram ete viparīte viṣūcī avidyā yā ca vidyā iti jñātā"[23] iti śruteḥ | "vidyāṃ ca avidyāṃ ca" iti vacanād avirodha iti cen na | hetu-sva-rūpa-phala-virodhāt | vidyâvidyā-virodhâvirodhayor vikalpâsambhavāt samuccaya-vidhānād avirodha eva iti cen na | saha-sambhavânupapatteḥ | krameṇa ekâśraye syātāṃ vidyâvidye iti cen na | vidyôtpattau avidyāyā hy astatvāt tad-āśraye 'vidyânupapatteḥ | na hy agnir uṣṇaḥ prakāśaś ca iti vijñānôtpattau yasminn āśraye tad-utpannaṃ tasmin eva āśraye śīto 'gnir aprakāśo vā ity avidyāyā utpattiḥ | na api saṃśayo 'jñānaṃ vā | "yasmin sarvāṇi bhūtāny ātmā eva abhūd vijānataḥ | tatra ko mohaḥ kaḥ śoka ekatvam anupaśyataḥ" iti śoka-mohâdy-asambhava-śruteḥ | avidyâsambhavāt tad-upādānasya karmaṇo 'py anupapattim avocāma | "amṛtam aśnute" ity āpekṣikam amṛtam, vidyā-śabdena paramâtma-vidyā-grahaṇe hiraṇmayena ity-ādinā dvāra-mārgâdi-yācanam anupapannaṃ syāt | tasmād upāsanayā samuccayo na paramâtma-vijñānena iti yathā asmābhir vyākhyāta eva mantrāṇām artha ity uparamyate || 18 ||

Interlocutor: "Crossing over death by the ignorance, one tastes by the knowledge the nectar of immortality," and "By the dissolution [one] crosses beyond death, by the unmanifest tastes the nectar of immortality"—some of us hearing these two sacred texts may be doubtful about what they mean.

Śaṅkara: For that reason we'll undertake briefly some reflection to dispel the worry. Just what gives rise to the doubt in the first place?

Interlocutor: The word *vidyā*—"knowledge"—in its primary sense refers to knowledge of the supreme self. Why, then, is that not what's meant when it is used along with "nectar of immortality" (in the first verse quoted, verse 11)? The problem is putting the meanings of the verses together which seems impossible because knowledge of the supreme self, as has been explained, is incompatible with "works."

Śaṅkara: True. However, the nature of the opposition is not something to be so easily inferred because *śāstra* is here, too, the authority about the incompatibility or its lack. As *śāstra* is the authority for the practices of spiritual ignorance as well as for the meditative engagement that leads to spiritual knowledge, so its authority extends to incompatibility or its absence in these matters too.

There are, furthermore, other examples of this: "One should not kill (*ahiṃsā*) any being," a teaching learned from *śāstra*. But there is another śāstric teaching that overrides it, indeed a teaching that is nothing but *śāstra*, "For the Adhvara (Soma sacrifice) one should kill (*hiṃsā*) an animal." The case with spiritual knowledge (*vidyā*) and spiritual ignorance (*avidyā*) could be expected to be similar.

Interlocutor: Then knowledge and works can be combined.

Śaṅkara: No. There is the sacred text, (*Kaṭha Upaniṣad* 2.4) "Wide apart are those two, standing opposed, disparate: ignorance and what is called 'knowledge', *vidyā* and *avidyā*."

Interlocutor: Then the statement asserting "knowledge and ignorance," *vidyā* and *avidyā*, does not capture an opposition, an incompatibility.

Śaṅkara: Wrong. The opposition is in the result of practices supporting it naturally, by what the practices are.

Interlocutor: Then, since it is impossible to have a precise conception of what is knowledge and what is not, nor of what is opposition here and what is not, there would be no opposition at all in a teaching that the two should be combined.

Śaṅkara: No. It is unreasonable to think that they could occur together.

Interlocutor: A single person could bear the two, *vidyā* and *avidyā*, one after the other, serially.

Śaṅkara: No. For, since upon an arising of *vidyā*, "knowledge," *avidyā*, "ignorance," is banished, a person with spiritual knowledge cannot experience *avidyā*. For, a person who really knows that fire is hot and luminous does not think *ignorantly*, "Fire is cold and not luminous," not in the face of the knowledge. Nor would there be, for such a person, any doubt about the matter nor an absence of knowledge.

In line with this, there is the verse above about the *impossibility* of grief, delusion, and the like,

> **When 'Nothing but myself has come to be,' when in this way someone knows all beings,/ How then can there be delusion? What grief can there be? For a person realizing oneness?**

Since *avidyā* cannot occur, action that depends on it is also absolutely ruled out, as has been explained. "One tastes the nectar of immortality" is about a "nectar" that is dependent on action. If in that verse the word *vidyā*, "knowledge," referred to knowledge of the supreme self, the prayer would be incoherent as about a means, a path with a "golden lid" and the rest.

Therefore, to combine paths of knowledge and works would not be to be proceeding to experience the supreme self—so we have made plain in our comments above on the meaning of the mantras of the Upaniṣad. Hence we desist. || 18 ||

> iti śrīmat-parama-haṃsa-parivrājakâcāryasya śrī-govinda-bhagavat-pūjya-pāda-śiṣyasya śrī-śaṅkara-bhagavataḥ kṛtau vājasaneya-saṃhitôpaniṣad-bhāṣyaṃ sampūrṇam |

> Here ends the commentary on the Upaniṣad which belongs to the (Vedic) *Vājasaneya-saṃhitā*, the effort belonging to that glorious renunciant teacher (*ācārya*) of the highest order, the blessed Śrī Śaṅkara, the disciple of Śrī Govinda (Kṛṣṇa) whose very feet are blessed, worthy of worship.

Addendum

Śaṅkara's Commentary on *Bṛhadāraṇyaka* 5.15.1
(*Bṛ* 5.15.1 is identical to *Īśā* 15–18 but glossed by Śaṅkara slightly differently)

hiraṇmayena pātreṇa satyasya apihitaṃ mukham |
tat tvaṃ pūṣann apāvṛṇu satya-dharmāya dṛṣṭaye ||

The face of truth is covered by a golden lid.
Pūṣan! Nourisher! Make it open, for one whose *dharma* is truth, for experience.

pūṣann ekarṣe yama sūrya prājāpatya vyūha raśmīn samūha tejas |
yat te rūpaṃ kalyāṇatamaṃ tat te paśyāmi yo 'sāv asau puruṣaḥ so 'ham asmi ||

Pūṣan! Nourisher! Sole Seer! Death, Yama the Controller! Sun! Child of Prajāpati, Father of Creatures! Disperse your (blinding) rays. Concentrate your energy (*tejas*).
The form of yours that is the most auspicious, that I would see. That yonder Person, I am He (*so 'ham*).

vāyur anilam amṛtam atha idaṃ bhasmāntaṃ śarīram |
oṃ krato smara kṛtaṃ smara krato smara kṛtaṃ smara ||

Air to Wind, to the Immortal; then there is this body that will turn now to ash (let it be an offering).
Om! Doer! Remember the deeds, remember. Doer! Remember the deeds, remember.

agne naya supathā rāye asmān viśvāni deva vayunāni vidvān |
yuyodhy asmaj juhurāṇam eno bhūyiṣṭhāṃ te nama-uktiṃ vidhema ||

Fire! Show us the true path to happiness. Divine Being! You know us, you know every state of mind.
Fight, please, to separate us from deviating evil and sin. Salutations, extreme salutations to you we urge.

yo jñāna-karma-samuccaya-kārī so 'nta-kāle ādityaṃ prārthayati | asti ca prasaṅgo, gāyatryās turīyaḥ pādo hi saḥ | tad-upasthānaṃ prakṛtam ataḥ sa eva prārthyate | hiraṇmayena jyotirmayena pātreṇa, yathā pātreṇa iṣṭaṃ vastv apidhīyate evam idaṃ satyâkhyaṃ brahma jyotirmayena maṇḍalena apihitam iva asamāhita-cetasām adṛśyatvāt | tad ucyate—satyasya apihitaṃ mukhaṃ mukhyaṃ sva-rūpaṃ, tad-apidhānaṃ pātram apidhānam iva darśana-pratibandha-kāraṇaṃ tattvaṃ he pūṣan jagataḥ poṣaṇāt pūṣā savitā 'pāvṛṇv apāvṛtaṃ kuru darśana-pratibandha-kāraṇam apanaya ity-arthaḥ | satya-dharmāya satyaṃ dharmo 'sya mama so 'haṃ satya-dharmā tasmai tvad-ātma-bhūtāya ity-arthaḥ | dṛṣṭaye darśanāya | pūṣann ity-ādīni nāmāny āmantraṇârthāni savituḥ | ekarṣe, ekaś ca asāv ṛṣiś ca ekarṣir darśanād ṛṣiḥ | sa hi sarvasya jagata ātmā cakṣuś ca san sarvaṃ paśyati | eko vā gacchati ity ekarṣiḥ "sūrya ekākī carati" iti mantra-varṇāt | yama, sarvaṃ hi jagataḥ saṃyamanaṃ tvat-kṛtam | sūrya, suṣṭhu īrayate rasān raśmīn prāṇān dhiyo vā jagata iti | prājāpatya, prajāpater īśvarasya āpatyaṃ hiraṇyagarbhasya vā he prājāpatya | vyūha vigamaya raśmīn | samūha saṅkṣipa ātmanas tejo yena ahaṃ śaknuyāṃ draṣṭum | tejasā hy apahata-dṛṣṭir na śaknuyāṃ tvat-sva-rūpam añjasā draṣṭum | vidyotana iva rūpāṇām ata upasaṃhara tejaḥ | yat te tava rūpaṃ sarva-kalyāṇām atiśayena kalyāṇaṃ kalyāṇatamaṃ tat te paśyāmi | paśyāmo vayaṃ vacana-vyatyayena | yo 'sau bhūr-bhuvaḥ-svar-vyāvṛtty-avayavaḥ puruṣaḥ puruṣâkṛtitvāt puruṣaḥ so 'ham asmi bhavāmi | ahar aham iti ca upaniṣada uktatvād āditya-cākṣuṣayoḥ tad eva idaṃ parāmṛśyate | so 'ham asmy amṛtam iti sambandhaḥ | mama amṛtasya satyasya śarīra-pāte śarīra-stho yaḥ prāṇo vāyuḥ so 'nilaṃ bāhyaṃ vāyum eva pratigacchatu | tathā anyā devatāḥ svāṃ svāṃ prakṛtiṃ gacchantu | atha idam api bhasmântaṃ sat pṛthivīṃ yātu śarīraṃ |

Śaṅkara: Someone having practiced a combination of the paths of knowledge and of action ("works") is, at the time of death, praying to the Sun, as is appropriate, since "Sun" is the fourth foot of the Gāyatrī mantra ("Om. May we mediate on the most auspicious form of the god Sāvitri, the Sun, that which will enlighten us, illumining our minds, raising our consciousness.")[24] The Sun's sacred nearness is in focus. So it is just He to whom the prayer is directed. The verse (= *Īśā* 15) says, "by a golden lid," meaning "by a lid made of light." Like something wanted that is covered by a lid, so Brahman, called here "truth," is hidden, covered by a globe of light, as it were, in that for want of properly concentrated consciousness there is no "sight." So the verse says, "the face of truth is covered," the "face" (*mukha*) being the "principal" (*mukhya*) feature, that is to say, its essential nature (*sva-rūpa*). In that there is a covering, it is a "lid," a cause, as it were, something blocking mystical vision.

The next verse (= *Īśā* 16) says, "Pūṣan!" The Sun, *sāvitri*, is the Nourisher (*pūṣan*), because it nourishes the world. "Make it open" means "Do please remove the lid," that is to say, "Take away the cause, the blocking, that prevents vision." This is the sense.

The verse continues, "for one whose *dharma* is truth." (In Sanskrit) this is a compound word to be analyzed: "a person whose *dharma* is truth," for that person, that is, belonging to that person, belonging to me—"I am He"—I am the one whose *dharma* is truth, for that person, who is your very self, remove the lid. This is the sense. "For experience" means "for vision."

The names "Pūṣan" and the rest are for addressing the Sun. And "Sole Seer!" is said because of the vision of that one, the one being a "rishi," the one *ṛṣi*. For he is the self of the entire world; furthermore, (as a faculty) sight sees all that there is to see. Alternatively, it's because he goes alone (the sun travels alone) that the verse says "*ekarṣiḥ*" (then not "Sole Seer," but "Solo Traveler"); for there is a mantra that spells it out, "The Sun moves along alone."

"Death, Yama the Controller!" is said because for everyone and everything in the world there is the controlling that you perform.

"Sun!": most naturally, most agreeably (as suggested by '*su*' embedded in '*sūrya*') the Sun excites our sensibilities, the "rays" mentioned in the verse, our "vital energies," *prāṇa*, or, possibly, our thought, for us all.

"Child of of Prajāpati, Father of Creatures!": the Lord's progeny is said to be from Prajāpati, "Father of Creatures," or it could be that Hiraṇyagarbha is meant by "Child of Prajāpati!"

"Disperse," that is to say, "Make go away," "(blinding, blocking) rays." "Concentrate," that is, "bring together," spiritual energy (*tejas*), that is, the energy of the self (*ātman*) whereby I can have mystic vision. For, it is that energy that has cut off vision such that right now your true nature I am unable to see. It is like lightning with things' colors and shapes (so blinding they cannot be seen). So unify your energy (*tejas*).

"The form of yours that is the most auspicious," in other words, of all things that are wondrous and blest, the exceedingly auspicious is the "most auspicious," "that I would see," in effect with a change of number, "*we* would see."

"That yonder Person," it's a person because of having the form of a person but whose members include the worlds, earth (*bhūr*), the intermediate realm (*bhuvas*), and heaven (*svar*), as in the sacred chant, *om bhūr bhuvaḥ suvaḥ*. "I am He" (*so 'ham asmi*), that is, I have so become.

And since the Upaniṣad says "day" (*ahar*) and "I" (*aham*) together, meaning respectively the Sun and vision, just that (namely, the two together) is the reference. The connection (with the next verse = *Īśā* 17) is that the "Immortal" (*amṛta*) is referred to with the statement, "I am He."

When the body falls away, the truth, the Immortal, which I am, well, let my life energy (*prāṇa*) return to "Wind" (universal *prāṇa*); let the air in my lungs go back to the external air. Likewise, all my other faculties—the divinities of sensation and action—let them go to their respective natures. Then also this body, "which will turn to ash," may it go to earth.

> atha idānīm ātmanaḥ saṅkalpa-bhūtāṃ manasi vyavasthitām agni-devatām prārthayate—om krato | om iti krato iti ca sambodhanârthāv eva | oṃkāra-pratīkatvād om | manomayatvāc ca kratuḥ | he om he krato smara smartavyam | anta-kāle hi tvat-smaraṇa-vaśād iṣṭā gatiḥ prāpyate | ataḥ prārthayate yan mayā kṛtaṃ tat smara | punar-uktir ādarârthā | kiñ ca he 'gne naya prāpaya supathā śobhanena mārgeṇa, rāye dhanāya karma-phala-prāptaye ity-arthaḥ | na dakṣiṇena kṛṣṇena punar-āvṛtti-yuktena kiṃ tarhi śuklena supathā | asmān viśvāni sarvāṇi he deva vayunāni prajñānāni sarva-prāṇīṇāṃ vidvān | kiñ ca yuyodhy apanaya viyojaya asmad asmatto juhurāṇaṃ kuṭilam enaḥ pāpaṃ pāpa-jātaṃ sarvam | tena pāpena viyuktā vayam eṣyāma uttareṇa pathā tvat-prasādāt | kin tu vayaṃ tubhyaṃ paricaryāṃ kartuṃ na śaknumaḥ | bhūyiṣṭhāṃ bahutamāṃ te tubhyam nama-uktiṃ namaskāra-vacanaṃ vidhema namaskārôktyā paricarema ity-arthaḥ, anyat kartum aśaktāḥ santi iti ||

Now the speaker saying "Om! Doer!" makes a prayer to the divinity Agni, "Fire," who is manifest as the mind formed by intentions (*saṅkalpa*). And "Om!" and "Doer!" are (in Sanskrit) two words, both in the vocative case ("doer" obviously, "om" not so), since the syllable "om" is a symbol standing for itself—Om—and the "doer" is made of mental stuff (*manomaya*). "Om! Doer! Remember," that is, remember that which is worthy of remembering. For here I am at the end of life wanting after death to go on the route secured by what you remember. Therefore, I pray that what has been done by me, please, that remember. The repetition in the verse is to show respect.

And then (in the next verse = *Īśā* 18) there is "Fire! Show us," that is, "lead us along," by a splendid path, which is what is meant by "true path," followed by the words "to happiness," which mean to the wealth that is obtained as the result of karma. This is the sense. So let me not be one yoked to the southern, dark way in being reborn but rather to the bright way, the "true path."

"Divine Being!" You know us, you know "every," that is to say, "absolutely all," every state of mind of every living being.

Then there is "Fight, please," which means take it away, from whom, "from us"—the accusative (in Sanskrit) having here the sense of the ablative, "from us"—or, let us say, "separate us from." From what? From "deviating," that is to say, from crooked, "evil and sin," from the bad, all of it, from everything connected with what's bad. Freed from wrong-doing, we would travel the northern route, by way of grace, by your favor.

May we add that we are not capable of serving you further. That's why we say "extreme," that is, to the fullest extent, "to *you*," to *thee*, "salutations," more precisely, statements of salutation, "we urge," that is, we would serve by making statements of salutation. This is the sense. By us now there is nothing more that can be done. || 5.15.1 ||

• • •

Appendix C

Part One

Bhagavad Gītā 6.10–32
The Yoga of Meditation

(Bhagavān Śrī Kṛṣṇa speaking:)

6.10. In a secluded place, a yogi should practice uninterruptedly, solitary, controlled in thought, without expectation or sense of possessiveness.

6.11–12. Finding a clean spot, sitting in a steady āsana not too high, not too low, on a cloth, pelt, or *kuśa* grass, fixing heart and mind on a single point, working to bring thought as well as the body's organs and faculties under control, one should practice yoga for self-purification.

6.13–14. Holding still the body, head, and neck, drawing the vision in to fix it on a midline and not looking in any direction, steady, bringing the mind under control, untroubled, fear departed, settled in a vow of sexual restraint, one should, to practice yoga, sit with thought directed to me, intent on me.

6.15. Practicing yoga in this way constantly, the yogi with fixed heart and mind attains the supreme peace of Nirvāṇa, that is to say, attains to my station, my consciousness.

6.16. Yoga is not for one who eats too much, nor for one who does not eat at all. Arjuna, it is not for one who sleeps too much, nor for one who does not sleep at all.

6.17. Yoga banishes suffering for one who practices asleep and awake, eating and playing, in working, always behaving like a yogi.

6.18. Insofar as thought is directed solely to the self, *ātman*, the person is rightly called a yogi, free of wishfulness, practicing with respect to all desire.

6.19. As a lamp set down out of the wind does not flicker—this analogy is used for one whose thought is restrained, practicing yoga for self-realization.

6.20–1. Checked by yoga practice, thought having become still, seeing self by self, a yogi, being satisfied in self, experiences a supreme and endless pleasure, graspable by the intelligence though it is beyond the senses; the yogi in it becomes fixed and stable, never moving away from the reality.

6.22. It is that which once gotten a person would not regard getting anything else as better. Fixed in it, a person is not disturbed by occasions even for the fiercest grief.

6.23. This is what should be realized, called yoga ("union"), the disjunction ("disunion") from all connection with pain and misery. Such yoga should be practiced with determination, never despairing, with thought and mind engaged.

6.24–5. Rejecting desires born of intentions, all of them without exception, with the *manas* alone, the attention, completely checking the pack of sense organs, then gradually, step-by-step, one should become still, holding the attention (*manas*) in the self (*ātman*) by means of the intelligence (*buddhi*); the intelligence itself held tight with fortitude, one should think of nothing at all, nothing whatsoever should come into consciousness.

6.26. Wherever the attention would roam, restless and not steady or firm, just there checking it, one should put it in the control of the self alone.

6.27. For, a pacified mentality carries the yogi to the highest pleasure and happiness, passion quietened, absorbed in Brahman, without flaw.

6.28. A yogi practicing constantly in this way, flaws departed, effortlessly enjoys the supreme happiness that is the touch of Brahman.

6.29. Seeing the same everywhere, disciplined through yoga practice, one perceives the self seated in all beings and all beings in the self.

6.30. A person who sees me everywhere and everything in me is never lost to me and I am never lost to that person.

6.31. However the yogi may live who, stationed in oneness, is devoted to me who is set in the heart of all beings, that yogi lives in me.

6.32. Who sees by way of likeness to self the same everywhere, Arjuna, whether pleasure and happiness or pain and suffering, that yogi is deemed the very best.

Part Two

From the *Bhagavad Gītā*
The Yoga of Action (*Gītā* chapter 3)
The Yoga of Knowledge and Renunciation of Action (*Gītā* chapter 4)
The Yoga of Renunciation (*Gītā* chapter 5)

(Arjuna:)

3.1. Kṛṣṇa, if you consider mental attitude (*buddhi*) superior to action, why then do you urge me on to an action so terrible?

3.2. It seems you would confuse my mind (*buddhi*) with contradictory words. So tell me definitely that whereby I can attain the supreme good.

(Bhagavān Śrī Kṛṣṇa:)

...

3.17. Yet the person delighting only in the true self (*ātman*) and satisfied living in it—for such a person, thoroughly contented in the self alone, there is nothing that must be done.

3.18. Nor is there for him any gain in what he has done or has not done. Nor do his interests depend in any way on anyone or anything else.
3.19. Therefore, ever unattached do the work that has to be done. For the person who is unattached in performing action attains the supreme good.
3.20. For by work alone did Janaka and others attain perfection. Considering also the holding together of the worlds of society, you should be doing works.
3.21. Setting a standard that the world follows, whatever the superior person does that indeed is what others try to do.
3.22. For me, there is nothing whatsoever that has to be done, Arjuna, in the three worlds; nor anything unattained that I need to attain. Still I continue in action.
3.23. For if I did not continue ever tirelessly in action, my example people would follow, Arjuna, as they always do.
3.24. Societies would come apart if I were not to do works, and I would be the author of chaos. These creatures I would destroy.
3.25. The unenlightened, who are attached to their actions, proceed in works, Arjuna; so too should the enlightened, unattached, to hold together society.
3.26. One should not engender a division in the understanding of ignorant folk who are attached to their works; rather, knowing, one should inspire them, performing all actions, disciplined in yoga.
3.27. Works in every fashion are being done by the impulsions (modes, *guṇa*) of nature. The person deluded by egoism thinks, "I am the doer of this work."
3.28. But the one who knows what is real, strong-armed warrior, concerning those impulsions and the different types of action, realizing that the impulsions operate on themselves, he is not attached.

. . .

4.16. What action is, and what inaction, even rishis (seer-sages) are confused on the score. To you I will explain that kind of action which when understood you will be free from all ill.
4.17. For, action must be understood, and wrong action as well; inaction must be understood—deep, dark, and dense is the nature of action.
4.18. If one were to see inaction in action and action in inaction, that person among mortals would be wise; that one would be spiritually disciplined, yoked in yoga, in all works.
4.19. One whose instigations and undertakings are all free from the motive of personal desire, the wise see that person as the genuinely learned, the one whose karma has been burned up in the fire of knowledge.
4.20. Having abandoned attachment to the fruits of works, constantly satisfied, independent, one does nothing whatsoever even while thoroughly engaged in works.
4.21. Transcending hope and expectation, controlled in heart and mind, with all possessiveness renounced, one doing simply physical actions accrues no (karmic) adversity.
4.22. Satisfied with whatever gain comes, passed beyond oppositions and dualities, untouched by jealousy, equal-minded and balanced in the face of success and failure, such a person though acting is not bound.

4.23. All karmic dispositions dissolve and wash away when a person is free from attachment, liberated, with a mind firmly fixed in knowledge, acting in a spirit of sacrifice.

4.24. Brahman is the giving, Brahman the oblation; by Brahman into the Brahman-fire it is poured. It is just to Brahman where one goes achieving the ecstatic trance of Brahman-action.

4.25. Some yogis practice sacrifice directed to the gods. Others offer the sacrifice by the sacrifice into the fire of Brahman.

4.26. Others offer the sense organs of hearing and so on into the fires of control. Still others offer the sense objects of sound and so on into the fires of the senses.

4.27. And others all the actions of the sense organs and the actions of the life-breaths as well into the yogic fire of self-control kindled by knowledge.

4.28. Likewise, some perform material sacrifices, some sacrifices of austerity, and some sacrifices of yoga. There are seekers who with strict vows perform sacrifices both of religious study and of knowledge.

4.29. Similarly, some offer the incoming breath into the outgoing breath and the outgoing breath into the incoming. These restraining the courses of the breaths are devoted to the practice of breath-control (*prāṇâyāma*)....

4.32. In this way, numerous diverse sacrifices are spread wide in the mouth of Brahman. Know them all as born in action. Thus knowing, you will be enlightened, free.

...

5.8. The knower of the truth of things, disciplined in yoga practice, would think, "I do nothing whatsoever," while seeing, hearing, touching, smelling, eating, moving about, sleeping, breathing.

5.9. Conversing, ejecting, taking in, opening or closing the eyes, "The organs and faculties are working on their objects," contemplating (all the time).

5.10. Depositing actions in (the fire of) Brahman, giving up attachment, one who then acts is not stained by sin, like a lotus leaf by water (is not touched).

5.11. By the body, with the heart and mind, by the intelligence, even only with the organs and faculties, yogis perform actions, abandoning attachment, to purify themselves.

5.12. Disciplined through yoga practice, abandoning attachment, one finds the peace of the deepest foundation. A person who does no yoga practice, attached to the fruit of what has been done because of desire, is bound (by karma).

...

5.24. It is the one whose happiness is within, whose enjoyment is inner, and whose light is within only, who is the yogi. Having become Brahman, that person attains Nirvāṇa in Brahman.

5.25. Seer-sages (*ṛṣis*) gain Nirvāṇa in Brahman with their sins effaced, cutting through dualities, working for the good of all beings, delighted in the good of all.

5.26. Separating themselves from desire and anger, the disciplined, with their thought-streams under control, possess Nirvāṇa in Brahman here and now and all around, having knowledge of the self (*ātman*).

5.27–8. Outside having put external touches and directing the visual organ (to the inner center) between the eyebrows, making the upward and downward breaths (inhalations and exhalations, *prāṇa* and *apāna*) equal (in duration) moving through the nostrils (not the mouth), with organs and faculties, heart and mind, and higher intelligence (*buddhi*) all under control, the sage intent on liberation, with desire, fear, and anger gone, is (already) liberated forever indeed.

5.29. Such a person, knowing the sweet inner heart of all beings, comes to peace (*śānti*), comes to me, the enjoyer of sacrifice and asceticism, the great Lord (*īśvara*) of all the worlds.

Appendix D

Śaṅkara's Theodicy

From God and the World's Arrangement, by N. Guha, M. Dasti, and S. Phillips (2021: 71–5). Reprinted by permission of Hackett Publishing Company, Inc.

At *Brahma-sūtra* 2.1.33, Śaṅkara answers the objection that the world could not have been created by an *īśvara* ("Lord") because creation is an action and an action by a person requires a motive connected to an idea of something to be accomplished, something desired. And the Lord has no desires. Śaṅkara:

> Like activities on the part of a prince or minister who has no compelling desire, activities undertaken in playgrounds just for sport (*līlā*) without a particular motive, and like inhalation and exhalation of breath as activities that can occur on their own just from their own nature without regard to any exterior motive, so the creative activity of the Lord we may suppose to come about as nothing but play, sport (*līlā*), just naturally without depending upon any exterior motive whatsoever. For it is false that the Lord has some motive or purpose that is to be discerned either by reason or revelation. Nor is it implausible that the Lord's creative activity is simply a matter of the Lord's nature. Although the universe appears to us to be so intelligently arranged to require prodigious effort of a very weighty sort, to the Supreme Lord it would all be like mere play, because the Lord's power is immeasurable. Admittedly, in our experience a subtle motive might be detected even in play. Still, no motive whatsoever can be discerned with regard to the Lord's creative action; we know as much from scriptural revelations about those whose "desires are all satisfied." Nor should it be thought that the Lord is not active. Nor that the action is like that of a madman. Scriptural stories there are about creation that say the creative Lord is all-knowing. Moreover, it should not be forgotten that all that we cognize, including from scripture, is limited to that formulable in everyday speech which is a matter of (as the

Upaniṣads say) "name and form" (*nāma-rūpa*) conditioned by *avidyā*, "spiritual ignorance," and, furthermore, that the primary intent of the teaching about *avidyā* is that we get the right idea about the self and Brahman.

And so the best intellectual view for us who do not pretend to know precisely how the world looks to the Indeterminable is that there is a Creator who easily has the power and knowledge to bring forth this incredible world-arrangement. The question is, then, why is there not much less pain and suffering and a much more even distribution of pleasure and happiness than what we see out there in our real but often very unpleasant circumstances. To this question, there is an answer in the next sūtra, *Brahma-sūtra* 2.1.34. Śaṅkara:

> . . . the objection is that no *īśvara* could be the cause of the universe because of the difficulty of **inequality and cruelty** (as the sūtra says) as *īśvara*-perpetrated if it were so. The Lord would be conceived as making some beings—for example, gods and goddesses—exceedingly happy, knowing pleasures in the extreme, while the lot of others—for example, animals—is to have pain in the extreme. And although human beings and the like have pleasures and pains of intermediate varieties, the Lord's creation is such that it is lacking equality of distribution in their having them. Thus the Lord appears to be a particular individual with his or her own personal proclivities, likes and dislikes. The problem here is that the purported teaching of scripture and "sacred memory" (*śruti* and *smṛti*) would have to be wrong about the Lord's having a nature of purity and other attributes (compassion and so on). Similarly, there is a problem about cruelty even to the wicked being terribly bad if due to a "Lord." Therefore, so the objection goes, no *īśvara* is the cause of the universe because of the problems of **inequality and cruelty**.
>
> To this, we respond as follows. Inequality and cruelty do not problematize the way we understand the Lord. How so? Because of (as the sūtra says in its later portion) **dependence**. That is, if the Lord alone were responsible for this uneven creation, then the charges of inequality and cruelty would be flaws devastating our position. However, there is no creation without dependence. For, the *īśvara* fashions this uneven creation depending on something else. What, you may ask, could that be? Righteousness and unrighteousness, *dharma* and *adharma*, we answer, which, we say, the Lord respects, taking them into consideration in creating. Therefore, it is no fault for which the Lord is to blame in there being this uneven creation that depends on the *dharma* and *adharma* of emergent creatures.
>
> Now the *īśvara* is to be viewed as somewhat like Parjanya, the giver of rain. For as Parjanya is a causal factor had in common for the emergence of rice, wheat, and so on while unique capacities are also causal factors had just by the

> seeds of this and that species of plant, so the Lord is a cause had in common by the emergence of gods, humans, and so on while the unevenness among these kinds is due to different karma belonging to this and that individual. The distinct karma is a causal factor. So because the Lord fashions in accordance with karma, that is to say, because there is such dependence, our concept of an *īśvara* is not vitiated by the reality of what appears to be inequality and cruelty. There are scriptural statements (*śruti*) to this effect ... and also teachings of sacred memory (*smṛti*) that declare that the Lord's favor and its lack depend on the particular karma of creatures, as is said (*Gītā* 4.11, Kṛṣṇa speaking as the Lord), "As they approach me, so do I receive them to my love" and similar statements.

Then at *Brahma-sūtra* 2.1.35, the next sūtra, there is a question about the very first "emergence" (*sarga*, "creation"). Before there was any good and bad karma created by individuals in a previous round, before the cosmic dissolution that preceded a new round of emergence, that is, before there were any good and bad karma-making choices and karmic dispositions said to lie latent (like the seed Veda) during the dissolution, it does not seem possible that the Lord could be mindful of any moral deserts in creating and fashioning the manifest universe in a new round. In other words, what about the absolute beginning, before there was any good or bad karma for the Lord to depend upon? Śaṅkara:

> An objection is raised that there would be no karma to be depended upon on account of which the creation might have become uneven, because there would be no distinction to be discerned of deeds good and bad prior to the *first* creation. The objection finds support in a scriptural passage, to wit, "The existent alone, my dear, was this in the beginning, one, without a second" (*Chāndogya Upaniṣad* 6.2.1). For, karma is acquired at a time after creation. It presupposes diversity of individual bodies and company. And if it is said that the diversity of individual bodies and company depends on karma, circular reasoning is the vitiator. Therefore, we have to say that the Lord could act while considering karma only after a distribution of distinct effects. Because there could be no karma to account for diversity before such a distribution, the original creation would have to be nothing but equal (in the distribution of pleasures and pains, happiness and suffering).
>
> There is no flaw here, no real difficulty. The objection is rejected since the world of transmigration is (as the sūtra says at the end) **without a beginning**. The objection would be right if transmigration had a beginning. But, transmigration has no beginning; like seed and sprout, karma causes and is caused. Thus the idea of the Lord's proceeding to act in creation is not contradicted by the unevenness of the emergent world.

So, how is it established that transmigration is beginningless? We are given the answer in the next sūtra.

Thus Śaṅkara finds a natural order to the sūtras in this stretch of the treatise. There are only two more sūtras until the end of a major division of the *Brahma-sūtra*.

(Sūtra 2.136:) **It is rationally a good explanation, and it is found.**

Śaṅkara:

It is rationally a good explanation, that is, the beginninglessness of the transmigratory world recommends itself to reason. For, if it had a beginning, the difficulty would be that the transmigratory world's coming to be would make no sense and, further, that even the liberated might by chance come to be bound again within transmigratory existence. And we would have to live with the unfortunate consequence that what happens would be uncaused, as there would be nothing to account for the uneven distribution of pleasure and pain and like matters.

That it would be no *īśvara* that would bring about such inequality has, furthermore, already been said. We may add that *avidyā*, "spiritual ignorance," could not by itself cause the inequality, since it is uniform. However, *avidyā* could be said to be a factor in bringing about the inequality if it were considered dependent on karma embedding mental dispositions made by obstacles (to self-discovery) like passion (*rāga*). Furthermore, no living body would be formed in the way it is if there were no karma, while without a living body no karma would be formed. Indeed, there *would* be a circularity predicament, if we assumed a beginning. But if there is beginninglessness, then by the logic of seed and sprout it would all be explicable, **rationally a good explanation**, such that no vitiation of our view of the Lord's creative action would occur.

The sūtra also says, **and it is found**. The doctrine of the beginninglessness of transmigratory existence is found in both *śruti* and *smṛti*. . . . (*Gītā* 15.3) "(The extent of the tree of transmigratory existence) is not experienced as such here in this life. It has no end, and it has no beginning. Its permanence is established." This is a verse from *smṛti* where the doctrine is found of the beginninglessness of transmigratory existence. And in the Purāṇas as well, it is asserted that past and future "ages," *kalpa*, are innumerable.

(Sūtra 2.1.37) **And because all the properties (needed for creation) are rationally explained (in viewing Brahman as the Lord).**

Śaṅkara:

Having shown that it is a Vedic teaching (i.e., a Vedāntic teaching), the teaching, namely, that a conscious Brahman is the cause of the universe as well as its material, our esteemed teacher Bādarāyaṇa proceeded to defend the view against failings alleged by others such as the radical differences found in the manifest world. Now about to begin a new section with a new topic—which will be refutations of the positive positions advanced by others in opposition to this view—he summarizes with the current sūtra the main topic of the prior section. This is the topic of why his, and our, own view should be accepted (to wit, that is taught by the Upaniṣads and withstands rational scrutiny). Given that the view being accepted is that Brahman is the cause of the world, all the properties needed to be that cause are to be rationally endorsed in line with the thesis—to quote our sacred inheritance—"All-knowing, all-powerful, endowed with the great power of delimitation (*mahā-māyā*) is Brahman." Thus is this our Upaniṣadic philosophy beyond reproach.

• • •

Glossary of Sanskrit Words

ābhāsa appearance, semblance

abhimāna identity, personal identity, self-regard

ācārya revered teacher, guru

adharma wrong-doing

adhikāra prerequisite, yogic prerequisite

adhikārin person who is qualified, entitled, "fit" (for rituals, or by yogic practice, etc., for meditational experience)

adhyāsa superimposition

adṛṣṭa Unseen (moral) Force, impersonal cosmic force of karmic payback

advaita non-dual

agni fire, psychic fire

aham I

ahaṃkāra egoism; the individuating principle (*tattva*) in Sāṃkhya

ahiṃsā non-injury, nonharmfulness

ahiṃsika one who practices *ahiṃsā*

ājñā-cakra "third-eye" *cakra* associated in tantra with mentality, the "command" center, purportedly felt in the middle of the forehead

ākāśa ether, sky, space, a pervasive element

alaṃkāra-śāstra aesthetics, the "science of ornament," the tradition of literary criticism in particular

alaṁkārika literary critic, aesthetics theorist

amṛta nectar of immortality

anāhata-cakra the "heart" *cakra* associated in tantra with the higher emotions of love and generosity

ānanda bliss, spiritual ecstasy (or *en*stasy); the affective side of Brahman and self-knowledge, according to Vedānta

ānandamaya-kośa body made of bliss, *ānanda*

anātman "no self," "no soul"; an important Buddhist doctrine

anavasthā infinite regress

anirvacanīya "impossible to explain"

annamaya-kośa body made of matter, "food," *anna*, the physical body

anta end, goal

antar-yāmin inner controller

anubhava awareness, experience

anumāna inference; a knowledge source, *pramāṇa*, according to practically all the classical schools

āpta trustworthy testifier, one who knows the truth and wants to communicate it without deception

artha (1) meaning; (2) goal, aim, purpose, value; (3) object, thing

asamprajñāta-samādhi yogic trance without meditational prop according to the *Yoga-sūtra*; equivalent to self-discovery, *brahma-vidyā*, according to some Vedāntins

āsana poses and meditational postures taught as part of yoga

āśrama (1) yogic retreat; (2) stage of life

aṣṭâṅga-yoga the "Eight-limbed" yoga taught in the *Yoga-sūtra* (1) *yama*, ethical restraints (*ahiṃsā*, non-injury, *satya*, truth-telling, *asteya*, non-stealing, *brahmacarya*, sexual restraint, and *aparigraha*, non-possessiveness), (2) *niyama*, personal restraints (*saucya*, cleanliness, *santoṣa*, contentment, *tapas*, austerity, *svādhyāya*, study of a yogic text, and *īśvara-praṇidhāna*, meditation on the Lord) (3) *āsana*, postures, (4) *prāṇâyāma*, breath-control, (5) *pratyāhāra*, attending to sensory presentations as opposed to sensory objects, (6) *dhāraṇā*, concentrated attention, (7) *dhyāna*, meditation, and (8) *samādhi*, self-luminous trance

ātman "self"; the Upaniṣadic term for a truest self or consciousness; cosmic self

avatāra divine "descent"; a special incarnation of the Lord, *īśvara*

avidyā spiritual ignorance; lack of direct awareness of the true self

bādhaka epistemic "defeater," for example, experiential sublation, as a veridical perception of a rope correcting an illusory perception of a snake

bhagavad blessed, divine

bhakti devotional love

bhakti-yoga yoga of love and devotion

bhāṣya commentary

bhoga enjoyment

bodhisattva the ideal person in Mahāyāna Buddhism, possessing awesome characteristics, *pāramitā*

brahma-carya sexual restraint, celibacy

brahman the Absolute; the One; God, the "Lord," *īśvara*; the key concept of Vedānta metaphysics

brāhmaṇa priest, member of the highest caste of Hinduism

brahma-sākṣātkāra immediate awareness of Brahman; *brahma-vidyā*

brahma-vidyā enlightenment, self-discovery; the *summum bonum*, according to Vedānta

buddha "the Awakened"; an epithet of Siddhartha Gautama, the founder of Buddhism, after his enlightenment or *nirvāṇa* experience

buddhi rational intelligence; cognition, knowledge

buddhi-yoga discipline for the higher intelligence

caitya-puruṣa psychic being ("psychic" in Aurobindo's sense)

cakra occult center of consciousness, "wheel" of occult energy

cit consciousness
citta thought and emotion
citta-vṛtti-nirodha stilling of the fluctuations of thought and emotion; *yoga* as defined in the *Yoga-sūtra*
dama self-control
dāna generosity, munificence
darśana worldview, philosophy, a "viewing"
dayā compassion
devatā "divinity," occult force
dharma duty, right way of action
dhyāna meditation
duḥkha pain, suffering, unhappiness
ekāgratā one-pointedness of mind, "exclusive concentration"
gāyatrī a meter in twenty-four syllables found as early as the *Ṛg Veda*; a popular mantra from the *Ṛg Veda* (3.62.10) beseeching the "Sun" for higher consciousness
gītā song
gopī cowgirl (*gopī*s famously love Kṛṣṇa and are taken to symbolize individual souls)
guṇa quality, property; mode or strand of nature, according to Sāṃkhya (see *sattva*, *rajas*, and *tamas*)
guru teacher
haṃsa crane, swan, goose; symbol of the transmigrating individual, *jīvâtman*
hiraṇya-garbha the "Golden (Seeded) Womb," the causal Brahman from which things finite emerge
iṣṭa-devatā "preferred divinity"
īśvara "Lord," Brahman viewed as creator
jīvan-mukti "living liberation," a person's living in self-knowledge
jīvâtman, jīva person, individual soul
jñāna cognition, consciousness, knowledge
jñāna-karma-samuccaya simultaneous practice of a path of "knowledge" with one of "works"
jñāna-yoga yoga of meditation
kārikā concise statement in verse
karman (1) "action"; (2) habit; the psychological law that every act creates a psychic valency to repeat the act; (3) sacrifice, ritual; (4) karma; "Unseen (moral) Force," *adṛṣṭa*
karma-yoga yoga of action and sacrifice, yoga of offering
karuṇā compassion
kārya what ought to be done
kavi seer-poet; author of one or more Vedic *stotra*
kośa sheath, body
kriyā action
kṣānti patience, endurance, acceptance

kuṇḍalinī occult "serpent-power"; divine energy said to be asleep in the lowest *cakra*, the awakening of which is in tantra taken to be equivalent to self-discovery

līlā play, sport; in Vedānta, the world as the Lord's play

loka world; field of vision

mahā-vākya "great statement"; one of eighteen or so Upaniṣadic statements taken by Śaṅkara and other Vedāntins to have special import for philosophy

manas sense-mind, animal mind, inner sense, the internal organ, the conduit of sensory information to the perceiving self, according to several schools

maṅgala "doing something auspicious," such as chanting *om*, making a flower offering, etc.

manomaya-kośa body or "sheath" made of sensuous intelligence, *manas*

mantra verse of the Veda; words or sounds with power to aid meditation

marga way, path

māyā illusion; cosmic illusion, according to many Advaita Vedāntins; "delimitation," according to Vedāntic theists, the Lord's power of emanation

mokṣa = mukti

mukti (= mokṣa) "liberation" (from rebirth); enlightenment, self-discovery

mumukṣu desiring liberation

nāḍi in tantric psychology, a "channel" for occult energies

nêti nêti "not this, not that," an Upaniṣadic formula for the inexplicability of the essential nature of Brahman

nididhyāsana intense meditation

nirguṇa without attributes

nirvāṇa extinction (of suffering); enlightenment; the experience of the "Void" (of desire and attachment); the *summum bonum* in Buddhism (although in Mahāyāna the goal is to become a Bodhisattva)

nirvikalpaka indeterminate, "concept-free," non-propositional

niṣṭhā yogic path, faith "stand"

nyāya critical reasoning, rational proof

parama-puruṣârtha "supreme personal good"

pāramitā perfection; quality or mark of a Bodhisattva, according to Mahāyāna Buddhism, six being commonly mentioned: (1) charity, (2) uprightness, (3) energy, (4) patience, (5) meditation (*samādhi*), and (6) wisdom (*prajñā*)

parinirvāṇa in Buddhism, the experience of the enlightened at death, *mahā-samādhi*

paryudāsa-pratiṣedha broad-scope negation, e.g., a ballgame is not blue in that it is not something that could be blue or not-blue; cf. *prasajya-pratiṣedha*

phala "fruit," goal, end for which an action is undertaken

pradhāna root form of nature, *prakṛti*, according to Sāṃkhya

prajñā wisdom; spiritual insight

prakṛti "nature," in Sāṃkhya philosophy conceived as operating mechanically, without intrinsic consciousness

prakṛti-laya a type of deep meditation or yogic trance, *samādhi*, that is thought to insure *sāmadhi* in the next incarnation
pralaya cosmic dissolution
pramā "knowledge," everyday knowledge as produced by a knowledge source such as perception, testimony, or inference
pramāṇa source of knowledge; justifier
prāṇa breath; life or vital energy
prāṇamaya-kośa body made of life-energy
prāṇâyāma breath-control
praṇidhāna devotion, meditation
prapañca worldly display
prasāda graciousness, kindness; divine grace
prasajya-pratiṣedha narrow-scope negation, e.g., "Devadatta is *not* eating," that is, he could be; cf. *paryudāsa-pratiṣedha*
prasthāna-trāyi "triad of support"; for Vedāntic philosophy an epithet for the classical Upaniṣads, the *Gītā*, and the *Brahma-sūtra* taken together
pratītya-samutpāda "interdependent origination"; the Buddhist doctrine that each event comes to be in interdependence with other events
pratyāhāra "withdrawal" from the sense-organs to cognize only sense-data
pratyakṣa perception; a source of knowledge, *pramāṇa*, according to practically all the classical philosophies
pratyeka-buddha a solitary Buddha
puruṣa conscious being, person
pūrva-pakṣa (1) prima facie position, the opponent's position; (2) text devoted to exploring views and arguments not accepted by the author whose own views are expressed in a correlate *siddhānta*
rajas the *guṇa* of passion and activity
rasa "flavor," "juice," essence; aesthetic experience, aesthetic relishing
ṛṣi seer-poet, author of mantras of the *Ṛg Veda*; enlightened seer who originates a tradition of yoga or a skill or a craft
sac-cid-ānanda "Existence-Consciousness-Bliss," a longstanding Vedāntic characterization of Brahman; *sat* = being, *cit* = consciousness, *ānanda* = delight, bliss, self-delight
sādhana yoga practice considered instrumental to self-discovery
saguṇa with attributes
sahasradala "thousand-pedaled" *cakra* said to situated roughly three finger thicknesses above the back of the head
śākhā branch of Vedic recension
sākṣin witness
śakti energy; Divine Energy, power of the Lord; the Goddess
śama calm
samādhi yogic trance, deepest meditation, "enstasy," enlightenment

sāmagrī collection of causal factors together sufficient for an effect
saṃkalpa intention
sāṃkhya "analysis"; meditation emphasizing disidentification
sampradāya "tradition," yogic lineage; a lineage of teachers and students who become teachers in turn
samprajñāta-samādhi samādhi "with prop"; the penultimate stage of yogic accomplishment according the *Yoga-sūtra*
saṃsāra transmigratory existence, the wheel of birth and rebirth, worldly existence
saṃskāra mental disposition, memory-impression housing information acquired through experience
sandhi euphonic combination; the running together of the ending of one word with the beginning of another, a complex feature of written as well as spoken Sanskrit, with numerous rules (compare "com-mere" said instead of "come here" in English)
sannyāsa renunciation
śānti tranquility, peace
sarga creation, "loosing forth," emanation
śāstra science or craft; scientific textbook
sat being
sattva guṇa of intelligence and purity, of calm, control, and compassion; character traits that are "sattvic" are said to contribute to the general happiness and welfare of everyone as well as to be conducive to enlightenment
seśvara-sāṃkhya theistic Sāṃkhya, prominent in the *Mahābhārata* and elsewhere
siddhānta (1) the "right view" answering a correlate "*prima facie* view"; an author's "own position" and that of his school; (2) a portion of a text devoted to elaborating an author's own views in relation to a correlate *pūrva-pakṣa*
siddhāntin the "proponent of the right view" answering a correlative opponent, *pūrvapakṣin*
siddhi occult power, perfection
śīla good character
smṛti (1) memory; (2) second order of sacred texts in epistemological contrast with a first order, *śruti*
soma a plant esp. the juice of a plant used in Vedic times in shamanic ceremonies which is said to provide visions in the chapter of hymns to the god Soma in the *Ṛg Veda*
śramaṇa ascetic
śruti (occult) "hearing"; scripture; the revealed Veda, including the Upaniṣads, according to much Vedānta as well as other schools
stotra hymn, poem
sukha pleasure, happiness
sūkṣma-śarīra subtle body comprising subtle elements transmigrating as a *jīva* or individual soul, according to most Vedānta
sukta "hymn," poem, comprising an entry in the *Ṛg Veda*
śūnyatā "Emptiness"; the Void vibrant with compassion, according to Mahāyāna Buddhism

suṣumṇa in tantric psychology the central channel, connecting vertically seven (or eight or ten) main *cakra* centers of consciousness

sūtra "thread"; an aphorism and summary statement expressing succinctly a position or argument to be explained and fleshed out by commentary by a teacher or expert

sva-prakāśa "self-illuminating"; a Vedāntic doctrine of self-consciousness

sva-prāmāṇya cognition as "self-authenticating," a Mīmāṃsaka and Vedāntic view of confirmation contrasting with the Nyāya view that cognition is certified "through another"

sva-rūpa essential nature, "own form"

svarga heaven

svayam-bhū "self-existent," *causa sui*, being by and through itself

svayam-prakāśamāna "irreflexively self-illumining"; an Upaniṣadic doctrine of the nature of self-consciousness championed by certain Mīmāṃsakas as well as Vedāntins

svayaṃvara "self-selection," as of a bride of a husband on her own, not by her parents

tamas guṇa of dullness and inertia

tantra systematic instruction; "web" or "woven fabric" of belief; family of related religious and philosophic systems using feminine imagery in ceremonies and stories, tending to find nature as an expression of *śakti*

tapas heat; asceticism, yogic heat

tapasyā asceticism, yoga in general

tattva reality, "that-ness"; principle or type of being

tejas heat and warmth; enthusiasm, energy; spiritual energy, energy of the *ātman*

tvam "you," second-person personal pronoun

upaniṣat "secret doctrine"; various prose and verse texts originally appended to the Vedas, with mystic themes centered on an understanding of the self and its relation to Brahman, the Absolute; the primary sources for Vedānta philosophy and the first texts of yoga practices

upāsanā worshipful meditation

upāya-kauśala "skill in means," the reputed ability of the Buddha or another guru to specify a yogic discipline appropriate for a particular student or audience

vaiśvānara the universally human

vāsanā saṃskāra spanning lifetimes

veda "(revealed) knowledge"

vedānta epithet for the Upaniṣads ("end of the Veda"); school of philosophy basing itself on Upaniṣads, the *Bhagavad Gītā*, and the *Brahma-sūtra* and centered on a concept of Brahman and the importance of self-discovery

vibhu pervasive, omnipresent

vidyā knowledge, spiritual knowledge

vijñānamaya-kośa "sheath" or body made of higher intelligence, *vijñāna*

virodha contradiction; a trope used mainly for emphasis

vīrya strength, energy

vivarta turning, change; illusory change; transmogrification
vṛtti modification (usually, of awareness)
vyavahāra conventional discourse; everyday speech and activity; conventional wisdom
yama restraints (the first limb of the "Eight-limbed Yoga" of the *Yoga-sūtra* in five parts) (1) non-injury, (2) truth-telling, (3) non-stealing, (4) sexual restraint, (5) non-possessiveness
yaugika-pratyakṣa yogic perception, alleged special perceptual capacities said to be brought about by yoga practices
yoga connection, relation; self-discipline; conscious "union" with the true self or Brahman

Classical Authors, Schools, and Texts

Abhinava (Gupta) premier philosopher of Kashmiri Śaivism, a leading literary critic, *alaṃkārika*, as well as a famous tantric guru

Advaita Vedānta "Non-dual" classical subschool of Upaniṣadic philosophy of Brahman that becomes a whole school to itself, subscribing to a monism and cosmopsychism, "All is Brahman (the Absolute)," including—and especially—the seemingly individual consciousness or self that knows, or can know, itself non-dualistically

Aitareya Upaniṣad short, prose Upaniṣad of the *Ṛg Veda*; not as old as the *Bṛhadāraṇyaka* or *Chāndogya* but belonging to the oldest prose group

Ānandagiri (*c.* 1300) Advaita author of a long commentary on Śaṅkara's *Brahma-sūtra-bhāṣya*

Bādarāyaṇa (*c.* 200 CE) legendary author of the *Brahma-sūtra*

Bhagavad-gītā (*c.* 200 BCE?) A small portion of the massive epic poem, the *Mahābhārata*, where the warrior Kṛṣṇa employing ideas of the Upaniṣads teaches yogic paths to enlightenment, especially the three paths of "knowledge" (*jñāna*, *sāṃkhya*), "works" (*karman*), and "devotional love" (*bhakti*)

Bhāgavata-purāṇa (*c.* 700–900 CE?) a Purāṇa, which is a genre of texts not much in evidence in Śaṅkara's corpus but later becoming sources for much Vedānta philosophy and psychology—written in verse and popular Sanskrit and later in regional vernaculars—the *Bhāgavata* being a long Purāṇa especially dear to Vaiṣṇavism, which is a major branch of modern Hinduism, and telling the story of Kṛṣṇa as an *avatāra*, "divine incarnation"

Bhāmatī the commentary on Śaṅkara's *Brahma-sūtra-bhāṣya* by Vācaspati, who is said to have named it after his wife in amends for not having children due to his yoga practice including *brahmacarya*; stresses theism and yoga practice

Bhartṛhari (*c.* 450 CE) grammarian and philosopher of language celebrated for an idealist metaphysics of a "word" Brahman

Brahma-sūtra (*c.* 200 CE) systemization in a few hundred interlocking sūtras of the teachings of the early Upaniṣads including arguments against rival worldviews and defenses of Vedāntic cosmopsychism and monistic theism

Brahma-sūtra-bhāṣya **(*BSB*)** the long commentary on the *Brahma-sūtra*—the oldest extant—by Śaṅkara

Bṛhadāraṇyaka Upaniṣad **(*BṛU*)** a long prose Upaniṣad considered the oldest, featuring the philosophic yogi Yājñavalkya in dialogue about Brahman or the self with his two wives or Janaka, a king, along with parables, jokes, and puns; the Upaniṣad quoted most often by Śaṅkara

Cārvāka classical philosophic school of materialism, religious skepticism, and hedonism

***Chāndogya Upaniṣad* (*Chā*)** a long prose Upaniṣad containing much archaic language (like the *Bṛhadāraṇyaka*) and several stories with lessons about Brahman and the self, including the *mahā-vākya*, *tat tvam asi*, "Thou art That"

Gauḍapāda (*c.* 650) author of a 215-verse commentary on the short *Māṇḍūkya Upaniṣad*, called *Kārikā*, commonly taken to show strong Buddhist influence in shaping Advaita metaphysics

Gītā see *Bhagavad-gītā*

Īśā Upaniṣad an old, eighteen-verse Upaniṣad about Brahman and the self and the possibility of mystical knowledge of Brahman

Kālidāsa (*c.* 450) poet of great renown including the delightful travelog, *Megha-dūta*, "The Cloud Messenger," also a dramatist of wide influence and recognition, whose *Śakuntalā* is probably the most widely translated and performed of classical plays

***Kārikā* (*Gauḍapadīya-kārikā*)** a 215-verse commentary on the *Māṇḍūkya Upaniṣad* by Gauḍapāda

Kaṭha Upaniṣad an old Upaniṣad mainly in verse with a prose introduction recounting the story of Naciketas who objects to the ritualism of his father and "goes to hell" at his father's command (in a brilliant pun) to dialogue with Death, Yama, the "Controller," about the self, *ātman*, and the meaning of life

Kena Upaniṣad an old and short verse Upaniṣad famous for the *anirvacanīya*, "inexplicability," doctrine of Brahman

Kumārila (*c.* 650) prominent Mīmāṃsaka philosopher

Mādhava (*c.* 1500) author of an elegantly written textbook and doxology, *Sarva-darśana-saṃgraha*, "Compendium of All Worldviews," delineating fifteen or so classical philosophies along with their best defenses and refutations and culminating in exposition of Advaita Vedānta as the best of all

Mādhyamika Buddhist "school of the Middle" (avoidance of extremes) founded by Nāgārjuna; famous for philosophic skepticism

Mahābhārata (*c.* 400 BCE–200 CE) "The Great Indian Epic," with more than 100,000 verses, usually counted as *smṛti*, "sacred memory," the main story-line of which (surrounded by numerous substories) concerns princely succession in one of the many city states whose urban and agricultural centers were carved out of dense forests along the Gaṅgā and other rivers of northeastern India; includes yogic/ philosophic sections, esp. the *Bhagavad-gītā* and the *Mokṣa-dharma*

Mahāyāna Northern Buddhism, the "Great Vehicle"

Maitrī Upaniṣad a later Upaniṣad not commented upon by Śaṅkara but recognized by other classical Vedāntins, remarkable for a doctrine of a formless and a formed Brahman, likewise *ātman*

Maṇḍana(miśra) (*c.* 700) Mīmāṃsaka author reputedly converted to Advaita by Śaṅkara; Advaita author of *Brahma-siddhi* which may be older than Śaṅkara's work, influencing it, especially with the doctine of the inexplicability of *avidyā*, "spiritual ignorance"

Māṇḍūkya Upaniṣad a short prose Upaniṣad espousing four states of the self, *ātman*, corresponding to an analysis of the mantra *om* into three feet (*a*, *u*, *m* inasmuch as *a* + *u* = *o* by *sandhi*) plus the whole as the fourth, *turīya*, symbolizing the highest state of consciousness which is Brahman

Mīmāṃsā "Exegesis"; long-running school devoted to interpreting and defending the revelation of the Veda and the importance and proper conduct of rituals considered Vedically prescribed; from of the root '*man*', "to think" (Verpoorten 1987: 1), thus "effort at intense reflection"; a realist school celebrated for philosophy of language and epistemology as well as principles of interpretation; the *Mīmāṃsā-sūtra* (*c.* 100 BCE) is the root text; a commentary by Śabara (*c.* 300) is expanded by Kumārila (*c.* 650) and in a second line by Prabhākara (*c.* 700), the two being the school's chief philosophic representatives

Mīmāṃsaka an advocate of Mīmāṃsā

Mīmāṃsā-sūtra (*c.* 100 BCE) the founding text of Mīmāṃsā

Muṇḍaka Upaniṣad a verse Upaniṣad of the *Atharva Veda*, proclaiming knowledge of Brahman as the aim of meditation on *om* and the self and encouraging renunciation and asceticism; probably influenced by Buddhism as shown by its use of Buddhist Hybrid Sanskrit (Cohen 2008: 189–90)

Nāgārjuna (*c.* 150 CE) prominent Buddhist philosopher commonly understood to be skeptical about philosophy including, especially, "knowledge sources," *pramāṇa*; founder of the Mādhyamika school of Buddhism

Naiyāyika an advocate of Nyāya

Nyāya "Logic"; a school of realism and common sense prominent throughout the classical period, from the *Nyāya-sūtra* (*c.* 200) on, developing out of canons of debate and informal logic; focused on issues in epistemology but also defending yoga practice

Padmapāda (*c.* 750) immediate disciple of Śaṅkara who wrote a sub-commentary on Śaṅkara's commentary on the first five sūtras of the *Brahma-sūtra*, the *Pañcapādikā*, on which Prakāśātman wrote the *Vivaraṇa* sub-subcommentary accounting for the common name of the Padmapāda/Prakāśātman Advaita subschool—Vivaraṇa—which insists that Brahman does not change but "transmogrifies" (like magic, *māyā*) in becoming (*vivarta*) our world of finite things

Patañjali (*c.* 400 CE) legendary author of the *Yoga-sūtra*

Prabhākara (*c.* 675) prominent Mīmāṃsaka philosopher

Prakāśātman (*c.* 975) author of the *Vivaraṇa* commentary on Padmapāda's *Pañcapādikā* giving rise to the Vivaraṇa subschool of Advaita which is opposed on numerous counts to Vācaspati's Bhāmatī subschool, especially Prakāśātman's *vivarta* vs the Vācaspati's *parināma*, illusory vs real change, on the part of Brahman as appearing as, or manifesting, the universe

Praśna Upaniṣad a prose Upaniṣad of the *Atharva Veda* with fifteen stanzas of verse, commencing with "questions," *praśna*, by six interlocutors put to yogi/philosopher Pippalāda, who discourses on Brahman and, especially, on "life energy," *prāṇa*, which he says arises from *ātman* and divides into five "breaths" in the body; knowledge and control of *prāṇa* are said to be the path to the realization of the *ātman* and then Brahman

Rāmānuja (*c.* 1100) author of *Śrī-bhāṣya*, a commentary on the *Brahma-sūtra* with a long Advaita "opponent's section," *pūrva-pakṣa*, within the commentary on the first sūtra that presumably captures Śaṅkara's views which are then refuted in a long *siddhānta* section; also author of a commentary on the *Gītā* and other works; taken to found, along with Yamuna (*c.* 1000), who wrote no *Brahma-sūtra* commentary, the Viśiṣṭādvaita Vedānta subschool, "Qualified Non-Dualism," which accepts much Mīmāṃsā teaching and puts much greater emphasis than Śaṅkara on *bhakti* and Kṛṣṇa as an "incarnation," *avatāra*, of the Lord

***Ṛg Veda* (*RV*)** (1500–800 BCE?) comprised of ten books of poetic "hymns," *suktas*, used in rituals—originally continuous with indoeuropean shamanic ceremonies—as specified in other Vedas and as interpreted by Mīmāṃsakas, presenting especially psalms to and stories of gods and goddesses viewed as animating natural phenomena or, in some neo-Vedāntic interpretations (such as Aurobindo's), the natural phenomena themselves viewed as symbolizing forces affecting stages of yogic accomplishment

Śabara (*c.* 300 CE) author of the earliest extant commentary on the *Mīmāṃsā-sūtra*

Śaiva "relating to Śiva," a family of theistic and mainly tantric traditions some of which are traditionally said to have been founded by Śaṅkara, the name *śaṅkara* ("maker of tranquility") itself being a common epithet for the god Śiva

Śākta from *śakti*, "energy" or "force," a Śaiva tradition focused on "Shakti" conceived as the "Goddess," *devī*, and the energy of the Lord that, in on-going fashion and through diverse "divinities," forms and directs the beings and events of everything in the universe

Sāṃkhya "Analysis"; an early school of metaphysical dualism analyzing nature (*prakṛti*) in the interests of psychological disidentification on the part of the conscious self (*puruṣa*) and proposing a state of primordial matter (*pradhāna*) where three basic components or "qualities," *guṇa*, are in equilibrium

Śaṅkara (Ādi Śaṅkara, the "original Śaṅkara") (*c.* 725) the most prominent philosopher of the Advaita Vedānta school, espousing a radical monism of Brahman, the Absolute, and the value of enlightenment conceived as immediate experience of Brahman as self, *ātman*

Saundarya-laharī "Torrent of Beauty"; a long tantric text traditionally ascribed to Ādi Śaṅkara

Śrī-bhāṣya the commentary on the *Brahma-sūtra* by Rāmānuja

Śrīharṣa (*c.* 1100) Advaita dialectician whose long *Khaṇḍana-khaṇḍa-khādya*, "Sweetmeats of Refutation," is directed principally against Nyāya

Śvetāśvatara Upaniṣad a prose Upaniṣad declaring itself, along with much explicit instruction in yoga, to be composed by yogi/theologian Śvetāśvatara who claims to have realized Brahman "by yogic heat along with divine grace" (6.21), teaching that *ātman*, "self," is not only the impersonal Brahman but also a personal agent, creator of the universe, that is, the higher *ātman*, which is enlightened, in contrast with the lower, which is unenlightened

Taittirīya Upaniṣad a middle-sized prose Upaniṣad of the *Yajur Veda*; dated as not as old as the *Bṛhadāraṇyaka* or *Chāndogya* but belonging to the oldest prose group; source of the "sheath" or *kośa* theory of five simultaneous embodiments along with stories of Brahman realization

Udayana (*c.* 1000) prolific Nyāya/Vaiśeṣika author of both commentaries and independent treatises, famous for natural theology, formulating more than two dozen theistic "proofs," as well as for merging the traditions of Nyāya and Vaiśeṣika to inaugurate what is commonly called by scholars "Navya Nyāya," "New Logic," with its argumentatively refined texts

Upadeśa-sahasrī "A Thousand Teachings," a text by Śaṅkara, part prose, part verse, laying out yogic prerequisites for self-discovery as well as philosophic and psychological theses

Upaniṣad "secret doctrine"; various prose and verse texts originally appended to Vedas, having mystic themes centered on a hidden self or consciousness in relation to the Absolute called "Brahman"; the primary sources for classical Vedānta philosophy as well as for yoga and meditation

Vācaspati Miśra (*c.* 950) prolific author of treatises in five distinct schools, Yoga, Nyāya, Sāṃkhya, Mīmāṃsā, and Advaita Vedānta, his *Bhāmatī* subcommentary on Śaṅkara's *Brahma-sūtra-bhāṣya* giving rise to the Bhāmatī subschool of Advaita which finds real emanations of Brahman who is conceived theistically but whose realization is said to depend on yoga and meditation as opposed to the Vivaraṇa subschool of Prakāśātman emphasing study of "scripture," *śruti*

Vaiśeṣika "Atomism"; a classical philosophy focusing mainly on ontological issues ("What kinds of things are there?") and defending a realist view of material things as composed of atoms as well as a realist ontology of universals or natural kinds

Veda there are four Vedas—*Ṛg*, *Yājur*, *Sāman*, and *Atharva*—comprised principally of hymns to gods and goddesses and instructions for rituals and ceremonies; the oldest texts in Sanskrit, some hymns possibly as early as 1500 BCE; the most sacred texts of Hinduism

Vedānta originally an epithet for Upaniṣads; in the classical period, the philosophy of the *Brahma-sūtra* and of several subschools defending Upaniṣadic views and practices

Vedāntin proponent of Vedānta

Vijñānabhikṣu (*c.* 1575) author of a long "Advaita" commentary not on Śaṅkara's *Brahma-sūtra-bhāṣya* but on Bādarāyaṇa's *Brahma-sūtra* itself; author as well of texts in the schools of Yoga and Sāṃkhya

Viśiṣṭādvaita Vedānta "Qualified Non-dualism" subschool of Upaniṣadic philosophy allied with Mīmāṃsā and denying that the individual is Brahman without qualification

Yoga the philosophic school launched by the *Yoga-sūtra* along with the commentary of Vyāsa

Yogācāra Buddhist Idealism; the school of the idealists Vasubandhu and company, as well as of the Buddhist logicians Dignāga and Dharmakīrti who lay out a pragmatist epistemology that is a principal rival of Mīmāṃsā and Nyāya in the early period of classical philosophy; a tradition in many ways cross-seminal with Vedānta

***Yoga-sūtra* (*YS*)** (*c.* 400 CE in its final redaction) a textbook on meditation and yoga practices by a legendary Patañjali utilizing much Sāṃkhya metaphysics and psychology

Notes

Introduction

1 See, for example, *Bhagavad Gītā* 6.24 and 6.25, translated in Appendix C, echoing *Śvetāśvatara Upaniṣad* 2.8–10 among other Upaniṣadic passages in teaching meditation. Both the early Upaniṣads and the *Gītā* precurse main ideas of the *Yoga-sūtra* on meditation.

2 Śaṅkara, who will be studied on point, agrees with the *Yoga-sūtra* warning: psychic powers are an inferior result of meditation practice (see in this book pp. 86–7 for elaboration).

3 This rather obvious point is made much of in my "Mysticism and Metaphor" (1988).

4 Nakamura (1983, 2004) traces the evolution of a variety of Upaniṣadic themes and theories, showing rich development of Vedānta views prior to Śaṅkara, whom Nakamura regards as a highly *un*original thinker. According to him, Śaṅkara collected and systematized positions of earlier Vedāntins whose works have been lost except for fragments in Śaṅkara or later authors or in the literature of rival schools. Much of Nakamura's tracing is doubtless correct, but Śaṅkara is not so concerned with consistency as Nakamura (and others) apparently think, whose overly intellectualist interpretation I will combat. (In an appendix on Śaṅkara and yoga practice, the great scholar mischaracterizes "Self-awareness" (2004: 742–4), but his treatment of meditation is much better in subsequent pages: 744–54. He does not miss its importance altogether.)

5 The *Bhagavad Gītā*—that later, "little Upaniṣad" distilling earlier Vedāntic teachings—calls this *buddhi-yoga*, discipline for the intellect, *buddhi*: *Gītā* 2.49, 10.10, and 18.57.

6 Clooney (2000: 341–2) identifies ten genre of Vedānta: two concerning ritual, one on meditation and instruction from a meditation master, the Upaniṣad itself as a fourth, systemization of Upaniṣadic philosophy in the *Brahma-sūtra*, five, and five more in commentaries, polemical texts, and manuals for practice. However, these dimensions, or themes, are often not delineated, some converging in both Śaṅkara's and Aurobindo's work on the *Īśā*.

7 The word "enlightenment" is commonly used in English to capture experiences or states going by several different names in Sanskrit depending on the advocating school (*apavarga*, *vidyā*, *brahma-sākṣātkāra*, *samādhi*, *parama-puruṣârtha*, *kaivalya*, *nirvāṇa*, *yoga*, *mukti*, *mokṣa*, *citta-vṛtti-nirodha*, and others). The word may be best

reserved to render the Mahāyāna Buddhist *bodhi*, which is supposed to be the highest state of consciousness available to a person. Nevertheless, to use it to render yogic *samādhi* is acceptable I think in some cases. For Vedānta, "self-discovery" is usually a better term for the idea of such an experience or state. Ambiguity with the word "enlightenment" as relevant to Vedānta and Sri Aurobindo are ably discussed by Banerji (2020).

8 (Kṛṣṇa:) "Veda-mongers, who are far from wise, proclaiming with flowery speech there is nothing other than all their many rituals, which, they say, have karmic results in reincarnation, are set on heavens of pleasure, of enjoyment and lordship. People attached to power and pleasure have their intelligence snatched away by the misleading speech. A resolved mind may find enlightenment, *samādhi*, but not such people, Arjuna."

9 Partly because of the prominence of a devotional path with later Vedāntins such as Rāmānuja and company who often take Śaṅkara to task, how to interpret Śaṅkara on *bhakti* is controversial. Mahadevan (1980), however, assumes that Śaṅkara is the author of many of the devotional poems so ascribed—some of which he translates (masterfully)—and the "hymns" themselves are nothing less than awesome in showing *bhakti* practice converging with Advaita metaphysics. In this way *bhakti* is not denigrated in the Advaita view, as has been made out, for instance, by Ram-Prasad (2013: 111–14).

10 Technically, later Advaita has *bhakti* as a manifestation of *sattva*, of a "purified mind," a product of yoga and meditation that is preparatory for enlightenment. Even in the midst of Kṛṣṇa at *Gītā* 2.47 enjoining Arjuna to be above all three *guṇa*s, the three "modes" of nature—*sattva*, *rajas*, and *tamas*—says that the self-knower "stands constantly in *sattva*," *nitya-sattva-stha*.

11 *Brahma-sūtra* 2.1.2.3 (*etena yogaḥ pratyuktaḥ*: "Thereby Yoga is refuted") is read by Śaṅkara not as a repudiation of the practices—nor, in the main, the psychology—laid out in the *Yoga-sūtra*. He makes clear (*Brahma-sūtra-bhāṣya* 2.1.2.3) that it is the text's *Sāṃkhya-like* metaphysics of an inconscient original cause that is refuted by the argument of the preceding sūtra, not the practices or the psychology. He writes: "'Thereby' means 'by the refutation of the Sāṃkhya teaching,' the Yoga teaching is refuted too. . . . In opposition to the Upaniṣads, an inconscient original cause, *pradhāna*, is supposed to unfold just on its own (which is impossible)." *etena sāṃkhya-smṛti-pratyākhyānena yoga-smṛtir api pratyākhyātā . . . śruti-virodhena pradhānaṃ sva-tantram eva kāraṇam . . .* Vācaspati's *Bhāmatī* commentary makes the point even more lucidly (Shastri 1980: 352).

12 It is apparently Śaṅkara who gets the credit for adding the *Gītā* to make the triad (Ram-Prasad 2013: 1–2).

13 Renou, *Hymnes Spéculatif du Véda* (1956), translates fifty hymns he sees as speculative including the *Īśā*, which he identifies as a *stotra* in the *Yajur Veda* before

its elevation to an Upaniṣad. (Certain verses of the *Īśā* appear also in earlier Upaniṣads, Renou points out, the *Bṛhadāraṇyaka* in particular.) And *Ṛg Veda* 10.129 is famous for skepticism about knowledge of an ultimate origin, in its last verse.

14 Despite varieties and differences, meditation in the classical Upaniṣads is the yoga practice *par excellence*, as it is in the *Yoga-sūtra* and other yogic texts including those one might think are more about *āsanas*, "postures," and physical fitness, such as the *Haṭha-yoga-pradīpikā*: as shown in my *Yoga, Karma, and Rebirth* (2009). And an ability to appreciate conveyances of poetry comes, in Vedānta, to be thought of as a meditational aid. A great example is found in the epic *Naiṣadhacarita* of the eleventh century Advaitin, Śrīharṣa, who, in another work, is famous for a brand of metaphysical skepticism, but who in his poem suggests a positive intellectual/meditational route. The heroine Damayantī finds the key to happiness in coming to understand the multiple, *poetic* meanings of the goddess Sarasvatī's introductions, in a *svayaṃvara* ceremony, "self-selection," of her suitors (Sarasvatī is the "Goddess of Speech").

15 *Gītā* 5.8–9: "The yogi who knows the truth of things has the attitude, 'I do nothing whatsoever,' even while seeing, hearing, touching, smelling, moving around, sleeping, eating, conversing, letting go, grasping, opening and closing the eyes, thus meditating with the idea, 'The faculties are operating on their objects.'"

16 *Upadeśa-sahasrī* 2.1.2: "[This teaching is to be given to one] with calm, control, compassion, and similar qualities . . ." *Upadeśa-sahasrī* 2.1.6 outlines the ideal yoga teacher (*ācārya*): "The teacher should be able to understand reasons pro and con, maintain theses in memory, and be endowed with the qualities of calm, control, compassion, and so on" (*ācāryas tu ūhâpoha-grahaṇa-dhāraṇa-śama-dama-dayânugrahâdi-sampanno*). Then in commenting on the first sūtra of the *Brahma-sūtra*, Śaṅkara argues that the prerequisites for "investigation into Brahman" do not include performance of rituals but rather: "discrimination of things constant and non-constant, freedom from desires for enjoyments of this world or another, accomplishment in maintaining calm, control, and other (yogic) methods, and being intent on liberation (*mumukṣutva*)." *nityânitya-vastu-vivekaḥ, ihâmutrârtha-virāgaḥ, śama-damâdi-sādhana-sampat, mumukṣutvaṃ ca* (*Brahma-sūtra-bhāṣya* 1.1.1, Shastri 1980: 36–7).

17 Dalal (2020: 54–5) lists a number of terms for yogic practices used by Śaṅkara in addition to the words for the three paths called in the *Gītā karma-yoga* ("the yoga of action"), *jñāna-yoga* ("the yoga of knowledge"), and *bhakti-yoga* ("the yoga of love and devotion"). These include "continuous flow of recognition" (*smṛti-santāna*), "non-contact" (*asparśa-yoga*), "absorbed concentration" (*saṃrādhana, samādhi*), "meditative worship" (*upāsana*), and "non-dual contemplation" (*nididhyāsana*). Bader (1990: 101) sums up with respect to the āsanas, the "postures" of yoga: "Śaṅkara accepts the validity of yoga practice as a means to both physical and psychical transformation. Although he rarely discusses disciplines relating to the physical body,

he makes a point of acknowledging some of the remarkable achievements yogis have made in this regard." Actually, Śaṅkara, like the *Yoga-sūtra*, sees the physical practices as continuous with meditation, the yogic practice par excellence.

18 Specific occurrences of the word *yoga* and cognates such as *tapasyā* and *upāsana* are discussed in my *Yoga, Karma, and Rebirth* (2009: 28–31 and 163–75).

19 *Śrī-bhāṣya*, ed. Karmarkar, vol. 1 (1959: 12), in, for example, a passage just before the beginning of the "small *siddhānta*" within the long commentary on the first sūtra (Thibaut 1904: 11–12). From a summary I did for Karl Potter:

> *Advaitin*: In sum, viewing things as distinct is the root of bondage. By knowledge it is eliminated. Such knowledge arises from (understanding) Upaniṣadic texts such as "Thou art That" (*Chāndogya* 6.8.7). Inquiry into works has no relevance.
>
> *Rāmānuja's answer*: What form does this knowledge of Brahman take that, we agree, means the end of spiritual ignorance, *avidyā*? It does not take, contrary to your assumption, the form of testimonial knowledge that arises from hearing statements (even those of the Upaniṣads), but rather the form of meditational knowledge (*upāsanâtmika-jñāna*).

20 Śaṅkara says as much near the beginning of his *Brahma-sūtra-bhāṣya* (*BSB* 1.1.4): "What you allege would be correct if mere hearing about the true nature of Brahman could dispel the error of being subject to reincarnation, like learning from another's statement the true nature of a rope that is not the snake one took it to be. But that view is false, since we find that persons who have heard and learned about the true nature of Brahman are, just as before, subject to pleasure and pain and other conditions of the transmigratory universe." *syād etad evaṃ, yadi rajju-sva-rūpa-śravaṇa iva sarpa-bhrāntiḥ, saṃsāritva-bhrāntir brahma-sva-rūpa-śravaṇa-mātreṇa nirvarteta | na tu nirvarteta, śruta-brahmaṇo 'pi yathā-pūrvaṃ sukha-dukhâdi-saṃsāri-dharma-darśaṇāt . . .* | (Shastri 1980: 69). This is placed within a long *pūrva-pakṣa*, an exploration of a wrong position, but is not part of what Śaṅkara finds there objectionable.

21 The failure is not universal among Advaita scholars, fortunately. Not making the mistake are Deutsch 1969, Potter 1981, King 1995, Marcaurelle 2000, Ram-Prasad 2001, 2002, 2013, Malkovsky 2001, Sharma 2004, Hirst 2005, and Dalal 2020 that I know of. Ram-Prasad 2013 uses "gnosis" for self-knowledge, overall commendably, I'd say. But that word is easily confused for the special belief touted by "Gnostics" in the West, and is, furthermore, uncommon in English whereas many of the terms in Sanskrit for mystical gnosis, *as determined by context*, are employed in everyday speech in an everyday way.

22 Mayeda (1992, v. 1: 23–30), although commonly missing the ambiguity in "knowledge" and its Sanskrit equivalents, substantiates with many references the fact that Śaṅkara's use of the word *avidyā*, "non-knowledge" or "spiritual ignorance," is

generally not, unlike that of several famous later Advaitins, "cosmological"; that is, the term is not used to explain how the world has come about.

23 At *Śāṅkara-bhāṣya* on *Brahma-sūtra* 1.4.14 (Shastri 1980: 319–20), the Advaitin says that the objection to Vedānta that the Upaniṣads teach different doctrines of creation misses the point of the passages that do indeed refer to Brahman as the cause of the world. The point, he says, is to assert Brahman as the cause, not to give details of how it happens. Śaṅkara admits that there are different Upaniṣadic accounts of how it happens, but in all Brahman is the first cause.

24 Nakamura (2004: 626) points out that the words *pariṇāma* and *vivarta* are synonyms with Bhartṛhari (*c.* 450 CE), who, he argues, was a forerunner of Śaṅkara, suggesting that the terms mean the same with the Vedāntin. And *vivarta* can mean just "change," not "illusory change."

25 *Māṇḍūkya* 7 echoes the *nêti nêti* of the *Bṛhadāraṇyaka Upaniṣad*:

> The fourth state [after the waking, dream, and deep-sleep states] is considered neither inwardly sensible not outwardly sensible, nor both together, nor a mass of sensibility, nor "conscious," nor "not conscious." It is unseen, not conventionally conceived (*avyavahārya*), ungraspable, without characteristic mark, unthinkable, unnameable, being essentially awareness of the single self, a calming of presentational appearances, tranquil, good (*śiva*); it is the *ātman*; it is what is to be mystically known (*vijñeya*).

26 Some scholars find a distinct voice in the *Gauḍapādīya Commentary* attributed to Śaṅkara or find doctrinal differences with Śaṅkara's *Brahma-sūtra Commentary* as indicating intellectual growth and change of opinion. King elaborates these and other positions with reference to arguments he finds in a dozen or so scholarly treatments (1995: 3–11).

27 The fourth of four chapters or groupings of the *kārikās* is full of ideas indicating that it was done later than Śaṅkara. Some scholars (e.g., King 1995) surmise that each of the first three chapters, too, may well have been done by different people. In any case, it is only part of the first chapter that Aurobindo translated, and it is unclear whether he read the other three.

1 Who is Addressed by Śaṅkara, Who by Aurobindo?

1 From Renou, "Études Védiques: Yoga" (1953) to Scharf, "Creation Mythology and Enlightenment in Sanskrit Literature" (2020), scholars have found traces of yogic ideas in the earliest strands of Vedic literature. The topic is beyond our purview, but it seems worth mentioning that the *soma* hymns, which comprise one of the ten books of the *Ṛg Veda*—each book having about a hundred "hymns," *suktas*—are shamanic and full of wild visions. The book on *soma* stands out, but there are several

suktas in the tenth book that also precurse yogic themes (e.g. *Ṛg* 10.129, the "Hymn of Creation"). Wasson (1968) argues that Vedic *soma* is the psychotropic mushroom, *amanita muscaria*, fueling speculation that meditation traditions in India may have been connected to early *soma* cults.

2 Vedic rituals are not part of the *Ṛg Veda* itself, except that its verses, its "mantras," are specified as to be voiced according to instructions that lie elsewhere: there are several layers to Vedic literature. The *Ṛg* itself is highly poetic with complex meters and poetic figures. Renou (1953) sees poetic quality as the principal unifying feature of the hymns.

3 Roebuck (2003: xv) provides a succinct note on the word's meaning which she gives as "esoteric teaching," Cohen (2018: 2–3) lays out conflicting etymologies proffered over the centuries, and Nakamura (1983: 101–3) settles on "secret meeting" in contrast to "public meeting" as both the word's oldest and most prevalent sense. In a telling example of usage in the early Upaniṣads, Prajāpati, the "Father of Creatures," is asked for an *upaniṣat* three times at *Bṛhadāraṇyaka* 5.2.1–3. His response appears to be code for how three distinct groups of yoga students are to proceed in their disciplines (cf., T.S. Eliot's portrayal in "The Wasteland," the section "What the Thunder Said").

4 Paul Deussen, *Sechzig Upanishad's des Veda* (1897); Deussen, *The Philosophy of the Upanishads* (1906: 35–8); R.D. Ranade, *A Constructive Survey of Upanishadic Philosophy* (1926: 12). An edition in print by J.L. Shastri (1970) has 188.

5 Sri Aurobindo, *Śrī-aravindôpaniṣad* (1987, composed in the years 1910 to 1914, according to editors who provided the title: pp. 3, 4).

6 The "golden age" of empire and the great poets such as Kālidāsa was over, and tantrism along with "Purāṇic" Hinduism were in full swing in competition with Buddhism and Jainism as well as with the traditional Brāhmanism of high-caste priests. Religious tolerance was apparently the rule among the various regional kings and princes. We know from Kālidāsa and others a little about both the rural *āśramas*, which were beloved of yogis, and urban life, which was quite different. The conflict of the peaceful and pastoral versus the raucously royal and urban is a main theme of several poets and playwrights. Bāṇa, who lived about the same time as Śaṅkara, had royal patronage but also idealized the simple life of the forest and countryside. The motifs in Śaṅkara's writing tend to be pastoral, not urban. Pande (1994: 55–71) has a chapter, "The Age of Śaṅkara," that portrays the politics and religious landscape. Tradition has it that Śaṅkara was a practicing tantric, but there is little evidence of tantrism in his writings outside of the *Saundarya-laharī*, "Torrent of Beauty," a poem traditionally ascribed to him but not by the mainstream of modern scholarship.

7 Gauḍapāda's *Kārikās* precurse in some ways Śaṅkara's Advaita, but all but the first chapter present special hermeneutical problems (for example, the relation to Buddhist teachings, extensively explored in King 1995).

8 By Śaṅkara's time, Sanskrit was no one's mother tongue but was an intellectual *lingua franca*. (Filliozat, *The Sanskrit Language: An Overview*, 2000: 72–3.)

9 Śaṅkara's commentary on the *Brahma-sūtra* is translated in two volumes in lucid English by the nineteenth-century French sanskritist Georg Thibaut (1890, 1896), who, in a long introduction, confesses outright a bias in favor of Rāmānuja's reading. This is a bias that in some places shows, unfortunately. Thibaut's subtle mistranslations may be the root of some misinterpretations by scholars, though probably not by Aurobindo, who never mentions the *Brahma-sūtra*.

10 At the end of his commentary on *Gītā* 3.4, Śaṅkara writes: "The path of works/action can be a causal factor for coming to be capable of the path of knowledge. It is effective for the highest end but it does not take one there by itself. The path of knowledge, in contrast, does take one there independently, by itself. Its character is as though the ways of the path of works have been already accomplished." *The Bhagavad-gītā with the Commentary of Śrī Śaṅkarācārya* (Gokhale 1950: 49): *karma-niṣṭhāyāḥ jñāna-niṣṭhā-prāpti-hetutvena puruṣârtha-hetutvaṃ, na svātantryeṇa; jñāna-niṣṭhā tu karma-niṣṭhôpāyalabdhâtmikā satī svātantryeṇa puruṣârtha-hetuḥ anyânapekṣā*. That karma yoga is valuable as preparatory for the path of knowledge is a theme running throughout Śaṅkara's *Gītā* commentary, as might be expected given how dominant the topic of knowledge and action is in the *Gītā* itself.

11 The *Īśā* commentary passes with flying colors Mayeda's criteria for determining authenticity for works ascribed to Śaṅkara (1973/2006: 22–64).

12 This is the spelling given by Aurobindo's father. Aurobindo changed it after moving to Bengal in 1906 (Heehs 2008: 417 n. 4).

13 *Sri Aurobindo Birth Centenary Library* ("*SABCL*"), v. 12, "The Upanishads: Texts, Translations and Commentaries." A new edition of Aurobindo's works in thirty-six volumes—many just recently released—has slightly different pagination and will not be used here except in a couple of instances: *Collected Works of Sri Aurobindo* (*CWSA*). From 1910 to 1920, Aurobindo revised his work on the *Īśā* and a few other Upaniṣads while still others, translated early in his studies, were not revised. Another book of Upaniṣadic translations, *Kena and Other Upanishads*, completed over a period of twenty years from around 1900, has been published separately from the *SABCL* and *CWSA*: 2001. The editors explain in "Note on the Texts," pp. 440 ff., that in addition to the *Īśā* only the translations of the *Kena*, *Kaṭha*, and *Muṇḍaka* were published during Aurobindo's lifetime.

14 Śaṅkara opens his *Commentary on the Brahma-sūtra* with a dramatic statement of a kind of dualism: "Objects and subjects, meant by our concepts of 'it' and 'I', are, like light and darkness, opposed in their essential natures. With their mutual incompatibility established, all the more are occurrences of their properties mutually incompatible too." *yuṣmad-asmat-pratyaya-gocarayor viṣaya-viṣayinos tamaḥ-*

prakāśa-vad viruddha-sva-bhāvayor itaretara-bhāva-anupapattau siddhāyām tad-dharmāṇām api sutarām itaretara-bhāvânupapattiḥ. *BSB* ed. Shastri (1980: 4–6). Ram-Prasad (2002: 31–2) presents the dualism lucidly in analyzing the passage, revealing the importance of "false identification," *abhimāna*, although he does not use that Sanskrit word.

2 "Blocked Out" by the Lord or "Integrated?"

1 There are two Sanskrit roots from which the gerundive *vāsyam* could plausibly be formed (a tenth-class root being rare): the second-class √*vas*, "(to) wear," and the first-class √*vas* "(to) dwell in." Root meanings are to be taken broadly and, specifically here in context, narrowed to three possible—still very broad—meanings: (a) "to be covered, enveloped, blocked out," (b) "to be dwelled in," and (c) "to be dressed up."

2 The original version of this commentary may go all the way back to Aurobindo's "Baroda period." A revised version was published in the *Karmayogin* (1907, that is, "pre-Pondicherry"). Then an edited version was published in 1914 in the *Arya*.

3 The long poem *Savitri* has a couple of hundred pages about non-physical worlds, "planes of being," ranging from "subtle matter" to "supramental" worlds inhabited by creatures with "spiritual knowledge" (*SABCL* v. 27: 94–302). These "worlds" are also supposed to be manifest in our lives and physical dealings with one another. Śaṅkara does not deny that there are after-death worlds, or occult forces in life, but nothing about them is nearly as important, he implies in commenting on verse 3, as the difference between having and not having self-knowledge.

4 This judgment on my part may flow, however, from my inability to free myself from the readings of a host of classical Vedāntins, not just Advaitins. Matthew Dasti communicated to me in conversation that if one looks at the Upaniṣads while blocking out classical Vedānta it seems natural to read the verses Aurobindo's way. I disagree.

5 On the last page, p. 1070, of the *SABCL* edition (v. 19): "or, if its [a "Self's," from the previous page and sentence] end as an individual is to return into its Absolute, it could make that return also . . ." If condemnation of "world withdrawal" is in tension with this, we should note that this statement from *The Life Divine* was written in the 1940s and the Aurobindo quotation explaining *Īśā* 3 may go all the way back to his "Baroda period": see note 13 of Chapter 1. Aurobindo's world-affirmativism may have become tempered in his later years. Note further that Medhananda (2021b) argues that "psychic consent" is integral to Aurobindo's theodicy. The Lord does not

coerce the psychic being to take a physical or any kind of body, allowing it the choice mentioned in the last pages of *The Life Divine*. This important point is taken up in Chapter 8.

6 Marcaurelle (2000) argues cogently that *sannyāsa*, "renunciation," as touted in certain Upaniṣads and especially the *Bhagavad Gītā* as part of a yogic path, is not understood by Śaṅkara as an outwardly "renunciant" life as exhibited by those commonly called "sannyāsins" (who wander from place to place with hardly a possession save a walking stick). He points out (2000: 8–10) that Potter (1981: 35) drew attention to the misinterpretation which Marcaurelle fleshes out in a book devoted to showing that the yogic requirement according to Śaṅkara is only "*inner* renunciation" (Marcaurelle's term).

7 In *Aurobindo's Philosophy of Brahman* (1986: 131–4), I explain what I took to be Western influence on Aurobindo's world-affirmativism (now I believe overstated):

> Aurobindo's depreciation of the "Nirvana" type of mystic experience because it appears to reveal the world to be an illusion should be noted in this regard. But also significant are his conceptual attacks on all illusionist philosophy as well as on the idea of an "extracosmic God." . . . Consistent with this condemnation is his belief—and teaching of yoga—that all experience contributes to the spiritual evolution of one's individual personality or "soul." . . . He himself says that the forerunners of his teleological views are ideas of the *Ṛg Veda* and the *Īśā Upaniṣad*. But his notion of a reintegration of the human and the divine in a transformed earth depends on a modern awareness of evolutionary and historical process, and is thus much more obviously Romantic [as influenced by the Western movement of that name].

8 From Aurobindo's *Thoughts and Aphorisms* (*SABCL* v. 17: numbers 106–8):

> 106. Sannyas has a formal garb and outer tokens; therefore men think they can easily recognize it; but the freedom of a Janaka does not proclaim itself and it wears the garb of the world; to its presence even Narada was blinded.
> 107. Hard is it to be in the world, free, yet living the life of ordinary men; but because it is hard, therefore it must be attempted and accomplished.
> 108. When he watched the actions of Janaka, even Narada the divine sage thought him a luxurious worldling and libertine. Unless thou canst see the soul, how shalt thou say that a man is free or bound.

9 Although associated with tantra, the idea may originate with the *Gītā*, especially the famous verse 3.23: "Human beings in every way follow a path that is mine."

10 Since nowhere does Aurobindo mention a tantric initiation, it is reasonable to assume that he did not have one. But some tantric initiations are secret, and so that is not ruled out altogether.

11 Aurobindo makes several summary statements to this effect, for example, from *The Synthesis of Yoga* (*SABCL* v. 20: 231):

> No matter whether by knowledge, works, love or any other means, to become aware of this truth of our being [*ātman*, the "Self," the "Master of Works"], to realise it, to make it effective here or elsewhere is the object of all yoga.

12 The Hume translation (1931: 110) of *Bṛhadāraṇyaka* 3.2.10:

> "Yājñavalkya," said he [Jāratkārava], when the voice of a dead man goes into fire, his breath into wind, his eye into the sun, his mind into the moon, his hearing into the quarters of earth, his body into the earth, his soul (*ātman*) into space, the hairs of his head into plants, the hairs of his body into trees, and his blood and semen are placed in water, what then becomes of this person (*puruṣa*)?"
>
> "Ārtabhāga, my dear, take my hand. We two only will know of this. This is not for us two to speak of in public."
>
> The two went away and deliberated. What they said was *karma*. What they praised was *karma*. Verily, one becomes good by good action, bad by bad action.

13 *Gītā* 4.14. Similar ideas are expressed in other verses of the *Gītā* as well as several passages of the old Upaniṣads.

14 Kṛṣṇa sums up at 4.38, "For here in this word there is no purifier that is the equal of knowledge."

15 In *Candide*, Voltaire has the character Pangloss—a grisly old man hunched over a cane, a caricature of a *philosôphe*—say after every disaster his group encounters, such as plague and shipwreck, "But it's the best of all possible worlds."

16 C.J. Ducasse, a prominent American philosopher sympathetic to the idea of reincarnation, who was a President of the American Philosophical Association, makes the point in *Nature, Mind, and Death* (1951: 498–9).

17 The notion of *saṃsāra*, "the transmigratory round," surely was culturally deep-set in Śaṅkara's time. Perhaps it was taken for granted by the Advaitin, although certain "Materialists," Lokāyatas, made fun of the idea along with rituals: "The Agnihotra, the three Vedas, the ascetic's three staves, and smearing one's self with ashes,/ Were made by Nature as the livelihood of those destitute of knowledge and manliness. If a beast slain in the Jyotishṭoma rite will itself go to heaven,/ Why then does not the sacrificer forthwith offer his own father? . . . When once the body becomes ashes, how can it ever return again?" *Sarva-darśana-saṃgraha*, by Mādhava (*c.* 1500). tr. Cowell and Gough (1906: 10).

3 The Whole in the Part

1 Thrasher (1993: 1–38) traces the concept of "inexplicability," *anirvacanīyatva*, in early Advaita, identifying a few places in Śaṅkara's corpus where the concept is employed but crediting Maṇḍana, Śaṅkara's contemporary, for using it in the later classical sense as an analysis of both perceptual illusion and the "transcendent illusion" that is taken to be the world appearing to be other than Brahman. All that *Śaṅkara* actually says, however, echoing Upaniṣads, is that Brahman is beyond "name and form," *nāma-rūpa*, and for this reason is "inexplicable," as Thrasher shows.

2 This is the upshot of the last part of Śaṅkara's introduction to his *Brahma-sūtra-bhāṣya* along with extended comments on sūtras 1.1.2 and 1.1.3. Upaniṣadic passages suggesting a kind of negative theology such as *Kena* 3 and following mitigate this with the idea that practice teachings—including teachings about metaphysical underpinnings—are possible, despite the self being intellectually unknowable, because, "So we have heard from the wise who to us have explained it all" (*Īśā* 10).

3 This is not quite the pragmatism of Yogācāra Buddhist philosophers but there is a shared presupposition, namely, that traditional teachings of yoga and meditation are in some cases successful. As the *Kena Upaniṣad* says (especially verse 3), echoing the *nêti nêti* of the *Bṛhadāraṇyaka*, the self's not being a sensory object means that the ways to self-discovery are themselves difficult to teach. Fortunately, Śaṅkara says, there are the specific instructions of the ancients who had *vidyā* and declared the ways to us in texts like the *Gītā* and the Upaniṣads.

4 Śaṅkara's *Gītā* commentary on 18.61, glosses *māyā* as *chadman*, "external covering," "deceptive dress," "disguise" (Shastri 1980: 279). Aurobindo, *The Life Divine*, *SABCL* v. 18: 101:

> Maya in its original sense meant a comprehending and containing consciousness capable of embracing, measuring and limiting and therefore formative; it is that which outlines, measures out, moulds forms in the formless . . .

In a long essay, Gonda (1959: 119–94) discusses the etymology and uses of the term in the *Ṛg Veda*, where, at least in some passages, Aurobindo's comment rings true, for instance (1959: 129):

> [at] ṚV 3, 61, 7 . . . the important event of the sun's appearance into the world is attributed to the great *māyā* of Mitra and Varuṇa, that is to say to their "power of creating or constructing objects characterized by forms and dimensions."

Of course, the "trickery" sense became prominent in later Advaita, but Śaṅkara himself does not miss altogether the theistic use of the word. Similarly, Aurobindo does not avoid the negative sense altogether, since, according to him, Brahman does not lose awareness of being Brahman in being you and me, whereas, I take it, we are not aware of being Brahman.

5 Well, not exactly as we have it: all Vedānta holds Brahman has our experience while still knowing itself as Brahman. There is a metaphysical knot here to be addressed in several subsequent chapters. Brahman does not have your experience exactly as you have it, since Brahman continually, for example, experiences bliss. So, Brahman is not, in a sense, "all-inclusive," as claimed, but a causal monism skirts the difficulty of an ignorant Brahman, and this is, I think, how Śaṅkara understands Brahman's unity: everything *derives* from Brahman and in this way everything is "made of" and "made from" Brahman.

6 Ram-Prasad (2001: 189) makes the point referring to "the process of recognizing that the individuated self is in reality the universal supporting consciousness," and says, "[Regarding this process] . . . the Advaitin [Śaṅkara] must be understood as not primarily interested in assimilating the world into consciousness . . . [but] is concerned to specify the process by which de-individuation occurs."

7 A summary statement on point by Medhananda (2022: 102–3): "According to [Aurobindo's] 'realistic Advaita' philosophy, the sole reality is the infinite, impersonal-personal DC [Divine Consciousness], but DC, in its personal-dynamic aspect as Consciousness-Force, playfully manifests as all our various ignorant conscious perspectives through a threefold process of self-variation, self-limitation, and exclusive concentration."

8 Ingalls 1953, "Śaṅkara on the Question: Whose is *avidyā*?" is often cited in this regard but to my mind confuses the issue.

9 *cetanaṃ brahma ekam advitīyaṃ jagataḥ kāraṇam iti yad uktaṃ tan na upapadyate | kasmāt | upasaṃhāra-darśanāt | iha hi loke kulālâdayo ghaṭa-paṭâdīnāṃ kartāro mṛd-daṇḍa-cakra-sūtrâdy-aneka-kārakôpasaṃhāreṇa saṃgṛhīta-sādhanāḥ santas tat tat kāryaṃ kurvāṇā dṛśyante | brahma ca asahāyaṃ tava abhipretaṃ tasya sādhanântarânupasaṃgrahe sati kathaṃ sraṣṭṛtvam upapadyeta | tasmān na brahma jagat-kāraṇam iti cet | na eṣa doṣaḥ | yataḥ kṣīra-vad dravya-sva-bhāva-viśeṣād upapadyate | yathā hi loke kṣīraṃ jalaṃ vā svayam eva dadhi-hima-bhāvena pariṇamate 'napekṣya bāhyaṃ sādhanaṃ tathā iha api bhaviṣyati | nanu kṣīrâdy api dadhy-ādi-bhāvena pariṇamamānam apekṣata eva bāhyaṃ sādhanam auṣṇyādikaṃ katham ucyate kṣīra-vad dhi iti | na eṣa doṣaḥ | svayam api hi kṣīraṃ yāṃ ca yāvatīṃ ca pariṇāma-mātrām anubhavati tāvaty eva tv āryate tv auṣṇyâdinā dadhi-bhāvāya | yadi ca svayaṃ dadhi-bhāva-śīlatā na syān na eva auṣṇyâdinā api balād dadhi-bhāvam āpadyeta | na hi vāyur ākāśo vā auṣṇyâdinā balād dadhi-bhāvam āpadyate |* (*Brahma-sūtra-bhāṣya* 2.1.24, Shastri 1980: 396–7.)

10 "Scriptural" passages aplenty support one side or another. Surprisingly, even the *Gītā* in one place says quite explicitly that the Lord does not create/emanate the nexus of actions and agents and connections with results but rather it all occurs naturally: *Gītā* 5.14. And at *Gītā* 9.8 the Lord is said to be compelled to create/emanate.

11 *oṃ pūrṇam adaḥ pūrṇam idam pūrṇāt pūrṇam udacyate | pūrṇasya pūrṇam ādāya pūrṇam eva avaśiṣyate ||*

12 *Bṛhadāraṇyakôpaniṣad-bhāṣya* 5.1.1: *pūrṇam adaḥ, pūrṇaṃ na kutaścid-vyāvṛttaṃ vyāpi ity etat | . . . tat sampūrṇam ākāśa-vad vyāpi nirantaraṃ nirupādhikaṃ ca | tad eva idam sopādhikaṃ nāma-rūpa-sthaṃ vyavahārâpannaṃ pūrṇam svena rūpeṇa paramâtmanā vyāpyā iva, na upādhi-paricchinnena viśeṣâtmanā | tad idaṃ viśeṣâpannaṃ kāryâtmakaṃ brahma pūrṇāt kāraṇâtmanaḥ udacyate udricyate udgacchati ity etat | yady api kārymâtmanā udricyate tathā api yat sva-rūpaṃ pūrṇatvaṃ paramâtma-bhāvaṃ tan na jahāti, pūrṇam eva udricyate | pūrṇasya kāryâtmano brahmaṇaḥ pūrṇam pūrṇatvaṃ, ādāya gṛhītvā ātma-sva-rūpa-eka-rasatvam āpadya vidyayā 'vidyā-kṛtaṃ bhūta-mātrôpādhi-saṃsarga-jaṃ, anyatvâvabhāsaṃ tiraskṛtya, pūrṇam eva anantaram abāhyaṃ prajñāna-ghana-eka-rasa-sva-bhāvaṃ kevalaṃ brahma avaśisyate* | (Śaṅkara 1964: 950–1.)

Just a few lines later, there is a great summary statement by Śaṅkara about "knowledge of Brahman" and the practices of "self-control, charity, and compassion," *dama-dāna-dayā*, which we might note despite the digression:

> The teaching of all Upaniṣads is Brahman. This mantra presents it again to introduce a new section. For, certain practices—in particular, chanting *om*, self-control (*dama*), charity (*dāna*), and compassion (*dayā*)—are to be recommended as means to *brahma-vidyā*, that is, are means that, as mentioned in this supplementary portion, form part of all meditations and spiritual practices.

yaḥ sarvôpaniṣad-artho brahma sa eṣo 'nena mantreṇa anūdyate uttara-sambandhârtham | brahma-vidyā-sādhanatvena hi vakṣamāṇāni sādhanāni oṅ-kāra-dama-dāna-dayâkhyāni vidhitsitāni, khila-prakaraṇa-sambandhāt sarvôpāsanâṅga-bhūtāni ca | (Śaṅkara 1964: 951.)

13 Some may think that materialism as a metaphysics is what rules out Vedānta and all views that posit a God-like being ("Brahman," "Emptiness," "God," "Tao," etc.). That is the *defeater* (the *bādhaka* in the terms of classical Indian epistemology), not conflicting mystic testimony or excessive evil. However, despite the common view that there is fundamentally a plurality of things, much mainstream materialism professes to be monistic, thus fitting in nicely with Vedāntic monism except on a single point: namely, positions taken on materialism's "mind/body problem" which has not been solved. Mental causation, particularly as demonstrated in extraordinary feats coming from yoga practice, challenges the thesis of *causal closure*, which is the main offending position in materialist outlooks from a Vedāntic perspective. Some causal processes originate in consciousness. This, which seems obvious in someone's, say, raising a hand, is argued in my *Yoga, Karma, and Rebirth* (2009: 50–9). It is even better argued now by Richard Grego (2020) whose citations include the most prominent names in contemporary philosophy of mind.

14 Maharaj (2018) shows that "infinite paths to the Infinite" is the core teaching of Sri Ramakrishna, also of Swami Vivekananda, as Aurobindo likely understood, seeing himself as sustaining their message through his own yoga and spiritual experience.

15 In criticism of atomism and elsewhere, Śaṅkara does anticipate the dialectics of the later Advaitins Śrīharṣa and company who argue that no two things can be entirely distinct for fear of an infinite regress of relations. This, the so-called "Bradley problem," is also discussed in Chapter 5.

16 I discuss several holisms in a modern context, in economics, environmental science, ethics, and other other dimensions of life, in *Yoga, Karma, and Rebirth* (2009: 67–78), in a section entitled, "Yogic Control and Integration: Spiritual Holism."

4 Mystical Knowledge of Unity

1 Emily Dickenson, "The Mind is wider than the Sky," is a familiar expression of the idea (Miller, 1968). Śaṅkara: "the mind as embodied right here in this world can go very far, all the way to the world of Brahmā (the Creator), through imagination in no more than an instant."

2 Aurobindo says as much in *The Life Divine*, in a chapter entitled "Knowledge by Identity and Separative Knowledge" (*SABCL* v. 18: 525).

3 For example, from the *Gītā*:

> 6.28. A yogi practicing constantly in this way, flaws departed, effortlessly enjoys the supreme happiness that is the touch of Brahman.
> 6.29. Seeing the same everywhere, disciplined through yoga practice, one perceives the self seated in all beings and all beings in the self.

Śaṅkara cites *Bṛhadāraṇyaka Upaniṣad* 3.4.1 ("This self lies within all"), 3.8.11 ("There is none other than this"), and 4.5.13 ("just a mass of 'intuitive consciousness,' *prajñāna*") on point, but many other similar statements pepper the Upaniṣadic corpus; similarly, the *Gītā* (esp. *Gītā* 4.35 and 13.27 ff.).

4 In a book on yoga (2009: 131–5), I discuss the epistemology of mysticism following not only the yoga literature but also a debate in analytic epistemology between "externalists" and "internalists," factions who dramatically disagree about the nature of justification. Though fine points of that discussion would be digressive if we are to keep our focus on the *Īśā*, let me just mention some fine analytic contributions to the modern debate about the "cognitive value of mystical experience" beginning with James (1902/1982) but including now: Stace (1961), Wainwright (1981), Gale (1991), Alston (1991), Yandell (1993), Gellman (1997), Fales (2001), Swinburne (2001, 2004), Taves (2009), Wettstein (2012), Webb (2015), and Maharaj (2018).

5 A Mīmāṃsaka "non-cognition" theory of illusion has, in one version, illusion as a mixture of a perceiving and a remembering with a failure to recognize the difference due to the strength of the memory (*smṛti-pramośa-akhyāti-vāda*): "That is silver" said of a piece of mother-of-pearl right in front of the speaker is true in its "thatness" portion, which is based on a perception—there is something there the demonstrative refers to—whereas in the "silverness" portion a remembering is expressed, and there is no awareness of the difference. Nyāya agrees that the "thatness" part is correct and not sublated.

6 James accepts a weak, phenomenological version of epistemic parallelism: the experiences in focus, he says, are, by the mystics themselves, *taken* to be "noetic," which is one of four defining marks of a mystical/religious experience that he discerns, *The Varieties of Religious Experience* (1902/1961: Lectures 16 and 17). That is, the mystic typically takes her experiences to reveal a God-like being or self or state of consciousness—"God" or "Brahman" or "Emptiness" or the like—but she is wrong to do so, James concludes, except in the minimal sense of his "piecemeal supernaturalism."

7 From consideration of the epistemology of yogic testimony in my *Yoga, Karma, and Rebirth* (2009: 134):

> the parallelism thesis and what we may call the charity view of testimony do not entail the truth of yogic claims. All claims are corrigible. The faith to sustain practice does not depend on absolutely precise content of beliefs nor on certainty. There may well emerge considerations that override the guru's teaching, as with an apparent perception of two moons. Nevertheless, we are to assume that meditation and other yogic experience has a noetic or cognitive quality, being both taken as informative about some pretty important matters, such as the death-spanning nature of our consciousness, and being informative in fact. There is no general reason why we should not trust our teachers' testimony.... The Nyaya definition of testimony as a knowledge source (going all the way back to the *Nyaya-sutra*, sutra 1.1.7) is that it is the conveyance of information by an expert, i.e., by one knowing the truth, who wants to communicate it with no intention to deceive.

8 Mircea Eliade in his classic study of yoga says *samādhi*, "yogic trance," is "enstasis," a word coined to bring out the ecstasy but also the inwardness of the yogic end (1973: 92, 93). Ram-Prasad (2001:191–4) shows that the Advaita holds out "an exalted view of happiness rather than merely the absence of suffering" (2001: 192) as the motivation for seeking self-discovery.

9 This is not to say that "existence monism" and the arguments for it are irrelevant. Vedāntic monism is indeed a main topic of the next chapter, and one important argument—for "non-distinctness"—is taken up in this essay.

10 *Śāṅkara-gītā-bhāṣya* on *Gītā* 6.32: "The one who is in this way an *ahiṃsika*, firmly settled in a vision of equality, is deemed, that is to say, considered, the very best yogin, preëminent among all": *yaḥ evaṃ ahiṃsikaḥ samyag-darśana-niṣṭhaḥ saḥ yogī paramaḥ utkṛṣṭaḥ mataḥ abhipretaḥ sarva-yogināṃ madhye* |

11 *Gītā* 13.24: "Some through meditation 'see' the self in the self by the self": *dhyāyena ātmani paśyanti kecid ātmānam ātmanā*. Note the use of the word *dhyāna*, which is the most common classical word for meditation.

12 Vedānta's self-illumination thesis is extracted from several Upaniṣads but perhaps most memorably from the *Bṛhadāraṇyaka*, the fourth chapter: Yājñavalkya charts the self's journey through sleep and dreaming—where it sees "by its own light"—to deep sleep and non-dual consciousness. The climax comes at verse 32 of the third section: "An ocean, a seer alone without duality, becomes the one whose world (*loka*) is Brahman . . . This is the supreme journey. This is the greatest achievement. This is the best *loka*. This is the supreme bliss. On just a portion of this bliss other beings have their living."

13 Named after the nineteenth-century British idealist, F.H. Bradley. In India, the argument can be traced to the Buddhist Nāgārjuna, whom the eleventh-century Śrīharṣa acknowledges along with Śaṅkara for pioneering onslaughts on any kind of "distinctness," *bheda*, that is, in helping one maintain the right perspective against Nyāya and other "descriptive philosophies." I trace classical use of the Bradley problem through a number of authors in *Classical Indian Metaphysics* (1995). All told, it seems to me to constitute more of a challenge to Nyāya realism and pluralism than a convincingly successful indirect proof of Vedāntic monism (the notion of distinctness being confused, non-distinctness is proved, some do argue, however).

14 And he advances what seems to me to be a possibly ingenious theory of perception based on "knowledge by identity," which deserves careful reconstruction (not yet undertaken, so far as I know).

15 I draw on a paper of mine, "Theoretic Minimalism Among (Advaita Vedānta) Defenders of the 'Self-Illumining Consciousness' Thesis" (1999).

16 However, in favor of the Vivaraṇa stance it should be remarked that Brahman could not be "all-inclusive" if there is retaining of its native awareness and bliss in comprising the experience of you and me, because that inclusion has to leave out our self-experience as limited, egoistic. Sensory experience in the egoistic mode would indeed, as Padmapāda claims, cease to exist with self-discovery. In other words, Brahman may share with me my experience but not as I have it in my limited way. Thus, it does not participate in the existence of Brahman except by way of its immediacy, it would seem, on the subject side, and, on the object side, presumably, its content in a radically different mode of presentation.

17 Note that a telos in nature is hardly a strange idea in the classical context, as even Sāṃkhya theories of an utterly inconscient *prakṛti* give her an aim, or aims; see, for

instance, *Yoga-sūtra* 2.18 and 2.21, which say that "nature" serves the two ends of the conscious being, the *puruṣa*, enjoyment and enlightenment.

18 In the eleventh century *Kāvya-prakāśa*, "Light on Poetry," Mammaṭa famously compares "aesthetic delight," *rasa*, to the touch of Brahman: the statement is translated in note 13 of Chapter 7, in the context of what I call Aurobindo's *"rasa* theodicy." Aurobindo reverses the analogy; that is, he proposes transformation of everyday experience, through the touch of Brahman, into aesthetic delight, *rasa*.

19 *Brahma-sūtra-bhāṣya* 2.1.33: *yathā loke kasyacid āptaiṣaṇasya rājño rājâmātyasya vā vyatiriktaṃ kiṃcit-prayojanam anabhisaṃdhāya kevalaṃ līlā-rūpāḥ pravṛttayaḥ krīḍā-vihāreṣu bhavanti, yathā ca ucchvāsa-praśvāsâdayo 'nabhisaṃdhāya bāhyaṃ kiṃcit-prayojanaṃ sva-bhāvād eva saṃbhavanti, evam īśvarasya apy anapekṣya kiṃcit-prayojanântaraṃ sva-bhāvād eva kevalaṃ līlā-rūpā pravṛttir bhaviṣyati | na hi īśvarasya prayojanântaraṃ nirūpyamāṇaṃ nyāyataḥ śrutito vā saṃbhavati | na ca sva-bhāvaḥ paryanuyoktuṃ śakyate yady apy asmākam iyaṃ jagad-bimba-viracanā gurutara-saṃrambhā iva ābhāti tathā api paramêśvarasya līlā eva kevalā iyam aparimita-śaktitvāt | yadi nāma loke līlāsv api kiṃcit sūkṣmaṃ prajoyanam utprekṣyeta tathā api na eva atra kiṃcit-prayojanam utprekṣituṃ śakyate, āpta-kāma-śruteḥ* | (Shastri 1980: 405–6.)

20 At the end of his *Īśā* commentary, Śaṅkara writes:

Interlocutor: A single person could bear the two, *vidyā* and *avidyā*, one after the other, serially.

Śaṅkara: No. For, since upon an arising of *vidyā*, "knowledge," *avidyā*, "ignorance," is banished, a person with spiritual knowledge cannot experience *avidyā*. For, a person who really knows that fire is hot and luminous does not think *ignorantly*, "Fire is cold and not luminous," not in the face of the knowledge. Nor would there be, for such a person, any doubt about the matter nor an absence of knowledge.

5 (K)nots of Metaphysics: The Causal Argument for the "Self-Existent," *svayam-bhū*

1 See Appendix B. The Sanskrit root √*bhū*, "(to) become," is often used in strict synonymy with √*as*, "(to) be," thus possibly "by and of itself being" would be better, but the shock value is carried mainly by the force of *svayam*, "by and of itself," in connection with the idea that everything stands in some kind of causal relationship.

2 In a dramatic scene in the *Bṛhadāraṇyaka Upaniṣad* where a causal series ending in Brahman has been laid down, the sage Yājñavalkya is asked by the princess Gārgī, "On what is Brahman woven warp and woof?" Yājñavalkya replies, "Do not question too far, Gārgī, lest your head fly off." (*Bṛ U* 3.6.1.)

3 Another statement of the *nêti nêti* idea, which is echoed by *Īśā* 8, comes at *Bṛhadāraṇyaka* 3.9.26, a refrain recurring at *Bṛ U* 4.2.4, 4.4.22, and 4.5.15: "This self (*ātman*) is *not this, not that* (*nêti nêti*). It is ungraspable, for it is not grasped; not divisible, for it cannot be divided; unattached, because it is not attached to anything. Unfettered it is, because it neither harms nor is harmed."

4 For example, the Islamic philosopher, Avicinna (Ibn Sīnā), utilizes a God-like conception that is extremely close to the Vedāntic "Brahman," "the One," as evidenced in the emanationism he purports to prove which is launched by a proof of God's oneness, *Avicenna on Theology*, tr. Arberry (1951), anthologized in Bonevac and Phillips (2009: 546–7).

5 There is also *Taittirīya Upaniṣad* 2.7, perhaps the most famous passage for the idea: "That made itself by itself," *tad ātmanaṃ svayam akuruta*.

6 Compare the position championed by Priest and company that there are true contradictions: Priest 2002. This is arguably the position of the Buddhist Nāgārjuna (Garfield 1995). Nāgārjuna is one of two authors cited favorably by Śrīharṣa. The other is Śaṅkara.

7 Granted, if reference is possible, Brahman would have to be distinct from other referents that are not Brahman—which imperils Vedānta's monism—and if not, then a story needs to be told about what sort of meaning there is for statements in which the word "Brahman" appears. This, the "effability" issue, is worth examining—especially given the *nêti nêti* doctrine—but I want to focus on other difficulties.

8 See, for instance, *Gītā* 4.11, 7.18, and 9.18.

9 *sarvasya ātmatvāc ca brahmâstitva-prasiddhiḥ | sarvo hy ātmâstitvaṃ pratyeti, na na aham asti iti* (Shastri 1980: 42–3).

10 Most prominently, Udayana, an eleventh century Naiyāyika, presents multiple teleological conceptions in support of the existence of an *īśvara*, thus combatting Buddhist atheism in particular.

11 Aurobindo uses the image: *The Synthesis of Yoga*, *SABCL* v. 20: 196.

12 In *The God of Love*, Hick (1978: 297–309, 333–6), having rehearsed the biologically instrumental value of pain along with character-building scenarios of suffering in the context of his "soul-making" theodicy says that "disteleological" pain and suffering—the pain of a newborn who dies right away, for example—is surmountable only by an appeal to the *mystery* of "God's plan." Mystery, then, reasons the theologian, is part of what's required to make soul-making possible. Perhaps. But is there not at least a little support in the inductive move that since so much pain has

evident biological purpose we have a reason to believe that when something's purpose is not evident it also makes for something good?

13 *asya jagato nāma-rūpābhyāṃ vyākṛtasya aneka-kartṛ-bhoktṛ-samyuktasya pratiniyata-deśa-kāla-nimitta-kriyā-phalâśrayasya manasā api acintya-racanā-rūpasya janma-sthiti-bhaṅgaṃ yataḥ sarvajñāt sarva-śakteḥ kāraṇād bhavati tad brahma iti vākya-śeṣaḥ* | (Shastri 1980: 47–8).

14 *na yathôkta-viśeṣaṇasya jagato yathôkta-viśeṣaṇam īśvaraṃ muktvā anyataḥ pradhānād acetanād aṇubhyo 'bhāvāt saṃsāriṇo vā utpatty-ādi saṃbhāvayituṃ śakyaṃ* | *na ca sva-bhāvataḥ viśiṣṭa-deśa-kāla-nimittānām iha upādānāt* | (Shastri 1980: 49–50).

15 *etad eva anumānaṃ saṃsāri-vyatiriktêśvarâstitvâdi-sādhanaṃ manyanta īśvara-kāriṇaḥ* | *nanv iha api tad eva upanyastaṃ janmâdi-sūtre* | *na* | *vedānta-vākya-kusuma-grathanârthatvāt sūtrāṇām* | *vedānta-vākyāni hi sūtrair udāhṛtya vicāryante* | *vākyârtha-vicāraṇâdhyavasāna-nirvṛttā hi brahmâvagatir na anumānâdi-pramāṇântara-nirvṛttā* | *satsu tu vedānta-vākyeṣu jagato janmâdi-kāraṇa-vādiṣu tad-artha-grahaṇa-dārḍhyāya anumānam api vedānta-vākyâvirodhi pramāṇaṃ bhavan na nivāryate, . . .* | (Shastri 1980: 50–1).

16 *kiṃ tu śruty-ādayo 'nubhavâdayaś ca yathā-saṃbhavam iha pramāṇaṃ, anubhavâvasānatvād bhūta-vastu-viṣayatvāc ca brahma-jñānasya* | (Shastri 1980: 52).

17 *dehêndriyâdiṣv ahaṃ-mamâbhimāna-rahitasya pramātṛtvânupapattau pramāṇa-pravṛtty-anupapatteḥ* | *na hi indriyāṇy anupādāya pratyakṣâdi-vyavahāraḥ saṃbhavati* | *na ca adhiṣṭhānam antareṇa indriyāṇāṃ vyavahāraḥ saṃbhavati* | *na ca anadhyastâtma-bhāvena dehena kaścid vyāpriyate* | *na ca etasmin sarvasminn asati asaṅgasya ātmanaḥ pramātṛtvam upapadyate* | *na ca pramātṛtvam antareṇa pramāṇa-pravṛttir asti* | *tasmād avidyāvad-viṣayāṇy eva pratyakṣâdini pramānāni śāstrāṇi ca* | From the *BSB avatāra* (Shastri 1980: 20–1).

18 See Appendix D. Here we may remark that while this karma-as-retribution doctrine may help the Lord "get off the hook" for *natural* evil, as a *moral* doctrine it faces difficulties. Why should a person suffering from, say, a birth defect be treated kindly if we know that the defect shows that a horrible deed must have been committed previously?

19 A poetic characterization of Brahman in *The Life Divine* (*SABCL* v. 18: 324) presents the "*iti iti*" idea echoing several Upaniṣadic passages:

> The Upanishads affirm that all this is the Brahman; Mind is Brahman, Life is Brahman, Matter is Brahman; addressing Vayu, the Lord of Air, of Life, it is said "O Vayu, thou art manifest Brahman"; and pointing to man and beast and bird and insect, each separately is identified with the One—"O Brahman, thou art this old man and boy and girl, this bird, this insect." Brahman is the Consciousness that knows itself in all that exists; Brahman is the Force that

sustains the power of God and Titan and Demon, the Force that acts in man and animal and the forms and energies of Nature; Brahman is the Ananda, the secret Bliss of existence which is the ether of our being and without which none could breathe or live. Brahman is the inner Soul in all; it has taken a form in correspondence with each created form it inhabits. The Lord of Beings is that which is conscious in the conscious being, but he is also the Conscient in inconscient things, the One who is master and in control of the many that are passive in the hands of Force-Nature. He is the Timeless and Time; he is Space and all that is in Space; he is Causality and the cause and the effect: He is the thinker and his thought, the warrior and his courage, the gambler and his dice-throw. All realities and all aspects and all semblances are the Brahman; . . .

20 Aurobindo could have picked up the reasoning from any number of Śaṅkara's Upaniṣadic commentaries or his commentary on the *Gītā*.

6 Knowledge of Self (*ātman*) and Knowledge of the Occult

1 This is true also for letters, where Aurobindo has a particular recipient in mind (there are four volumes of letters collected in the *SABCL*). The "Shankara" of the letters often seems like that in the recipient's mind, not Aurobindo's opinion about a historical figure.

2 Brown (1958: 29) in careful consideration of the evidence pro and con and concludes, "Its ascription to Śaṅkara was to win it prestige." Rukmani (2001: xv–xxxi) is convincing, as mentioned, that the *Vivaraṇa* commentary on Vyāsa's *Yoga-sūtra-bhāṣya* should not be accredited to Ādi Śaṅkara. The *Viveka-cūḍā-maṇi* ("Crest-Jewel of Discrimination") is another work traditionally ascribed to him that has been shown to be by someone else. Criteria for authenticity in this regard have been discussed, notably, by Hacker (1951), Ingalls (1952), Brown (1958), Mayeda (1973: 22-51), Potter (1981: 15, 115–16), Comans (2000), and Rukmani (2001) as well as by Pande (1994) and others prone to accept tradition.

3 Pande's best arguments are refutations of the reasons Brown (1958) and others give for denying ascription in the case of the *Saundarya-laharī* in particular. The occult poem translated by Brown was also translated earlier, exquisitely and with copious notes by S. Subramanya Sastri and T.R. Srinivasa Ayyangar (1937), who say that out of thirty-five commentaries known to them, thirty-four attribute the work to Śaṅkara (ibid.: xi). Pande argues that unless there is a good reason to deny the commentaries' practically unanimous accord—and the mere fact that the claim is made in Sanskrit commentaries is not a good reason—the traditional ascription

should be accepted. Furthermore, styles being distinctive constitutes no good reason in itself to divide authorship: precedents for excellence in diverse genre in classical India include the great names of Nāgārjuna (Lindtner 1986) and, within Advaita, Śrīharṣa (and how far apart stylistically are Śrīharṣa's long philosophic *Khaṇḍana-khaṇḍa-khādya*, "Sweetmeats of Refutation," and his equally long epic, *Naiṣadha-carita*, "Tales of King Nala"!).

4 A case could be made that Śaṅkara is the realist about worldly things, taking them to be the result of a distinct emanation from that of selves, and Aurobindo the illusionist in taking them to be bound up somehow with an expanding "self-discovery."

5 Medhananda (2021c) makes this point but still argues that Aurobindo's "experiential" critique of Śaṅkara is valid.

6 The "Copernican hypothesis" in contemporary cosmogony relies on the intuition that earth evolution is not unique, not special: anywhere life and consciousness could evolve, it will, so the thesis goes. Aurobindo, too, speculated, consistently with his metaphysics, that consciousness emerges in other parts of the material universe: "there is no reason to suppose that there is not life in any part of the material cosmic system except earth. No doubt the suns and nebulae cannot harbour material life because there is not the necessary basis, but wherever there is a formed world, Life can exist" (*CWSA* v. 28: 326).

7 From *The Life Divine*, the chapter "The Origin and Remedy of Falsehood, Error, Wrong and Evil" (*SABCL* v. 18: 597): "if that [Divine] Reality is what we have supposed it to be, there must be some necessity for the appearance of these contrary phenomena, some significance, some function that they had to serve in the economy of the universe."

8 Aurobindo often connects poetry and yoga. From *Savitri*, the section entitled, "The Yoga of the Soul's Release": "Oft inspiration with her lightning feet . . . / Traversed the soundless corridors of his mind/ Bringing her rhythmic sense of hidden things" (*SABCL* v. 28: 38).

7 A Theistic Way to Self-Discovery

1 Radhakrishnan (1953: 577): "Even today they [the four verses] are used by the Hindus in their funeral rites."

2 From Appendix B: "And a person having practiced meditation on Brahman and having performed works as laid out prays at the time of death to the self for the door to self-realization to open." Also note that Śaṅkara explicitly glosses the word "now" in verse 17 in this way too, namely, that the speaker knows death is near.

3 Radhakrishnan, *Indian Philosophy* (1923/1956) v. 2, pp. 627–8, is cited as favoring this hypothesis.

4 Deutsch (1969: 99–100) is cited for this.

5 The classical authors Kumārila, Prabhākara, and Maṇḍana are mentioned as advocating *jñāna-karma-samuccaya* as the superior way to the supreme good.

6 Among moderns, I am hardly alone in this emphasis. Bader (1990), De Smet (2013), and others have seen the preëminence, including Nakamura (2004: 734–55).

7 Gerow (1971: 266) points out that a common variety of the trope feeds a sense of hyperbole "to exaggerate one . . . at the expense of the other."

8 Compare William Blake, from his essay, "A Vision of the Last Judgment": "'What,' it will be Questioned, 'When the Sun rises do you see a round Disk of fire somewhat like a Guinea?' O no no, I see an Innumerable company of the Heavenly host crying 'Holy, Holy, Holy is the Lord God Almighty.'"

9 Compare *Muṇḍaka Upaniṣad* 3.2.3 (repeated at *Kaṭha* 2.23): "The 'self,' *ātman*, is not to be realized by talking, not by intelligence, not by pouring over sacred texts. Only by one whom the self chooses is it to be realized; the self determines to whom it reveals its true form."

Among recent scholarly treatments, Malkovsky (2001), notably, is sensitive to the theistic turn here and elsewhere in Śaṅkara's corpus, including his *Brahma-sūtra-bhāṣya*: (the theme of his title is borne out in copious citation) *The Role of Divine Grace in the Soteriology of Śaṅkarācārya*. *Īśā* 15-18 Malkovsky takes to be in accord with Śaṅkara's overall views and are discussed lucidly (2001: 308–10). His conclusion (310): "Thus, in his *Īśā-Upaniṣad-bhāṣya* Śaṅkara clearly teaches the efficacy of the grace of the highest Self for the Self-realization of the seeker."

10 From Renou (1968: 10):

> I imagine that the works which have survived [as the hymns of the *Ṛg Veda*] are those which fulfilled the requirements of a poetic competition. . . . The aim was to compose on a given theme, or perhaps according to a given plan, not introducing direct accounts of the lives of the gods so much as veiled allusions, occult correspondences between the sacred and the profane, . . . These correspondences, and the magic power they emanate, are called *brahman*: this is the oldest sense of the term. They are not intellectual conceptions but experiences which have been lived through at the culmination of a state of mystic exaltation conceived as revelation. The *soma* is the catalyst of these latent forces. The designation *kavi* is given to the poet who can seize and express these correspondences, and to the god who sends him inspiration.

11 Defenses of Aurobindo's interpretation of the *Ṛg Veda* have been written in Sanskrit in the twentieth century—most notably by Kapali-Sastry (1952), a short study translated into English in the same book—but academic sanskritists have tended to

see Aurobindo's work as anachronistic. Again Renou (1968: 17): "[According to Aurobindo, the Veda would be] symbolism representing the passions of the soul and its striving after higher spiritual planes: thus the Veda, we are told, ceases to be a barbarous and unintelligible hymnary. I fear that it also ceases to be a document of pre-history and becomes a manual of modern theosophy."

12 The other three are the dream state, the dreamless-sleep state, and the "fourth," *turīya*, which is indescribable.

13 This is to echo a famous statement in the *Kāvya-prakāśa* ("Light on Poetry") by the renowned critic Mammaṭa of the eleventh century. Here is about half of a long Sanskrit sentence explaining *rasa*, rendered by the prolific Victorian translator, Ganganatha Jha (1924/1967: 57–8):

> though the said emotion actually subsists in the particular spectator himself, yet, by reason of the generalised form in which it is presented, the man loses, for the moment, all sense of his separate personality and has his consciousness merged in the universal; and this representing the mental condition of all men of poetic sensibility, he apprehends the said emotion; though, having been manifested in its most general form, it has no existence apart from its own apprehension; in fact its sole essence consists in its *being relished*, and it lasts as long as the [dramatic, fictional] Excitants, Ensuants and Variants [the tools of the dramatic art] continue to exist; . . . and when it is relished, it appears as if it were vibrating before the eyes, entering the inmost recesses of the heart, inspiriting the entire body, and eclipsing everything else; it makes one feel the rapturous bliss of Brahman; the emotion thus manifested becomes the source of transcendent charm and is spoken of as '*rasa*.'

14 This theme runs throughout *The Life Divine*, but a particularly dramatic statement and explicit mention of *rasa* occurs in the chapter entitled, "The Double Soul in Man" (*SABCL* v. 18: 222–3): "The subliminal soul is conscious inwardly of the *rasa* of things and has an equal delight in all contacts; it is conscious also of the values and standards of the surface desire-soul and receives on its own surface corresponding touches of pleasure, pain, and indifference, but takes an equal delight in all. In other words, our real soul within takes joy of all its experiences . . ."

15 There are other possible influences, Western Romanticism, for instance, or even the *Gītā*. The *Gītā*'s ninth chapter, for example, opens with Kṛṣṇa saying he is about to lay out a path for freedom from *aśubha*, literally, the "non-beautiful."

16 He had, however, a well-known tantric writer as a disciple, M.P. Pandit, who wrote in English numerous small pamphlets explaining tantric ideas and practices, many published by the Sri Aurobindo Ashram in Pondicherry. M.P. Pandit also translated—elegantly, I may add, though often abridging—the *Kulārṇava Tantra*

(1965), a well-known Sanskrit text of approximately the tenth century (the publication erroneously attributed to Sir John Woodruffe who wrote the introduction but only that).

17 The biographer Heehs writes (2008: 84): "[Aurobindo] saw [Ramakrishna] as a modern representative of a tradition of spiritual experience going back to the Upanishads and earlier." Maharaj (2018) shows several lines of continuity from Ramakrishna and Vivekananda through Aurobindo.

18 Heehs 2008: 14–15. We may note that Aurobindo's *The Future Poetry* (*SABCL* v. 9) ranges widely—in a few hundred pages—over both Western and Sanskrit literatures but concentrates on Western epics along with the work of Shelley, Browning, Keats, Wordsworth, some other Romantics, and a few for Aurobindo more contemporary bards including Walt Whitman. From Heehs (2008: 27) on Aurobindo's career at Cambridge University where he excelled as a student: "In 1891 he was named joint winner of the annual Rawley Prize for the best composition in Greek iambics." *The Future Poetry* is supplemented by long letters mainly from the later period of Aurobindo's life which are published in the same volume (*SABCL* v. 9), all revealing a lover of nature poetry in English. Aurobindo read plenty of it and admired, especially, he seems to say, that bringing out enchantment, a certain "spiritual expressiveness" in nature. Shakespeare, for example, is downgraded as a master only of the craft of depiction without the uplifting quality of the best verse. For another example, consider the opening lines of Aurobindo's own "Ahana": "Vision delightful alone on the hills whom the silences cover,/Closer lean to mortality; human, stoop to thy lover." In rhyming couplets like this, the poem continues for hundreds of lines of evocative nature imagery. Aurobindo's corpus includes a volume of short and middle-sized poems (*SABCL* v. 5) in addition to the long epic *Savitri* (*SABCL* v. 28 and 29). Ghosal (2020) makes such poetry out to be, in the words of his title, "at the Center of Human Knowledge."

8 Aspiration and Surrender

1 The renderings are trimmed to present only the most important lines for Śaṅkara's views about action and the path of knowledge.

2 Mircea Eliade (1982: 241–3) has a lucid discussion, pointing out (241), "Kṛṣṇa reveals that man, too, can collaborate in the perfection of the divine work, not only by sacrifices properly speaking (those that make up the Vedic cult) but by *all his acts*, whatever their nature." Actually, Kṛṣṇa rules out the Vedic sacrifices, "sacrifices properly speaking," and it is not clear that an immoral or ugly act could meet the requirements of the *karma-yoga* of the *Gītā*.

3 *Gītā* 5.4: "Students may speak of meditation and (karma-)yoga as distinct but not those in the know."
4 A further word about "*om*," which occurs in verse 17 and in many other places in the early Upaniṣads and in the *Gītā*. The *Yoga-sūtra* says that *om* designates the *īśvara* (*YS* 1.27) and encourages chanting it as a way to self-discovery (*YS* 1.28), like many Vedāntic texts. Since Buddhists intone the sacred syllable without endorsing an idea of an *īśvara*, or *ātman*, for that matter, it seems that the common meaning is whatever the chanter takes to be the best in herself or the universe. That meaning at a minimum seems present here in the *Īśā*.
5 In *Savitri*, in the section entitled, "The Entry into the Inner Countries," Aurobindo uses "Fire burning on the bare stone" as a symbol of the ensoulment of matter: "There in the silence few have ever reached,/Thou shalt see the Fire burning on the bare stone/And the deep cavern of thy secret soul" (*SABCL*v. 28: 501).
6 Freud 1926/1961: *The Future of an Illusion.*
7 Kant 1788/1956, *Critique of Practical Reason.*
8 I argue this in "Ethical Skepticism in the Philosophy of Sri Aurobindo" (2006).
9 Compare the lines from Rimbaud, "Ô saisons, ô châteaux": "Ah! je n'aurai plus d'envie:/ Il ce chargé de ma vie./ Ce charme a pris âme et corps/ Et dispersé les efforts."
10 In *Essays on the Gita*, which is a compilation of essays written for a monthly journal that do not neatly correspond to the chapter divisions of the *Gītā*, Aurobindo devotes the essay entitled, "The Theory of the Vibhuti," to a meliorist interpretation of, it seems, *Gītā* chapter 10, in particular where Kṛṣṇa identifies the "Divine" as the best exemplar of a category, the Himalayas of mountain ranges, for example. The general point is that the Divine is identified with excellence. Other *Gītā* verses express similar ideas, *Gītā* 7.10–11, for instance, where Kṛṣṇa says he is the strength of the strong and the intelligence of the wise. Aurobindo seems to look upon the *vibhūti*s listed in the *Gītā* as symbolic of a psychecized life (*SABCL* v.13: 363–73).
11 *Letters on Yoga 1*, *SABCL* v. 22: 473.

Appendix A

1 Sri Aurobindo Birth Centenary Library (*SABCL*), v. 12: 63–8.
2 Euphonic combination of Sanskrit letters between words is like "com'ere" in English meaning "come here." To read the Sanskrit sentences, breaking this so-called *sandhi* ("combination") is necessary, but to chant or read a verse as poetry with meter, etc., *sandhi* must be in place. In the Sanskrit grammarian literature, there is a long list of rules governing *sandhi*.

3 For the editions used, see the first footnote of Appendix B. The punctation here follows Śaṅkara's reading, Aurobindo's, too, as opposed to the Granthāvalī edition which puts the *daṇḍa* (period) before *tejas*.
4 This punctation follows Śaṅkara's reading as opposed to the Granthāvalī edition which puts the *daṇḍa* after *samūha*.

Appendix B

1 The Granthāvalī edition (Śaṅkara 1964, 1979), which is reproduced here with a few exceptions, has *loka-buddhi-siddhaṃ karmāṇi vihitāni*. Most of the variants with respect to the Kāṇva recension transcribed on the GRETIL website: http://gretil.sub.uni-goettingen.de/gretil.html are minor, like this one, and, unlike this one, will not be marked. The punctuation in the two editions, however, is often different, and invariably I follow the Granthāvalī editor in that regard, that is, in the transliteration though not invariably in the English renderings where paragraph breaks are sometimes added.
2 The GRETIL website has *svābhāvikam ajñānaṃ nivartayantaḥ*, "making our native ignorance cease."
3 The GRETIL edition adds *svena* to read *svena paramâtmanā*.
4 The GRETIL edition adds: *nivṛtti-mārgeṇa eṣaṇā atra yasya tyāgaḥ*.
5 This seems to be reference to Śaṅkara's opening statement above, his *avatāra* to the Upaniṣad as a whole: "And that the teaching about the self stands opposed to a doctrine of works is the only view that fits." But it could be a reference to his commentary on the *Bṛhadāraṇyaka Upaniṣad* which often sounds the theme according to Śaṅkara's reading.
6 *Taittirīya Upaniṣad* 2.8.1.
7 *Bṛhadāraṇyaka Upaniṣad* 3.4.1.
8 *Bṛhadāraṇyaka Upaniṣad* 4.5.13.
9 *Bṛhadāraṇyaka Upaniṣad* 3.8.11.
10 *Bṛhadāraṇyaka Upaniṣad* 1.4.17.
11 *Bṛhadāraṇyaka Upaniṣad* 1.4.17.
12 *Bṛhadāraṇyaka Upaniṣad* 4.4.22.
13 *Śvetāśvatara Upaniṣad* 6.21.
14 *Bṛhadāraṇyaka Upaniṣad* 1.5.16.
15 *Bṛhadāraṇyaka Upaniṣad* 1.5.16.
16 *Bṛhadāraṇyaka Upaniṣad* 1.5.16.
17 The explanation supplied by the editor, p. 8, slightly elaborated, runs as follows. The seven kinds of "fruition" mentioned by Śaṅkara amount to distinct kinds of food and corresponding bodies for (1) animals, (2) humans, (3) and (4) gods/goddesses, two

kinds, then (5) mind, (6) speech, and (7) breath ("vital energy," *prāṇa*) for the self as an individual.

18 *Bṛhadāraṇyaka Upaniṣad* 1.5.16.

19 *Bṛhadāraṇyaka Upaniṣad* 1.5.16.

20 It is common in Sanskrit to elide an initial letter *a*, which at the beginning of a compound means "not" or "non-," and Śaṅkara's amending the text to conform to his reading is not as outrageous as it may seem.

21 *Bṛhadāraṇyaka Upaniṣad* 5.5.2.

22 This punctation follows Śaṅkara's reading as opposed to the Granthāvalī edition (p. 11) which puts the *daṇḍa* after *samūha*.

23 *Kaṭha Upaniṣad* 2.4.

24 In Sanskrit, the word *sāvitṛ* spans the fourth foot of the meter, *gāyatrī*, for which the famous mantra is named. But why is it that the *fourth* foot is singled out by Śaṅkara? At least part of the answer is that the immediately preceding section of the *Bṛhadāraṇyaka* (not of the *Īśā*) is about the Gāyatrī mantra. There may also be an allusion to the *Māṇḍūkya Upaniṣad* which has spiritual knowledge as the fourth state of the self, beyond waking, dreaming, and deep sleep.

Bibliography

Abhinava (Abhinavagupta). See Mueller-Ortega 2000: "Abhinava's *Anubhava-nivedana-stotra*, 'The Song of Praise Intended to Communicate the Direct Experience of the Absolute.'"

Abhinava (Abhinavagupta). See Gnoli 1968. *The Aesthetic Experience According to Abhinava Gupta*.

Abhinava (Abhinavagupta). See Pandey 1963. *Abhinavagupta*.

Abhinava (Abhinavagupta). See Sharma 1983. *Abhinavagupta: Gītārthasaṅgraha*.

Abhinava (Abhinavagupta). See Silburn 1970. *Hymnes de Abhinava*.

Acharya, Narayan Ram, ed. 1986. *Naiṣadhacarita of Śrīharṣa*. New Delhi: Nārāyaṇa Bedarakara.

Alston, William. 1991. *Perceiving God: The Epistemology of Religious Experience*. Ithaca, New York: Cornell University Press.

Arberry, Arthur, tr. 1951. *Avicenna on Theology*. London: J. Murray.

Aurobindo, Sri (Arabinda Ghose). 1914–19, rev. ed. 1951/1973. *The Life Divine. Sri Aurobindo Birth Centenary Library* (*SABCL*) v. 18 and 19. Pondicherry: Sri Aurobindo Ashram Trust.

Aurobindo, Sri (Arabinda Ghose). 1914–21, rev. ed. 1951/1973. *The Synthesis of Yoga*. *SABCL* v. 20 and 21. Pondicherry: Sri Aurobindo Ashram Trust.

Aurobindo, Sri (Arabinda Ghose). 1916–20, rev. ed. 1922/1973. *Essays on the Gita*. v. 13. Pondicherry: Sri Aurobindo Ashram Trust.

Aurobindo, Sri (Arabinda Ghose). 1917–1920, rev. ed. 1953/1973. *The Future Poetry*. *SABCL* v. 9. Pondicherry: Sri Aurobindo Ashram Trust.

Aurobindo, Sri (Arabinda Ghose). 1951/1973. *Savitri*. *SABCL* v. 28 and 29. Pondicherry: Sri Aurobindo Ashram Trust.

Aurobindo, Sri (Arabinda Ghose). 1973. *Letters on Yoga 1*. *SABCL* v. 22. Pondicherry: Sri Aurobindo Ashram Trust.

Aurobindo, Sri (Arabinda Ghose). 1973. *The Upanishads*. *SABCL* v. 12. Pondicherry: Sri Aurobindo Ashram Trust (see note 13 of Chapter 1, on Aurobindo's *Īśā* translation).

Aurobindo, Sri (Arabinda Ghose). 1987. *Śrī-aravindôpaniṣad*. Pondicherry: Sri Aurobindo Ashram Trust.

Aurobindo, Sri (Arabinda Ghose). 1997. *Letters on Yoga 1*. *Collected Works of Sri Aurobindo* (*CWSA*) v. 28. Pondicherry: Sri Aurobindo Ashram Trust.

Aurobindo, Sri (Arabinda Ghose). 2001. *Record of Yoga*, 2 vols. Pondicherry: Sri Aurobindo Ashram Trust.

Aurobindo, Sri (Arabinda Ghose). 2001. *Kena and Other Upanishads.* Pondicherry: Sri Aurobindo Ashram Trust.

Avalon, Arthur (Woodroffe, John, q.v.), ed. 1965. *Kularnava Tantra.* Summarized by M.P. Pandit; Sanskrit text ed. by Taranatha Vidyaratha. Delhi: Motilal Banarsidass.

Bader, Jonathan. 1990. *Meditation in Śaṅkara's Vedānta.* New Delhi: Aditya Prakashan.

Banerji, Debashish. 2020. "Sri Aurobindo, Enlightenment, and the Bengal Renaissance." In Debidatta Aurobinda Mahapatra, ed., *The Philosophy of Sri Aurobindo.* London: Bloomsbury.

Bonevac, Daniel and Stephen Phillips, eds. 2009. *Introduction to World Philosophy.* New York: Oxford University Press.

Brown, W. Norman, tr. 1958. *The Saundaryalaharī or Flood of Beauty.* Cambridge: Harvard University Press.

Chan, Wing-Tsit, tr. 1963. *The Way of Lao Tzu (Tao-tê ching).* Indianapolis: Bobbs-Merrill.

Clooney, Francis X. 2000. "On the Style of Vedānta." In Ayon Maharaj, ed., *The Bloomsbury Research Handbook of Vedānta.* London: Bloomsbury.

Cohen, Signe. 2008. *Text and Authority in the Older Upaniṣads.* Leiden: Brill.

Cohen, Signe, ed. 2018. *The Upaniṣads: A Complete Guide.* New York: Routledge.

Comans, Michael. 2000. *The Method of Early Advaita Vedānta.* Delhi: Motilal Banarsidass.

Cornelissen, Mattjijs. 2008. "The Evolution of Consciousness in Sri Aurobindo's Cosmopsychology." In Helmut Wautischer, ed., *Ontology of Consciousness.* Cambridge, Massachusetts: M.I.T. Press.

Cowell, E.B. and A.E. Gough, tr. 1906. *Sarva-darśana-saṃgraha.* Varanasi: Chowkhamba Sanskrit Studies, vol. 10.

Dalal, Neil. 2020. "Contemplating Duality: The Method of *Nididhyāsana* in Śaṅkara's Advaita Vedānta." In Ayon Maharaj, ed., *The Bloomsbury Research Handbook of Vedānta.* London: Bloomsbury.

De Smet, Richard. 2013. *Understanding Śaṅkara,* ed. Ivo Coelo. Delhi: Motilal Banarsidass.

Deussen, Paul. 1912. *The System of the Vedānta,* tr. Charles Johnston. Chicago: Open Court.

Deussen 1966. *The Philosophy of the Upaniṣads,* tr. A.S. Geden. New York: Dover.

Deussen 1980. *Sixty Upaniṣads of the Veda.* 2 vols, tr. V.M. Bedekar and G.B. Palsule. Delhi: Motilal Banarsidass (originally published in German, 1883/1897).

Deutsch, Eliot. 1969. *Advaita Vedānta.* Honolulu: University Press of Hawaii.

Dharmarāja Adhvarin, *Vedānta-paribhāṣā.* See Suryanarayana Sastri.

Dickenson, Emily. 1968. *The Poetry of Emily Dickenson,* ed. Ruth Miller. Middletown, Connecticut: Wesleyan University Press.

Ducasse, C.J. 1951. *Nature, Mind, and Death.* La Salle, Illinois: Open Court.

Eliade, Mircea. 1973. *Yoga: Immortality and Freedom,* tr. W. Trask. Princeton, N.J.: Princeton University Press.

Eliade, Mircea. 1978 and 1982. *A History of Religious Ideas*, vols. 1 and 2, tr. W.R. Trask. Chicago: University of Chicago Press.

Eliot, T.S. 1928. *Selected Poems*. London: Faber & Faber.

Fales, Evin. 2001. "Do Mystics See God?" in *Contemporary Debates in the Philosophy of Religion*, Michael L. Peterson, ed. Oxford: Blackwell.

Filliozat, Pierre-Sylvain. 2000. *The Sanskrit Language: An Overview*, tr. T.K. Gopalan. Varanasi: Indica Books.

Fort, Andrew O. and Patricia Y. Mumme, eds. 1996. *Living Liberation in Hindu Thought*. Albany, New York: State University of New York.

Frankfurt, Harry G. 1971. "Freedom of the Will and the Concept of a Person." *Journal of Philosophy* 68.1: 5–20.

Freud, Sigmund. 1926/1961. *The Future of an Illusion*, tr. James Strachey. New York: Norton.

Gale, Richard M. 1991. *On the Nature and Existence of God*. Cambridge: Cambridge University Press.

Garfield, Jay. 1995. *The Fundamental Wisdom of the Middle Way: Nāgārjuna's Mūla-madhyamika-kārikā*. New York: Oxford University Press.

Gellman, Jerome. 1997. *Experience of God and the Rationality of Theistic Belief*. Ithaca: Cornell University Press.

Gerow, Edwin. 1994. "Abhinava's Aesthetics as a Speculative Paradigm." *Journal of the American Oriental Society* 114.2: 186–208.

Gerow, Edwin. 1971. *A Glossary of Indian Figures of Speech*. The Hague: Mouton.

Ghosal, Goutam. 2020. "Poetry at the Center of Human Knowledge." In Debidatta Aurobinda Mahapatra, ed., *The Philosophy of Sri Aurobindo*. London: Bloomsbury.

Gnoli, Raniero. 1968. *The Aesthetic Experience According to Abhinava Gupta*. Chowkhamba Sanskrit Studies vol. 62. Varanasi: Chowkhamba Sanskrit Series Office.

Gokhale, Dinkar Vishnu, ed. 1950. *The Bhagavad Gita with the Commentary of Shankaracharya*. Poona Oriental Series 1. Pune: Oriental Book Agency.

Gonda, Jan. 1959. *Four Studies in the Language of the Veda*. The Hague: Mouton.

Gonda, Jan. 1963. *The Vision of the Vedic Poets*. The Hague: Mouton.

Göttingen Register of Electronic Texts in Indian Languages (GRETIL) http://gretil.sub.uni-goettingen.de/gretil.html.

Grego, Richard. 2020. "Mapping Sri Aurobindo's Metaphysics of Consciousness onto Western Philosophies of Mind." In Debidatta Aurobinda Mahapatra, ed., *The Philosophy of Sri Aurobindo*. London: Bloomsbury.

Guha, Nirmalya, Matthew Dasti, and Stephen Phillips, tr. 2021. *God and the World's Arrangement: Readings in Vedānta and Nyāya Philosophy of Religion*. Indianapolis: Hackett.

Hacker, Paul. 1951. *Untersuchungen über Texte des frühen Advaitavada*. Wiesbaden: Franz Steiner.

Halbfass, Wilhelm. 1983. *Studies in Kumārila and Śaṅkara*. Reinbek: Inge Wezler.

Handiqui, Krishna Kanta, tr. 1965. *The Naiṣadhacarita of Śrīharṣa*. Pune: Deccan College.

Hartshorne, Charles. 1984. *Omnipotence and Other Theological Mistakes*. Albany, New York: State University of New York Press.

Heehs, Peter. 2008. *The Lives of Sri Aurobindo*. New York: Columbia University Press.

Hick, John. 1978. *Evil and the God of Love*. New York: Harper & Row.

Hirst, J.G. Suthren. 2005. *Śaṃkara's Advaita Vedānta: A Way of Teaching*. London: RoutledgeCurzon.

Hume, David. 1776. *Dialogues Concerning Natural Religion*.

Hume, Robert, tr. 1887/1831, 2nd ed./1971. *The Thirteen Principal Upanishads*. Oxford: Oxford University Press.

Ingalls, Daniel H.H. 1953. "Śaṅkara on the Question: Whose is *avidyā*?" *Philosophy East and West* 3:69–72.

Īśvarakṛṣṇa. See Virupakshananda 2003. *Sāṃkhya-Kārikā of Īśvarakṛṣṇa*.

Jacob, Colonel. 1891/1963. *A Concordance to the Principal Upanishads and Bhagavadgita*. Delhi: Motilal Banarsidass.

Jagadananda, Swami, ed. and tr. 1970. *Upadeśasāhasrī* (of Śaṅkara). Madras: Sri Ramakrishna Math.

James, William. 1902/1961. *The Varieties of Religious Experience*. New York: Penguin.

Jha, Ganganatha. 1911/1978. *The Prābhākara School of Pūrva Mīmāṃsā*. Delhi: Motilal Banarsidass.

Jha, Ganganatha. 1924/1967. *The Kāvyaprakāsha of Mammaṭa* (rev. ed.). Varanasi: Bharatiya Vidya Prakashan.

Jha, Ganganatha. 1942/1964. *Pūrva-mīmāṃsā in Its Sources*. Varanasi: Benaras Hindu University Press.

Jha, Ganganatha. 1986 (reprint). *The Khaṇḍana-khaṇḍa-khādya of Śrīharṣa* ("Sweetmeats of Refutation"). Delhi: Sri Satguru Publications.

Jha, Navikanta, ed. 1970. *Khaṇḍana-khaṇḍa-khādya by Śrīharṣa*. Kashi Sanskrit Series 197. Varanasi: Chowkhamba.

Jones, Richard H. 1981. "Vidyā and Avidyā in the Īśā Upaniṣad." *Philosophy East and West* 31.1:79–87.

Kant, Immanuel. *Critique of Practical Reason* (1788), tr. Norman Kemp Smith. 1956. New York: St. Martin's Press.

Kapali-Sastry, T.V. 1952. *Rig-Bhashya Bhumika*. Pondicherry: M.P. Pandit.

Karmakar, R.D., ed. and tr. 1959, 1962, and 1964. *Rāmānujaviracitaṃ Śrībhāṣyam*, 3 vols. Poona: University of Poona.

King, Richard. 1995. *Early Advaita Vedānta and Buddhism*. Albany: State University if New York Press.

Leggett, Trevor, tr. 1981. *Śaṅkara on the Yoga-sūtrā-s: The Vivaraṇa Sub-commentary to Vyāsa-bhāṣya on the Yoga-sūtra-s of Pātañjali*. London: Routledge & Kegan Paul.

Leibniz, Gottfried Wilhelm. 1710. *Théodicée*.

Lindtner, Christian. 1986. *Nagarjuniana*. Delhi: Motilal Banarsidass.

Magnone, Paolo. 2012. "*Aho kauśalam apūrvam*: Hermeneutical Wrigglings about the *Īśopaniṣad*." In Piotr Balcerowicz, ed. *World View and Theory in Indian Philosophy*. Delhi: Manohar.

Mahadevan, T.M.P. 1969. *The Philosophy of Beauty*. Bombay: Bharatiya Vidya Bhavan.

Mahadevan, T.M.P. 1980. *The Hymns of Śaṅkara*. Delhi: Motilal Banarsidass.

Mahapatra, Debidatta Aurobinda, ed. 2020. *The Philosophy of Sri Aurobindo*. London: Bloomsbury.

Maharaj, Ayon (see also Medhananda, Swami). 2018. *Infinite Paths to Infinite Reality: Sri Ramakrishna and Cross-cultural Philosophy of Religion*. New York: Oxford University Press.

Maharaj, Ayon. 2020. "Seeing Oneness Everywhere: Sri Aurobindo's Mystico-Immanent Interpretation of the Īśā Upaniṣad." In Ayon Maharaj, ed., *The Bloomsbury Research Handbook of Vedānta*. London: Bloomsbury.

Malkovsky, Bradley J. 2001. *The Role of Divine Grace in the Soteriology of Śaṅkarācārya*. Leiden: Brill.

Marcaurelle, Roger. 2000. *Freedom Through Inner Renunciation: Śaṅkara's Philosophy in a New Light*. Albany: State University of New York Press.

Mammaṭa. See Jha, Ganganatha. 1924/1967: *The Kāvyaprakāsha of Mammaṭa*.

Mayeda, Sengaku. 1973/2006. *Śaṅkara's Upadeśasāhasrī*. Vol. 1. Delhi: Motilal Banarsidass.

Mayeda, Sengaku. 1979/1992. *A Thousand Teachings: The Upadeśasāhasrī of Śaṅkara*. Tokyo: University of Tokyo Press.

Medhananda, Swami (see also Ayon Maharaj). 2021a. "Why Sri Aurobindo's Hermeneutics Still Matters: Philology and the Transformative Power of Scripture," *Religions* 12.484: 1–14.

Medhananda, Swami (see also Ayon Maharaj). 2021b. "'A Great Adventure of the Soul': Sri Aurobindo's Theodicy of Spiritual Evolution." *International Journal of Hindu Studies* 25:1–29.

Medhananda, Swami (see also Ayon Maharaj). 2021c. "Cutting the Knot of the World Problem: Sri Aurobindo's Experiential and Philosophical Critique of Advaita Vedānta." *Religions* 12.9: 1–21.

Medhananda, Swami (see also Ayon Maharaj). 2022. "The Playful Self-Involution of Divine Consciousness: Sri Aurobindo's Evolutionary Cosmopsychism and His Response to the Individuation Problem." *The Monist* 105: 92–109.

Misra, Sri Narayana, ed. 1971. *Pātañjalayogadarśana* (with Vyāsa's *Bhāṣya*, Vācaspati Miśra's *Tattva-Vaiśāradi* and Vijñānabhikṣu's *Yoga-Vārttikā*). Varanasi: Chowkhamba.

Monier-Williams, Monier. 1851. *Sanskrit-English Dictionary*. London: W.H. Allen.

Mueller-Ortega, Paul, tr. 2000. "Abhinava's *Anubhava-nivedana-stotra*, 'The Song of Praise Intended to Communicate the Direct Experience of the Absolute.'" In David White, ed. *Tantra in Practice*. Princeton: Princeton University Press.

Murty, K. Satchidananda. 1959/1974. *Reason and Revelation in Advaita Vedānta*. Delhi: Motilal Banarsidass.

Nāgārjuna. See Garfield 1995. *The Fundamental Wisdom of the Middle Way: Nāgārjuna's Mūla-madhyamika-kārikā*.

Nāgārjuna. See Lindtner 1986. *Nagarjuniana*.

Nāgārjuna. See Westerhoff 2010. *Nāgārjuna's Vigrahavyāvartanī: Translation and Commentary.*

Nakamura, Hajime. 1983. *A History of Early Vedānta Philosophy.* Part One. Trevor Leggett, Sengaku Mayeda, Taitetz Unno, and others, tr. Delhi: Motilal Banarsidass.

Nakamura, Hajime. 2004. *A History of Early Vedānta Philosophy.* Part Two. Hajime Nakamura, Trevor Leggett, and others, tr. Delhi: Motilal Banarsidass.

Nozick, Robert. *Philosophical Explanations.* Cambridge: Harvard University Press.

Pande, Govind Chandra. 1994. *Life and Thought of Śaṅkarācārya.* Delhi: Motilal Banarsidass.

Pandey, K.C. 1963. *Abhinavagupta*, rev. ed. Varanasi: Chowkhamba.

Patañjali: See Misra 1971. *Pātañjalayogadarśana.*

Phillips, Stephen. 1986. *Aurobindo's Philosophy of Brahman.* Leiden: Brill.

Phillips, Stephen. 1987. "Padmapāda's Illusion Argument." *Philosophy East and West* 37.1: 3–23.

Phillips, Stephen. 1988. "Mysticism and Metaphor." *International Journal for Philosophy of Religion* 23.1: 17–41.

Phillips, Stephen. 1995. *Classical Indian Metaphysics.* Chicago: Open Court.

Phillips, Stephen. 1999. "Theoretic Minimalism Among (Advaita Vedānta) Defenders of the 'Self-Illumining Consciousness' Thesis." Eastern Division of the American Philosophical Association, Boston.

Phillips, Stephen. 2002. "The Mind-Body Problem in Three Indian Philosophies, Śaṅkara's Advaita Vedānta, Gaṅgeśa's Navya Nyāya, and Aurobindo's Theistic Monism." *Proceedings of the International Conference on Mind and Consciousness.* Kharagpur, West Bengal: Indian Institute of Technology.

Phillips, Stephen. 2006. "Ethical Skepticism in the Philosophy of Sri Aurobindo." In Purushottama Bilimoria, Joseph Prabhu, and Renuka Sharma, eds., *Indian Ethics: Classical Traditions and Contemporary Challenges.* Aldershot: Ashgate.

Phillips, Stephen. 2008/2016. "God's Last World: Sri Aurobindo's Argument for Divine Life." *Jadavpur Journal of Philosophy* 18.2: 1–12. Reprinted in *Essays on Sri Aurobindo*, ed. Aparajita Mukhopadhyay. Kolkata: Centre for Sri Aurobindo Studies, Jadavpur University.

Phillips, Stephen. 2009. *Yoga, Karma, and Rebirth: A Brief History and Philosophy.* New York: Columbia University Press.

Potter, Karl H. 1981. *Advaita Vedānta up to Śaṅkara and His Pupils: Encyclopedia of Indian Philosophies*, vol. 3. Delhi: Motilal Banarsidass.

Priest, Graham. 2002. *Beyond the Limits of Thought.* Oxford: Clarendon.

Priest, Graham and Jay Garfield. 2002. "Nāgārjuna and the Limits of Thought." In Graham Priest, *Beyond the Limits of Thought.* Oxford: Clarendon.

Radhakrishnan, Sarvepalli. 1923/1956. *Indian Philosophy*, 2 vols. London: G. Allen & Unwin.

Radhakrishnan, Sarvepalli. 1953. *The Principal Upanishads.* London: G. Allen & Unwin.

Rāmānuja. See Karmakar 1959, 1962, and 1964. *Rāmānujaviracitaṃ Śrībhāṣyam*, 3 vols.

Rāmānuja. See Thibaut 1904: *Vedanta Sutras with Ramanuja's Commentary.*
Rambachan, Anantanand. 2006. *The Advaita Worldview.* Albany: State University of New York Press.
Rimbaud, Jean-Arthur. 1943. *Oeuvres de Jean-Arthur Rimbaud.* Montréal: Éditions Bernard Valiquette.
Ram-Prasad, Chakravarthi. 2001. *Knowledge and Liberation in Classical Indian Thought.* New York: Palgrave.
Ram-Prasad, Chakravarthi. 2002. *Advaita Epistemology and Metaphysics.* London: RoutledgeCurzon.
Ram-Prasad, Chakravarthi. 2013. *Divine Self, Human Self: The Philosophy of Being in Two Gītā Commentaries.* London: Bloomsbury.
Ranade, R.D. 1926/1968. *A Constructive Survey of Upanishadic Philosophy.* Bombay: Bharatiya Vidya Bhavan.
Rau, Srinivasa. 1985. *Advaita: A Critical Investigation.* Bangalore: The Indian Philosophy Foundation.
Renou, Louis. 1953. "Étude Védiques: *Yoga.*" *Journal Asiatique* 241.1: 177–80.
Renou, Louis. 1953/1968. *Religions of Ancient India.* New York: Schocken.
Renou, Louis. 1956. *Hymnes Spéculatif du Véda.* Paris: Gallimard.
Roebuck, Valerie. 2003. *The Upanisads.* New York: Penguin Books.
Rukmani, T.S. 2001. *Yogasūtrabhāṣyavivaraṇa of Śaṅkara.* Vol. I. New Delhi: Munshiram Manoharlal.
Śaṅkara. 1964. *Ten Principal Upanishads* (with the commentary of Śaṅkara). Delhi: Motilal Banarsidass (Granthāvalī edition, no editor listed).
Śaṅkara. See Gokhale 1950: *The Bhagavad Gita with the Commentary of Shankaracharya.*
Śaṅkara. See Jagadananda 1970: *Upadeśasāhasrī* (of Śaṅkara).
Śaṅkara. See Mahadevan 1980: *The Hymns of Śaṅkara.*
Śaṅkara. See Mayeda 1973/2006. *Śaṅkara's Upadeśasāhasrī.* Vol. 1.
Śaṅkara. See Mayeda 1979/1992. *A Thousand Teachings: The Upadeśasāhasrī of Śaṅkara.*
Śaṅkara. See Shastri. 1980: *Brahmasūtra-Śāṅkarabhāṣyam.*
Śaṅkara. See Thibaut. 1962. *The Vedanta Sutras of Badarayana.* With Shankara's commentary.
Sastri, S. Subramanya and T.R. Srinivasa Ayyangar, tr. 1937. *Saundarya-Laharī,* "The Ocean of Beauty." Chennai: Theosophical Publishing House.
Satyananda Saraswati, Swami. 1989. *A Systematic Course in the Ancient Tantric Techniques of Yoga and Kriyā,* 2nd ed. Munger: Bihar School of Yoga.
Scharf, Peter M. 2020. "Creation Mythology and Enlightenment in Sanskrit Literature." *Journal of Indian Philosophy* 48: 751–66.
Sharma, Arvind, tr. 1983. *Abhinavagupta: Gītārthasaṅgraha.* Leiden: Brill.
Sharma, Arvind. 2004. *Sleep as a State of Consciousness in Advaita Vedānta.* Albany: State University of New York Press.
Shastri, J.L., ed. 1970. *Upaniṣat-Saṃgrahaḥ.* Delhi: Motilal Banarsidass.

Shastri, J.L. 1980. *Brahmasūtra-Śāṅkarabhāṣyam* (with the Commentaries *Bhāṣyaratnaprabhā* of Govindānanda, *Bhāmatī* of Vācaspatimiśra, *Nyāyanirṇaya* of Ānandagiri). Delhi: Motilal Banarsidass.

Silburn, Lilian. 1970. *Hymnes de Abhinava*. Paris: Institut de Civilisation Indienne.

Sivaramkrishna, M. and Sumita Roy. 1996. *Poet-Saints of India*. New Delhi: Sterling Publishers.

Śrīharṣa. See Acarya 1986: *Naiṣadhacarita of Śrīharṣa*.

Śrīharṣa. See Jha, Ganganatha 1986 (reprint). *The Khaṇḍana-khaṇḍa-khādya of Śrīharṣa*.

Śrīharṣa. See Jha, Navikanta 1970. *Khaṇḍana-khaṇḍa-khādya by Śrīharṣa*.

Stace, Walter T. 1961. *Mysticism and Philosophy*. London: Macmillan.

Suryanarayana Sastri, S.S., ed. and tr. 1971. Dharmarāja Adhvarin, *Vedāntaparibhāṣā*. The Adyar Library Series 34. Madras: The Adya Library and Research Centre.

Swinburne, Richard. 2001. *Epistemic Justification*. Oxford: Clarendon.

Swinburne, Richard. 2004. *The Existence of God*. Oxford: Clarendon.

Taves, Ann. 2009. *Religious Experience Reconsidered*. Princeton: Princeton University Press.

Tagare, G.V., tr. 1978. *Bhāgavata Purāṇa*. 4 vols. Delhi: Motilal Banarsidass.

Thibaut, Georg, tr. 1904. *Vedanta Sutras with Ramanuja's Commentary*. Vol. 48 of *The Sacred Books of the East*, ed. M. Mueller. Oxford: Oxford University Press.

Thibaut, Georg, tr. 1962. *The Vedanta Sutras of Badarayana*. With Shankara's commentary. New York: Dover (first published as vol. 34 and 35, *The Sacred Books of the East*, ed. M. Mueller, 1890 and 1896).

Thieme, Paul. 1965. "*Īśopaniṣad* (= Vājaseyani-Saṃhitā 40) 1–14." *Journal of the American Oriental Society* 85.1: 89–99.

Thrasher, Allen Wright. 1993. *The Advaita Vedānta of Brahma-siddhi*. Delhi: Motilal Banarsidass.

Tripurari, Swami B.V. 1996. *Aesthetic Vedānta: The Sacred Path of Passionate Love*. Eugene, Oregon: Mandala.

Vācapati(miśra). See Misra, Sri Narayana 1971. *Pātañjalayogadarśana* (with Vyāsa's *Bhāṣya*, Vācaspati Miśra's *Tattva-Vaiśāradi* and Vijñānabhikṣu's *Yoga-Vārttikā*).

Vācapati(miśra). See Shasti 1980. *Brahmasūtra-Śāṅkarabhāṣyam* (with the Commentaries *Bhāṣyaratnaprabhā* of Govindānanda, *Bhāmatī* of Vācaspatimiśra, *Nyāyanirṇaya* of Ānandagiri).

Vācapati(miśra). See Virupakshananda. 2003. *Sāṃkhya-Kārikā of Īśvarakṛṣṇa* (with the *Tatta-Kaumudī* of Śrī Vācaspati Miśra).

Valiaveetil, Chacko. 1980. *Liberated Life*. Madurai: Arun Anandar College Dialogue Series.

Virupakshananda, Swami, ed. and tr. 2003. *Sāṃkhya-Kārikā of Īśvarakṛṣṇa* (with the *Tattva-Kaumudī* of Śrī Vācaspati Miśra). Chennai: Sri Ramakrishna Math.

Vivekananda, Swami. 1977. *The Complete Works of Swami Vivekananda*, 8 vols. Calcutta: Advaita Ashrama.

Voltaire. 1759. *Candide ou l'Optimisme*.

Webb, Mark Owen, 2015. *A Comparative Doxastic-Practice Epistemology of Religious Experience*. New York: Springer.

Wainwright, William J. 1981. *Mysticism: A Study of its Nature, Cognitive Value, and Moral* Implications. Madison: University of Wisconsin Press.

Wasson, R. Gordon. 1968. *Soma: Divine Mushroom of Immortality*. New York: Harcourt Brace Jovanovich.

Westerhoff, Jan. 2010. *Nāgārjuna's Vigrahavyāvartanī: Translation and Commentary*. Oxford: Oxford University Press.

Wettstein, Howard. 2012. *The Significance of Religious Experience*. New York: Oxford University Press.

Whicher, Ian. 1998. *The Integrity of the Yoga Darśana*. Albany, New York: State University of New York Press.

Whitehead, Alfred North. 1929/1969. *Process and Reality*. New York: Macmillan.

Whitman, Walt. 1855. *Leaves of Grass*.

Wittgenstein, Ludwig. 1951. *Philosophical Investigations*, tr. G.E.M. Anscomb. New York: Macmillan.

Woodroffe, John (Avalon, Arthur, q.v.). 1913/1969. *Śakti and Śakta*. Madras: Ganesh.

Woodroffe, John (Avalon, Arthur, q.v.). 1928. *The Serpent Power*, 3rd ed. Madras: Ganesh.

Vyāsa. See Misra 1971. *Pātañjalayogadarśana* (with Vyāsa's *Bhāṣya*, Vācaspati Miśra's *Tattva-Vaiśāradi* and Vijñānabhikṣu's *Yoga-Vārttikā*).

Yandell, Keith. 1993. *The Epistemology of Religious Experience*. New York: Cambridge University Press.

Yeats, W.B. 1938. *The Collected Poems of W.B. Yeats*. New York: Macmillan.

Index

Pages followed by "n" refer to notes in the text.

ābhāsa (appearance) 26, 27, 48, 54, 62, 99, 138–9, 201n4
abhimāna (self and identity) 2, 5, 66, 74, 101–2, 198n14; Brahman and 8–10, 105; disidentification 12; experiential deficiency 27; false 88; individual 44, 47; self-knowledge 39; yogic practice 10
Abhinava Gupta, 35, 103, 105
Absolute, the *see* Brahman
ācāryāḥ (teachers) 11, 148, 159, 193n16
action 9–11; *see also karma*
actual entity 38, 71
adharma (unrighteousness) 144, 152, 172
adṛṣṭa (unseen force) 132
Advaita Vedānta 6, 11, 15, 20, 42, 47, 85; emanationist theism 85; metaphysics 15; nirvana and 89; promoting self-discovery 35; self-awareness in 61; subschools 66, 70; tantric 85; transmigratory realm 45; Upaniṣadic vidyā 11; Vedānta 15, 20, 47
aesthetics 4, 64; delight 103, 207n18; excellence of verse 15 100; heightened imagery 79; justification 114; turn 103; unity 97
agni (fire) 102–3, 112, 118, 135–6, 155
aham ('I') 74, 106, 162
ahiṃsā (non-injury) 21, 39, 61, 86, 109, 118
Aitareya Upaniṣad 18
Alighieri, D. 115
Alston, W. *Perceiving God* 59
anāhata cakra (heart chakra, heart center) 94, 103
ānanda (supreme worth/bliss) 27, 56, 60, 64, 74, 79–80, 88, 91, 103, 110, 113–14, 116, 118
Ānandagiri 16, 24
anātman (no-self) 10
anavasthā (no stopping place) 77
anirvacanīya (inexplicability) 6, 42, 69, 78, 201n1
antar-yāmin (inner controller) 74
anubhava (experience) 52, 69, 76
apperception 61
Aristotle 72, 74, 116
The Arya (Aurobindo) 24
āsana 165
asocial instincts 1
aspiration 9, 39; and surrender 107–19
āśrama (hermitage) 38
Atharva Veda 17
ātman (self or Self) 1–4, 6, 8, 10, 30, 32, 35, 42, 68, 78, 81–95, 108, 110, 132, 144, 162, 166, 168, 215n4
atomism 73, 204n15
Aurobindo, Sri (Arabinda Ghose) 4–5, 17, 22, 30, 41–2, 48–9, 53–5, 62, 67, 80, 82, 89, 97, 107, 123, 126, 214n18; *Collected Works of Sri Aurobindo* (*CWSA*) 197n13; *The Arya* 24; biography of 23; on birth and non-birth 127; cosmic consciousness 44; *Essays on the Gita* 119, 215n10; on fire 129; *The Future Poetry* 214n18; on habitation by the Lord 122; on immortal life 129; integral yoga 83; *Karmayogin* 198n2; knowledge by identity 62; *The Life Divine* 14, 22, 24–5, 33–4, 43, 45, 48–9, 62, 68, 70, 78, 84, 89, 92, 198n5, 201n4, 209n19, 213n14; meliorist theory 117; as neo-Vedāntic author 23; on nirvana 65; psychic element in 118; Śaṅkara *vs.* 14–16; *Savitri* 22, 24, 34–5, 119, 211n8, 214n18; on self-being 124; on self in existences 124–5; separative knowledge 62; *Sri Aurobindo Birth Centenary Library* ("*SABCL*") 197n13; *The Synthesis of Yoga* 22, 24, 35, 83, 111,

116, 119, 200n11; tantric teachings of 35, 83, 93–4, 103; theodicy of 114; *Thoughts and Aphorisms* 83, 199n8; on true individual 90; on truth 128; yogic teachings of 11, 14, 35, 50, 89, 117
Sri Aurobindo Birth Centenary Library ("*SABCL*") 197n13
Austin, J. L. 98
avidyā (spiritual ignorance) 14, 31, 44–5, 48, 63, 76–8, 81, 125, 137–8, 144, 147–8, 158–9, 172, 194n22, 207; Aurobindo views on 81; Brahman's relation to 69; inequality 174; nature and 150; in Śaṅkara's usage 14; spiritual knowledge and 148; *see also vidyā*

Bādarāyaṇa 175; *see also Brahma-sūtra*
Basu, A. 35
beauty 84, 88, 104, 116, 118
belief 4, 27, 57–8, 60, 194n21, 199n7, 205n7
Bhagavad Gītā 6–7, 14, 20, 34, 36–7, 57, 88, 108, 117–18, 132, 173, 193n15, 197n10, 199n6, 204n3; Brahman's power of "self-delimitation" 43; *karma-yoga* 27, 109; mystic knowledge 21; *seśvarasāṃkhya* 26; Veda-mongers condemned in 20; yoga of action 21, 100, 109, 166–9; yoga of meditation 61, 165–6
Bhāgavata Purāṇa 117–18
bhakti (devotion) 7, 101, 103, 110–11, 117–18, 192n9
Bhattacharya, K.C. 22
bliss *see ānanda*
body(ies): causal 144; limitation of 155; mind and 26, 32; physical 42, 94, 111, 144; subtle 9, 32–3, 108, 111, 144, 155
Bradley problem, the 61, 204n15, 206n13
Brahmā 139
Brahman (God, the Absolute, the One) 2, 5–6, 20, 27, 33, 42, 43–4, 50, 69, 70, 91, 155, 202n5, 203n13; changeless 140; desire and 114; meditating on Hiraṇyagarbha 87; motionless 44, 139; omnipresence of 88; psychic being 33; Upaniṣadic view 91; views of in relation to the world (*pariṇāma* and *vivarta*) 70; *see also* Infinite, logic of the
brahma-sākṣātkāra 63, 87
Brahma-sūtra 6, 11–12, 18, 20, 22, 73–5, 85, 171–4, 191n6, 192n11, 195n23, 197n9; Vedāntic metaphysics and 7–9
Bṛhadāraṇyaka Upaniṣad 14, 21, 34, 38, 55, 56, 68, 69, 78, 85, 86, 97, 102, 104, 107–8, 134, 144, 147–8, 153, 195n25, 196n3, 200n12, 201n3, 204n3, 206n12, 208n2
Brown, W. N. 210n2–3
Buddha 3, 34
buddhi (intelligence) 3, 166, 169
Buddhism 9, 10, 19, 27, 36, 57, 65, 77, 83–7, 115, 215n4; Bodhisattva 3, 34, 88–9; Mahāyāna Buddhism 10, 14, 34, 51, 63, 192n7; *tathā-gata-garbha* 10; Yogācāra 57, 201n3
buddhi-yoga (intellectual yoga) 3, 7–8, 191n5

Caitanya 103
caitya-puruṣa (psychic being) 9
causality 46, 72, 210n19; causal closure 203n15
chakras (*cakras*) 85, 94, 119
Chāndogya Upaniṣad 18, 56, 69, 72–3, 78, 102
cit (consciousness) 27, 79
citi-śakti (power of consciousness) 105
classical Indian philosophic schools 12, 18, 38, 57–8, 73–4, 84, 203n13; *see also* Mīmāṃsā, Nyāya, Sāṃkhya, Yogācāra
Clooney, F. 191n6
compassion 10, 60–1, 76, 80, 172, 193n16, 203n12
Confucius 116
consciousness 205n6, 211n6; block of 47; cosmic 44; discipline 4, 7, 17; dualism of 7, 26; immediacy of 44, 91, 206n16; Mahāyāna Buddhist *bodhi* 192n7; meditation and 3; non-duality of 56, 61; occult centers of 85; from physical and mental reality 5; power of 105; of self 56; spheres of embodiment 93; surface 38; transformations of 2, 149; *see also cit*; self-illumining consciousness
contradiction *see virodha*

Copernican hypothesis 211n6
cosmopsychism 3, 5, 84
creation (*sarga*, "emanation") 75, 113, 173; action and 171; Brahman 46; stories 8, 68; uneven 172; of world 69, 72; *see also* emanationism
creativity 37, 38, 103, 116, 118

Dalal, N. 193n17
Dao/Daoism 42
Dasti, M. 198n4; *God and the World's Arrangement* 171, 198n4
delight *see ānanda*
desire 193n16; action and 21; born of intentions 166; emanating from Brahman 27; for liberation 9, 39; to live a hundred years 40, 135; natural 83, 114; for nirvana 118; for personal continuity 115; renunciation of 85, 86, 99, 146; second-order 113; self-interest and 113; for wealth 27
Deussen, P. 31
devotion *see bhakti*
dharma (righteousness) 27, 98, 100, 127, 136, 144, 154, 156, 161, 172; dharmic yoga (right action) 39
dhyāna (concentration, meditation) 89
dhyāna-yoga 61
disidentification 5, 12, 26
disposition, mental *see saṃskāra*
divinities 3, 83; knowledge of 85–6, 147, 149; of sensation and action 107; Vedāntic 85
dualism 198n14; of consciousness and nature 7, 26; phenomenological 6
duty 20–1; *see also dharma*
Dvaita Vedānta 110

earth 29, 50, 74, 104, 107, 133–4, 162, 199, 200n12, 211n6
egoism 10, 88, 92, 114, 115
ekāgratā (one-pointedness of mind) 44
Eliade, M. 214n2
emanationism 3, 5, 15, 26, 37, 44, 46, 51, 68, 91, 100, 108, 208n4, 211n4; *see also* creation (*sarga*, "emanation")
emotion 7, 32, 90, 94, 105, 110, 118, 213n13
epistemology 12, 18; analytic 58, 204n4; metaphysics and 19, 23; of mystical experience 54; of mysticism 54, 204n4; of yogic testimony 205n7
ethics 18, 23, 98–9
evil 6, 9; balance of good and 92; habits 37; instrumental value of 80; moral 112; nescience of matter 114; novel cosmology 78; on panentheist premises 32; sin and 163; theodicy and 112
existentialism 37, 103

Frankfurt, H. G. 113
Freud, S. 115

Gandhi, M. 22
Gauḍapāda 15–16, 19, 20, 24, 106, 196n7; *Kārikās* 15, 19, 24, 106, 195n27, 196n7
Gāyatrī mantra 97–8, 161, 217n24
Gītā see Bhagavad Gītā
God *see* Brahman; natural theology; theodicy
Gonda, J. *The Vision of the Vedic Poets* 102
Guha, N.: *God and the World's Arrangement* 171

habit *see* karma; *saṃskāra*
Hartshorne, C.: *Omnipotence and Other Theological Mistakes* 71
Haṭha-yoga-pradīpikā 193n14
Heehs, P. 24, 214n17–18
hermeneutic circle 89
Hick, John, *Evil and the God of Love* 208n12
Hinduism 2, 196n6
holism 42, 52, 204n16
Hume, D.: *Dialogues Concerning Natural Religion* 71, 113
Hume, R. 30–1, 108; *The Principal Upaniṣads* 25

I *see aham*
idealism 15
identity *see abhimāna;* disidentification
illusion 14, 22, 91; multiplicity 88; non-cognition theory of 205n5; perceptual 58, 201n1; transcendent 201n1
imagination 93, 139, 204n1

individuality 32, 34, 35, 88, 111, 141
individual self (or soul, *jivâtman*) 39, 106, 111, 133
inference 75–6
Infinite, logic of the 43, 45–6, 49, 56, 68, 79, 91
infinite regress 61, 74, 77, 204n15
integral knowledge 89
integral yoga 83, 89
integration 68; *see also* transformation
intention 23, 111, 155, 163, 166
intersubjectivity 58–9
Īśā Upaniṣad 1–2, 4–6, 10–11, 14, 15, 18, 21, 28, 30, 45, 78, 88, 199n7, 208n3; verse 1-3 29–40; verse 4-5 41–52; verse 6-7 53–66; verse 8 67–80; verse 9-14 81–95; verse 15 and 16 97–106; verse 17 and 18 107–19
Islam, surrender in 117
iṣṭa-devatā (preferred divinity) 104
īśvara (Lord) 26, 33, 36, 51, 72, 91, 144, 169, 171–2, 174; as all-knowing (*sarvajña*) 71, 75, 79; capable of creation (*sarva-śaktitva*) 75, 79

Jainism 36, 196n6
James, W. 58–9, 205n6
Janaka (King) 34, 38, 83, 167, 199n8
Jha, G. 213n13
jīvan-mukti 44

Kālī (Mahakali) 104
Kālidāsa 196n6; *Megha-dūta* 104
Kant, I. 115
karma 33, 36, 135, 173, 197n10, 200n12; ethical nature 36; freedom from 36; mental dispositions 174; psychological theory of 35; reincarnation and 38; theodicy 113
karma-yoga (yoga of action) 21, 25, 27, 37, 109, 110
Kashmiri Shaivism *see* Shaivism, Kashmiri
Kaṭha Upaniṣad 5, 11, 18
kavi (seer-poet) 101, 108
Kāvya-prakāśa ("Light on Poetry" by Mammaṭa) 213n13
Keats, J. 33
Kena Upaniṣad 10, 18
King, R. 14, 15
knowledge: of divinities 85; by identity 54, 56, 60–2, 206n14; intellectual 12, 79; meditation and 11–13; sources of (*pramāṇa*) 76–7; *see also vidyā*
kośa 93, 94, 108, 111, 189
Kṛṣṇa 7, 13n15, 36–7, 88, 101, 165–6, 173, 192n8, 213n15, 214n2, 215n10
Kulārṇava Tantra 105, 213n16
Kumārila 21, 212n5

Lakṣmī (Mahalakshmi) 104
Leibniz, G. W. 37, 92
liberation 9–11; *see also mukti*/*mokṣa*
life *see prāṇa*
līlā (play) 64, 114, 171
liṅga-śarīra (subtle body) 32
Lord *see īśvara*

Mahābhārata 6, 109
Mahadevan, T.M.P. 39, 192n9
Maharaj, A. 14, 32, 37, 54–5, 56, 59, 204n14
mahā-samādhi 101
mahā-vākya ("great statement") 12, 76
Mahāyāna Buddhism *see under* Buddhism
Maheśvarī (Pārvatī) 104
Malkovsky, B. J. 27
Maṇḍana 68, 201n1, 212n5
Māṇḍūkya Upaniṣad 11, 15, 18–19, 102, 106, 195n25
maṅgala-vācana (auspicious statement) 47
manomaya-kośa 94, 111, 163
mantra 48, 146, 156; peace 47; *Soham* 105; *see also* Gāyatrī, oṃ
mātariśvā 50, 123, 140
materialism 79, 89, 203n13
māyā 22, 43, 91, 201n4
Māyāvādins 28, 45
Mayeda, S. 13, 20, 98–9, 194n22
meditation 191n6, 194n17; deep 87; knowledge and 7, 11–13; metaphysics of 28, 117; poetic symbols and rhythms 2; Vedāntic 1–2, 99; yoga and 23, 118, 201n3
Megha-dūta (Kālidāsa) 104
metaphysics 2–4; Advaita 192n9; dualist 105; epistemology and 19, 23; of illusionism 25; of individuation 44; on

meditation 11, 28; revisionist 67; of self 10; Vedāntic/Vedānta 7–9, 89–90
Mīmāṃsā 19, 20, 21, 57, 58, 78, 205n5; motivation for 58; ritualists 82, 85; rituals of 7, 26, 99
Mīmāṃsā-sūtra 21
mind *see buddhi* (intelligence)
mind/body problem 203n13
mindfulness 39
monism: Brahman 52; existence 205n9; theism and 67, 70–1; Vedāntic 73, 110, 203n13, 205n9, 206n13, 208n7
moral payback 9
Mueller-Ortega, Paul 105
mukti/mokṣa (freedom) 9, 38, 40
mumukṣatva (desire for liberation) 9–10, 39, 193n16
Muṇḍaka Upaniṣad 11, 18, 212n9
mystical knowledge of unity 53–66; epistemology of 54
mystic object 2, 49, 59–60

Nāgārjuna 208n6, 211n3
Nakamura, H. 13, 19, 191n4, 195n24, 196n3
nāma-rūpa (name and form) 6, 43, 75, 141, 172
natural theology 3, 52, 67, 69, 72–3, 75
nature *see prakṛti*
negation 10, 13, 42; types of 12; *see also anirvacanīya*
neo-Vedānta *see under* Vedānta
Nietzsche, F. 103
nirvāṇa 10, 65, 89, 118, 165, 199n7
niṣṭhā (faith-stand) 83
nonharmfulness *see ahiṃsā*
nonviolence *see ahiṃsā*
no-self *see anātman*
Nozick, R. 48
Nyāya 9, 12, 19, 25, 56, 57, 58, 61, 73, 205n5, 205n7
Nyāya-sūtra 26, 36

occult, knowledge of the 81–95
occult forces (divinities) 83
oṃ 106, 121, 131, 155, 163, 203n12, 215n4
One, the *see* Brahman
overbeliefs 58–9

Padmapāda 15, 63, 206n16
pain: disteleological 208n12; pleasures and 36, 172, 174; suffering and 9, 71, 74, 92, 95, 113, 115, 117, 172; unending 92; *see also* pleasure and pain
Pande, G. C. 13, 22, 39, 84, 196n6, 210n3
Pandit, M. P. 213n16
panentheism 3, 25, 27, 84
pantheism 25
parama-puruṣârtha (supreme personal good) 6, 34, 60, 69, 72, 87, 99
pariṇāma 15, 70
parinirvāṇa 101
paryudāsa negation 12, 42
Patañjali: *Yoga-sūtra* 26
perception 3, 77, 205n5, 205n7, 206n14; value 57; yogic 8, 11, 50, 57–8, 89, 205n7
perceptual illusion *see* under illusion
phenomenology 2, 91, 102, 115; of self-discovery 22; yogic 14, 28
Phillips, S.: *Aurobindo's Philosophy of Brahman* 199n7; *Yoga, Karma, and Rebirth* 193n14, 194n18, 203n13, 204n16, 205n7
Plato 67, 73, 94
pleasure and pain 174, 194n20; *see also* pain
poetry 2, 4, 39, 69, 88, 99, 104, 193n14, 214n18
pradhāna ("primordial matter") 6, 75, 79; Sāṃkhya 5–6
Prakāśātman 15, 43
prakṛti (nature) 5–6, 26, 27, 105, 107
prakṛti-laya (for the mind) 87, 151–2
pralaya (cosmic dissolution) 77
pramāṇa (knowledge source) 57, 76
prāṇa (vital energies) 107, 161–2, 168
prapañca (cosmic becoming) 27, 115
Prapañca-sāra (The Quintessence of the World's Unrolling) 84
prasāda (grace) 100
prasajya negation 12
Praśna Upaniṣad 18
prasthāna-trāyi 7
pratītya-samutpāda ("interdependent origination") 51
pratyeka-buddha (solitary Buddha) 34

process philosophy 27, 71; *see also* Whitehead
psychecization 32, 33, 38, 39, 112, 115
psychic beings 32, 33, 38, 88, 113, 114, 116, 117–18
psychic entity 38
psychic personality 111
psychic transformation 102
puruṣa (consciousness) 5, 26
pūrva-pakṣa (prima facie positions) 51, 53, 84

Radhakrishnan, S. 13, 22, 23, 29, 30, 41, 47, 72, 73, 211n1, 212n3
Ramakrishna, Sri 104
Rāmānuja 12, 197n9
Ram-Prasad, C. 74, 198n14, 202n6
rasa 68, 103, 113, 116
realism 71, 206n13
reality: of Brahman 153–4; of mystic object 60; physical and mental 5; psychic 103; self-multiplication 48
rebirth *see* reincarnation
reincarnation (rebirth) 9, 34, 36–8, 83, 86, 88, 192n8, 194n20, 200n16
Renou, L. 102, 196n2, 212n10, 213n11
renunciation (*sannyāsa*) 29, 199n6; of desire 85–6, 99, 109, 114, 146
Ṛg Veda 8, 12, 14, 17, 55, 98, 108, 111, 193n13, 196n1, 196n2, 201n4, 212n10, 212n11
Roebuck, V. 196n3
Romanticism (Western) 33, 104, 199n7, 213n15
ṛṣi (rishi, seer/poet) 39, 67, 78, 97, 161, 167; *see also kavi*

Śabara 21
Sachchidananda/*sac-chid-ānanda* (existence-consciousness-bliss) 71, 79, 91, 95
sādhana (discipline) 4, 10, 83, 102, 117, 118
sahasra-dala (chakra above head) 94
sākṣi 103
śakti/shakti (power) 27, 46, 83, 94, 119
Śāktism 85, 103
śama-dama-dayā 10, 60, 61, 76
samādhi (yogic trance) 25–8, 60, 87, 205n8; *nirbīja* 87; *nirvikalpaka* 88
saṃkalpa see intention
Sāṃkhya 5–6, 8, 19, 26, 39, 79, 103, 118; *pradhāna* 5–6; "sattvacization" 39
Saṃkhya-kārikā 87, 151
sampradāya 3, 15, 19
saṃsāra 45, 200n17
saṃskāra 35–6, 77, 132
sandhi (euphonics) x, 215n2
Śaṅkara, Ādi 4–5, 8, 53, 107, 122–4, 126–7, 191n4, 193n17, 194n20; Aurobindo *vs.* 14–16; *avidyā* (spiritual ignorance) 137–8, 147–8, 150; *Brahma-sūtra-bhāṣya* 45–6, 48, 64, 68, 76, 192n11, 194n20, 201n2; *Bṛhadāraṇyaka Commentary* 58, 104–5, 159–63, 203n12, 204n3, 216n5; divinities 119; on energy (*tejas*) 128; on fire 129, 156–7; on *Īśā Upanisad* 131–59; knowledge and of action 161–3; knowledge of divinities 148; on mantras 132, 140–3; on the One is motionless 139–40; paths of knowledge and works 136–7; *Saundarya-laharī* (Torrent of Beauty) 84, 85, 93; "sees all beings" 141–2; on self 143–5; on self-slayers 32, 34, 137–9; on the Sun 154–5; tantra and 119; theodicy of 171–5; on true self 135; *Upadeśa-sāhasrī* (A Thousand Teachings) 4, 20, 22, 37, 85, 99, 193n15
Śāṅkara-gītā-bhāṣya 206n10
Sanskrit ix–x, 4, 20, 43, 112, 197n8, 198n1, 207n1, 217n24; classical 18, 84; grammarians 12; literature 8, 214n18
Sarasvatī (Mahasaraswati) 104
Saraswati, S.: *A Systematic Course in the Ancient Tantric Techniques* 105
sarvāṇi bhūtāni 66
sarva-śaktitva (full capability) 79
śāstra 19, 136, 147, 152, 158
sat (being) 27, 69, 73, 79
Śatapatha Brāhmaṇa 153
sattva (luminous intelligence, calm contentment) 118
sattvacization 39

satya (telling the truth) 109
Saundarya-laharī (Torrent of Beauty) 84, 85, 93
science 22, 34
scripture *see śruti*
self *see ātman*
self and identity *see abhimāna*
self-discovery 3, 4, 9, 10, 14, 22, 25, 27, 32, 34–5, 37, 49, 54, 55, 60–6, 81, 83, 97–106
self-ignorance *see avidyā*
self-illumining consciousness (*sva-prakāśamāna*) 42, 62–5
self-knowledge *see vidyā*
separative knowledge 62
seśvara-sāṃkhya (theistic Sāṃkhya) 26
sex 20, 27
Shaivism, Kashmiri 37, 39, 103
shakti (divine energy) *see śakti*
sheaths 93–4, 108; *see also kośa*
siddhānta 51, 194n19
siddhis (yogic powers) 83, 86–7
smṛti (sacred memory) 172–3
so'ham 105, 128, 153; *see also* mantra
soul *see jīvâtman* (individual self)
soul-making 33–4, 74, 92, 112, 208n12
spiritual ignorance *see avidyā*
Śrīharṣa 39, 61, 70, 204n15
śruti (scripture) 3, 6, 30, 55, 69, 110, 172–3
sublation 54, 56, 62–3, 65
subtle body 9, 32–3, 108, 111, 144, 155; *see also* body
sūkṣma-śarīra see subtle body
summum bonum 10; *see also parama-puruṣârtha*
śūnya-vāda (nihilism) 83
supreme worth *see ānanda*
surrender 107–19
survival 31–2, 115
sūrya (Sun) 50, 55, 100–1, 104, 140, 153–4, 161–2
suṣumṇa (central channel) 94
svarga (heavens) 34
svayam-bhū (self-existent) 6, 67–80, 144
Śvetāśvatara Upaniṣad 11, 18, 146

Taittirīyaka Āraṇyaka 136
Taittirīya Upaniṣad 18–19, 93, 140
tantra 119, 199n9 tantric yoga 84, 85; *see also* chakras;
tejas (spiritual energy) 104, 162
teleology 74, 199n7, 208n10
telos 64, 72, 80, 92, 114, 117, 206n17
testimony 12, 49, 56–7, 59, 76, 203n13, 205n7
theism: monistic 30, 67, 70–1; Vedāntic 74, 80; *see also under* Vedānta
theodicy (theological explanation of evil) 37, 92, 103, 112–13, 115, 117, 208n12
Thibaut, G. 197n9
Thieme, Paul 29, 36, 41
Thrasher, A. W. 201n1
transformation 2, 27, 38, 64, 90, 94, 102, 193n17, 207n18; *see also* integration

Udayana 208n10
unity 25, 42, 45–6, 48, 51–2, 66; causal 68; essential 89; metaphysical 61; mystical knowledge of 53–66
Upaniṣads 2–4, 7, 17–18, 27, 54–5, 114, 118; *see also Aitareya*; *Bṛhadāraṇyaka, Chāndogya, Kaṭha, Kena, Māṇḍūkya, Muṇḍaka, Śvetāśvatara, Taittirīya Upaniṣad*
upaniṣat 1

Vācaspati(miśra) 15, 68–9, 87, 192n11
Vaiśeṣika19, 73
vaiśvānara (the self of everyone) 102
Vallabha 103
value, supreme *see paramârtha*
vāsanā 36
vāyu (air) 51
Veda 2, 17; *see also Ṛg Veda*
Vedānta 14, 16, 19, 25, 40, 42, 206n12; literature 20; meditation 1–2, 99; metaphysics7–9; modern studies of 13–14; monistic theism 30; neo-Vedānta 4, 13, 22, 23, 37, 39, 57, 78; philosophy 17; theism 80; *see also* Advaita Vedānta
Vedāntasāra 16
Vedānta-sūtra see Brahma-sūtra
neo-Vedāntins 22, 78, 93
Vedic rituals 20, 196n2
vibhūtis (psychic powers) 22

vidyā (self-knowledge) 8, 10, 17, 25, 33, 44, 48, 54, 76, 81, 108, 110, 118, 158–9; *see also avidyā*
Vijñānabhikṣu 16, 24
vijñānamaya-kośa 94
virodha (contradiction) 99
vivaraṇa (tranmogrification) 91, 206n16
vivarta 70
Viveka-cūḍā-maṇi 87, 88, 210n2
Vivekananda, Swami 22, 104

Wasson, R. 196n1
water 35, 41, 46, 55, 123, 134, 140, 200n12
wealth 27, 29, 86, 98, 119, 134, 136, 145, 147, 163
Whicher, Ian 39
Whitehead, A. N. 27, 37, 71, 103, 113
Wittgenstein, L. 12, 98
worlds, other 30–1, 93, 122, 137

Yājur Veda 17
yaugika-pratyakṣa see yogic perception
yoga *see āsana; bhakti; karma-yoga;* meditation
Yogācāra *see under* Buddhism
Yogasiksha Upanishad 105
Yoga-sūtra 1, 7, 26, 27, 66, 86–8, 105, 118, 119, 151, 191n2, 193n14, 215n4
Yoga-sūtra-bhāṣya 11
yogic perception (*yaugika pratyakṣa,* yogic experience) 8, 11, 50, 57–8, 89, 205n7
yogic powers (*siddhis*) 87, 151
yogic trance *see samādhi*

www.ingramcontent.com/pod-product-compliance
Lightning Source LLC
Chambersburg PA
CBHW071827300426
44116CB00009B/1469
* 9 7 8 1 3 5 0 4 1 2 4 4 6 *